CLASSIC READINGS IN ECONOMICS

to accompany David Colander's Economics

edited by

David Colander
Middlebury College

and

Harry Landreth
Centre College

Project Editor: Helen Reiff
Production Supervisor: Jenifer Gamber
Compositor : Jenifer Gamber
Art Director: Jenifer Gamber
Printer and Binder: McNaughton & Gunn, Inc.

MaxiPress, Box 152C, Dogteam Road, New Haven, VT 05472

Classic Readings in Economics
© MaxiPress, 1995

Printed in the United States of America.

ISBN 0-256-16816-4

*Dedicated to the authors whose work is included in
this volume; they make economics come alive.*

PREFACE

A while back we were sitting around talking about the dearth of classic literature assigned in economics and, to be truthful, in our own principles courses. With forms upon forms from libraries, it was simply easier to stick with the texts, but we weren't happy with ourselves. This book is our attempt to make amends—it is designed to make it easier for professors to assign classic literature. This is a labor of love, not profit. We did not take any royalties for this book and did whatever we could to hold the costs down. If, even at its low price, revenues exceed costs, the "profits" will be donated to an organization which furthers the appreciation of economic literature.

There are many people we want to thank for making this book a reality. First we want to thank *Irwin* who agreed to make no profit on this book in order to keep the costs low so that the book would be accessible and used. Second we want to thank the authors of the articles and the copyright holders—many of whom took no fee, or accepted a lower fee than they would normally receive for reprinting. These copyright holders are listed below.

Next we want to thank those people who helped select the articles in the manuscript. These include a number of our colleagues who made suggestions and Dave Colander's history of thought class at Middlebury College, which initially read through a mass of material and helped select what would be included.

After the selection process was complete, Mark Briggs, Helen Reiff, and Sandro Wulff helped to get the articles into a readable form by scanning, keyboarding, and proofing. Helen Reiff also handled the enormous task of getting permissions and played an important role in many of the infinite number of jobs associated with massaging the manuscript into a book.

Even then, there was an enormous number of things to check to see that we had the correct material and the correct information about the authors. Nicole Shown and Robert Alford played an important role at his stage. We also received assistance from three librarians, Mary Beth Garriott, Connie Klimke, and Judy Nystrom, who each did a superb job. We sincerely thank them all.

After the manuscript was in a reasonable, but not quite finished, form, we turned it over to Jenifer Gamber who took charge of the production process and prepared the manuscript into camera-ready form by editing, proofreading, and typesetting it. Elizabeth DeVault proofread the volume after it was typeset with her close eye for detail.

The final result of all these labors is something that we hope all of you will see as worthwhile. We're pleased to make the book available at such a low price and we thank all for their contributions to the project.

David Colander and Harry Landreth
October 1994

Acknowledgments to Copyright Holders

Abba Lerner's review of Milton Friedman's *Capitalism and Freedom*; and selections from Robert E. Lucas, Jr.; Franco Modigliani; and Paul Samuelson and Robert Solow by courtesy of *The American Economic Review* and the American Economic Association.

Selections from Frank Knight's *The Economic Organization* by courtesy of Augustus M. Kelley Publishers.

Selection from Joan Robinson reprinted by permission of BasicBooks, a division of HarperCollins.

Selections from R.A. Radford and Ronald Coase by permission of Blackwell Publishers, publishers of *Economica*.

Selection from Abba Lerner's "The Myth of the Parasitic Middleman" by courtesy of *Commentary*.

Selection from Thomas Malthus by courtesy of Everyman's Library and David Campbell Publishers, Ltd.

Milton Friedman and The University of Chicago for selections from *Capitalism and Freedom*.

Selections from John Maynard Keynes' *The General Theory of Employment, Interest, and Money* and from Adolph A. Berle's *The American Republic* by courtesy of Harcourt Brace & Company.

Selection from Robert Lekachman's "The Specter of Full Employment" copyright (c) 1977 by *Harper's Magazine*. All rights reserved. Reproduced from the February issue by special permission.

Selections from George J. Stigler reprinted by permission of the publishers from THE INTELLECTUAL AND THE MARKETPLACE by George J. Stigler, Cambridge, Mass.: Harvard University Press, copyright 1984 by the President and Fellows of Harvard College; 1936 by George J. Stigler.

Selection from Joseph Schumpeter reprinted by permission of HarperCollins Publishers, Inc.

Excerpt from THE AFFLUENT SOCIETY 4e. Copyright (c) 1958, 1960, 1976, 1984 by John Kenneth Galbraith. Reprinted by permission of Houghton Mifflin Co. All rights reserved.

Excerpt from PARKINSON'S LAW. Copyright (c) 1957, 1960, 1962, 1970, 1979 by C. Northcote Parkinson. Reprinted by permission of Houghton Mifflin Co. All rights reserved.

Excerpt from A CONTEMPORARY GUIDE TO THE ECONOMICS OF PEACE AND LAUGHTER by John Kenneth Galbraith. Copyright (c) 1971 by Houghton Mifflin Co. All rights reserved.

Selection from James M. Buchanan and Richard E. Wagner courtesy of The Institute of Economic Affairs.

Selection from Jack Hirschleifer by courtesy of *The Journal of Law and Economics*, copyright 1959 by the University of Chicago. All rights reserved.

Selection from Henry C. Simons by permission of *The Journal of Political Economy* and the University of Chicago Press. Copyright 1936 by The University of Chicago. All rights reserved.

Selection from Milton Friedman from *The Journal of Political Economy* by permission of *The Journal of Political Economy*, the University of Chicago Press, and Milton Friedman. Copyright 1977 by the University of Chicago. All rights reserved.

Macmillan London for selection from Sir John Hicks.

Selection from Alvin H. Hansen courtesy of McGraw Hill, Inc.

New Letters and the Curators of the University of Missouri-Kansas City for Abba Lerner's "Economic Steering Wheel," originally published in The University Review.

Selection from Bertrand de Jouvenel reprinted with permission from the February 1949 *Reader's Digest*, and by courtesy of *The Freeman*.

Selection from William Hutt courtesy of Regnery Publishing Co.

Selection from John Kenneth Galbraith's *A Survey of Contemporary Economics* courtesy of Richard D. Irwin.

Selections from John Maynard Keynes' *Essays in Persuasion* courtesy of St. Martin's Press.

The University of Chicago Press and Stephen Kresge, the Bartley Institute, editor, The Collected Works of F.A. Hayek, for selection from F.A. Hayek.

Selections from Henry Hazlitt and Frédéric Bastiat courtesy of Van Nostrand Publishing Company.

Selection from Lord Beveridge courtesy of W.W. Norton and Company.

Organization of Macro Readings by Topic

Introduction to Microeconomics
>Alfred Marshall: Economics
>Adam Smith: Of the Principle Which Gives Occasion to the Division of Labour

Supply and Demand
>Radford: The Price System in Microcosm: A P.O.W. Camp
>de Jouvenel: Rent Control: An Example of Price Fixing

Institutions and History of the Economy
>Marx and Engels: Selections from "Manifesto of the Communist Party"
>Hayek: Individualism vs. Collectivism
>Schumpeter: Can Capitalism Survive?
>Toynbee: The Chief Features of the Industrial Revolution
>Lerner: The "Unproductive Middleman"
>Berle: The American Political-Economic System

Inflation, Unemployment, and Growth
>Beveridge: Full Employment in a Free Society
>U.S. Government: The Full Employment and Balanced Growth Act of 1976

The Keynesian/Classical Debate
>Robert Lekachman: The Specter of Full Employment
>Henry Hazlitt: "Full Employment" as the Goal
>Robert E. Lucas, Jr.: Unemployment Policy
>Keynes: Preface and First Chapter to *The General Theory*
>Galbraith: How Keynes Came to America
>Keynes: Magneto Trouble
>Hansen: The American Economy on the March
>Hazlitt: The Multiplier
>Lerner: The Economic Steering Wheel: The Story of the People's New Clothes
>Milton Friedman: Fiscal Policy

Monetary and Financial Institutions
>Bagehot: Why Lombard Street is Often Very Dull and Sometimes Extremely Excited
>Fisher: 100 Per Cent Reserves
>Simons: Rules versus Authorities in Monetary Policy

Inflation
>John Law: The Importance of Money
>Keynes: Inflation and Deflation
>Samuelson and Solow: Policy Implications of the Phillips Curve
>Milton Friedman: The Stages of the Phillips Curve

International Dimensions of Macro Policy
>Hirshleifer: The Sumptuary Manifesto
>Malthus: The Theory of Population

Macroeconomic Policy Debates
>Buchanan and Wagner: The Consequences of Mr. Keynes
>Hutt: The Keynesian Episode
>Modigliani: The Monetarist Controversy, or Should We Forsake Stabilization Policies?
>Keynes: Concluding Notes on the Social Philosophy Towards Which the General Theory Might Lead

Organization of Micro Readings by Topic

Introduction to Microeconomics
Alfred Marshall: Economics
Adam Smith: Of the Principle Which Gives Occasion to the Division of Labour

Supply and Demand
Radford: The Price System in Microcosm: A P.O.W. Camp
de Jouvenel: Rent Control: An Example of Price Fixing

Institutions and History of the Economy
Marx and Engels: Selections from "Manifesto of the Communist Party"
Hayek: Individualism vs. Collectivism
Schumpeter: Can Capitalism Survive?
Toynbee: The Chief Features of the Industrial Revolution
Lerner: The "Unproductive Middleman"
Berle: The American Political-Economic System

Demand and Elasticity
Veblen: The Theory of the Leisure Class
Galbraith: The Dependence Effect

Cost Analysis and Supply
Robinson: Increasing and Diminishing Returns
Parkinson: Parkinson's Law or the Rising Pyramid
Coase: The Nature of the Firm

Competition and Monopoly and Monopolistic Competition and Oligopoly
Nassau Senior: Value and The Forces of Demand and Supply
Hayek: Economics and Knowledge
Marshall: Competition
Mill: Competition and Custom
Galbraith: The Development of Monopoly Theory

Factor Markets and the Distribution of Income
Hicks: Wage Theory: Basic Forces
Ricardo: Rent
Knight: Profit
Mill: Private Property Has Not Had A Fair Trial
George: Progress and Poverty: Preface

Microeconomics, Social Policy, and Economic Reasoning
Knight: The Price System and the Economic Process
Stigler: A Sketch of the History of Truth in Teaching
Mill: The Subjection of Women
Friedman: The Relation between Economic Freedom and Political Freedom
Lerner: Review of *Capitalism and Freedom* by Milton Friedman
Stigler: An Academic Episode

International Trade
Bastiat: Petition of the Candlemakers
Smith: Restraints on Trade and the Invisible Hand

Growth and the Microeconomics of Developing and Transitional Countries
Hirshleifer: The Sumptuary Manifesto

Index of Readings by Author

Bagehot, Walter: Why Lombard Street is Often Very Dull and Sometimes Extremely Excited, *86*

Bastiat, Frédéric: Petition of the Candlemakers, *198*

Berle, Adolph A.: The American Political-Economic System, *39*

Beveridge, Lord William: Full Employment in a Free Society, *43*

Buchanan, James and Richard E. Wagner: The Consequences of Mr. Keynes, *109*

Coase, Ronald: The Nature of the Firm, *162*

Fisher, Irving: 100 Per Cent Reserves, *89*

Friedman, Milton: Fiscal Policy, *81*
    The Relation Between Economic Freedom and Political Freedom, *189*
    The Stages of the Phillips Curve, *104*

Galbraith, John Kenneth: The Dependence Effect, *134*
    The Development of Monopoly Theory, *155*
    How Keynes Came to America, *65*

George, Henry: Progress and Poverty: Preface, *175*

Hansen, Alvin H.: The American Economy on the March, *72*

Hayek, F. A.: Economics and Knowledge, *144*
    Individualism and Collectivism, *24*

Hazlitt, Henry: "Full Employment" as the Goal, *50*
    The Multiplier, *75*

Hicks, Sir John: Wage Theory: Basic Forces, *165*

Hirshleifer, Jack: The Sumptuary Manifesto, *186*

Hutt, William H.: The Keynesian Episode, *113*

Jouvenel, Bertrand de: Rent Control: An Example of Price Fixing, *18*

Keynes, John Maynard: Concluding Notes on the Social Philosophy Towards Which General Theory Might
    Lead, *124*
    Inflation and Deflation, *100*
    Magneto Trouble, *69*
    Preface and First Chapter to *The General Theory*, *63*

Knight, Frank H.: The Price System and the Economic Process, *152*
    Profit, *172*

Law, John: The Importance of Money, *84*

Lekachman, Robert: The Specter of Full Employment, *47*

Lerner, Abba: The Economic Steering Wheel: The Story of the People's New Clothes, *78*
    Review of *Capitalism and Freedom* by Milton Friedman, *191*
    The "Unproductive Middleman," *36*

Lucas, Robert E., Jr.: Unemployment Policy, *55*

Malthus, Thomas R.: The Theory of Population, *196*

Marshall, Alfred: Competition, *147*
    Economics: *4*

Marx, Karl and Friedrich Engels: Selections from "Manifesto of the Communist Party," *20*

Mill, John Stuart: Competition and Custom, *150*
    Private Property Has Not Had A Fair Trial, *174*
    The Subjection of Women, *182*

Modigliani, Franco: The Monetarist Controversy, or Should We Forsake Stabilization Policy?, *117*

Parkinson, C. Northcote: Parkinson's Law or the Rising Pyramid, *158*

Radford, R. A.: The Price System in Microcosm: A P.O.W. Camp, *9*

Ricardo, David: Rent, *169*

Robinson, Joan: Increasing and Diminishing Returns, *138*

Samuelson, Paul A. and Robert Solow: Policy Implications of the Phillips Curve, *101*

Schumpeter, Joseph: Can Capitalism Survive?, *27*

Senior, Nassau: Value and the Forces of Supply and Demand, *128*

Simons, Henry C.: Rules Versus Authorities in Monetary Policy, *95*

Smith, Adam: Of the Principle Which Gives Occasion to the Division of Labour, *6*
    Restraints on Trade and the Invisible Hand, *201*

Stigler, George: An Academic Episode, *193*
    A Sketch of the History of Truth in Teaching, *178*

Toynbee, Arnold: The Chief Features of the Industrial Revolution, *31*

U.S. Congress: Full Employment and Balanced Growth Act of 1976, *59*

Veblen, Thorstein: The Theory of the Leisure Class, *131*

TABLE of CONTENTS

INTRODUCTION

Introduction
Alfred Marshall: Economics   4
Adam Smith: Of the Principle Which Gives Occasion to the Division of Labour   6

Supply and Demand
R. A. Radford: The Price System in Microcosm: A P.O.W. Camp   9
Bertrand de Jouvenel: Rent Control: An Example of Price Fixing   18

Economic Systems
Karl Marx and Friedrich Engels: Selections from "Manifesto of the Communist Party"   20
F. A. Hayek: Individualism and Collectivism   24
Joseph Schumpeter: Can Capitalism Survive?   27

Economic Institutions
Arnold Toynbee: The Chief Features of the Industrial Revolution   31
Abba Lerner: The "Unproductive Middleman"   36
Adolph A. Berle: The American Political-Economic System   39

MACROECONOMICS

The Question of Full Employment
Lord William Beveridge: Full Employment in a Free Society   43
Robert Lekachman: The Specter of Full Employment   47
Henry Hazlitt: "Full Employment" as the Goal   50
Robert E. Lucas, Jr.: Unemployment Policy   55
U.S. Congress: Full Employment and Balanced Growth Act of 1976   59

Keynesian Theory
John Maynard Keynes: Preface and First Chapter to *The General Theory*   63
John Kenneth Galbraith: How Keynes Came to America   65
John Maynard Keynes: Magneto Trouble   69
Alvin H. Hansen: The American Economy on the March   72
Henry Hazlitt: The Multiplier   75
Abba Lerner: The Economic Steering Wheel: The Story of the People's New Clothes   78
Milton Friedman: Fiscal Policy   81

Money and Monetary Policy
John Law: The Importance of Money   84
Walter Bagehot: Why Lombard Street is Often Very Dull and Sometimes Extremely Excited   86
Irving Fisher: 100 Per Cent Reserves   89
Henry C. Simons: Rules versus Authorities in Monetary Policy   95

Inflation and the Phillips Curve
John Maynard Keynes: Inflation and Deflation 100
Paul Samuelson and Robert Solow: Policy Implications of the Phillips Curve 101
Milton Friedman: The Stages of the Phillips Curve 104

The Keynesian Policy Legacy
James M. Buchanan and Richard E. Wagner: The Consequences of Mr. Keynes 109
William H. Hutt: The Keynesian Episode 113
Franco Modigliani: The Monetarist Controversy, or Should We Forsake Stabilization
  Policies? 117
John Maynard Keynes: Concluding Notes on the Social Philosophy Towards Which
  the General Theory Might Lead 124

MICROECONOMICS

Issues in Supply and Demand
Nassau Senior: Value and the Forces of Demand and Supply 128
Thorstein Veblen: The Theory of the Leisure Class 131
John Kenneth Galbraith: The Dependence Effect 134
Joan Robinson: Increasing and Diminishing Returns 137
F. A. Hayek: Economics and Knowledge 142

Competition, Market Structure, and the Firm
Alfred Marshall: Competition 145
John Stuart Mill: Competition and Custom 148
Frank H. Knight: The Price System and the Economic Process 150
John Kenneth Galbraith: The Development of Monopoly Theory 153
C. Northcote Parkinson: Parkinson's Law or the Rising Pyramid 156
Ronald Coase: The Nature of the Firm 160

Private Property, Factor Markets, and Distribution
Sir John Hicks: Wage Theory: Basic Forces 163
David Ricardo: Rent 167
Frank H. Knight: Profit 170
John Stuart Mill: Private Property Has Not Had A Fair Trial 172
Henry George: Progress and Poverty: Preface 173

Micro Policy Debates
George Stigler: A Sketch of the History of Truth in Teaching 176
John Stuart Mill: The Subjection of Women 180
Jack Hirshleifer: The Sumptuary Manifesto 184
Milton Friedman: The Relation between Economic Freedom and
  Political Freedom 187
Abba Lerner: Review of *Capitalism and Freedom* by Milton Friedman 189
George Stigler: An Academic Episode 191

International and Development
Thomas R. Malthus: The Theory of Population 194
Frédéric Bastiat: Petition of the Candlemakers 196
Adam Smith: Restraints on Trade and the Invisible Hand 199

INTRODUCTION

All too often students read their economics textbook and think that it conveys to them the entire principles of economics. Textbook writers try, but few would say that we succeed. In fact, what can fit in the text is just the tip of the iceberg—and that tip often does an injustice to the subtleties of arguments which give them real meaning. To convey those subtleties it is necessary to read original texts. Faculty know that, but because of copyright laws, time constraints, and costs of getting together a collection of readings, all too often the only assignments that appear on the reading list are those from the textbook. That's sad. Somehow, it just seems wrong to us for students to have gone through introductory economics and not have read a few pages of authors such as Adam Smith, Karl Marx, F. A. Hayek, John Maynard Keynes, Thorstein Veblen, Milton Friedman, and John Kenneth Galbraith. Their writings changed the direction of economic thinking and raise many questions that students should be considering when learning the principles of economics.

This collection is designed to make it a bit easier for faculty to assign some readings beyond the textbook. It is a collection of classic readings appropriate for the introductory economics course designed to accompany Colander's *Economics* textbook.

The Selection Process

There are thousands of articles and books which students could profitably read. How does anyone choose among them? With great difficulty, obviously. In our selection process, we specifically have stuck with what we call "classic readings" that we believe have an enduring quality. Other collections that focus on more recent articles, and *The Wall Street Journal* program that accompanies Colander's text cover up-to-date material.

Now clearly a short book of readings cannot do justice to these earlier writers, but we believe that it is better that they are unjustly treated than forgotten. We are sure that we will be accused of having left out many favorites and that we have not made the best selection possible. We plead guilty on both counts and simply ask that you recognize the enormous constraints we faced, and see this not as a complete collection of what students should read, but simply as an introduction for students to the broader literature in economics.

Our selection criteria were simple: first, we wanted to include a number of different economists, so the selections from each had to be short. Second, we had to like the selection, which adds a certain subjectivity to the process. Third, we had to capture a bit of the flavor of the writer. Fourth, we had to fit it into the course in a somewhat even manner. Thus, a writing on a topic in which not many writings existed had a much higher probability of being included than one on a topic in which many writings existed. And fifth, each reading had to represent the diversity of thought that has existed and continues to exist in economics.

We include many well-known economists, but we also include some lesser-known economists. Our general rule was that the lesser the importance of the writer, the more we had to like it. Thus, the "Economics of Organization of a P.O.W. Camp" is not by a well-known writer but it is in our view a classic. The opposite is the case with the Communist Manifesto—it's not very important for learning neoclassical economic principles, but it is a classic with which students should be acquainted. The selections are far too short, but we felt they had to be short (under 6 pages) so that it was possible that the students would read them and so that we could include the diversity of thought that we wanted.

We have 58 selections organized in the following manner: 10 in the introductory section; 23 in the macro section, and 25 in the micro section. These are rough divisions and there is much overlap. As a guide we list some chapters from the Colander text with which each of the readings might fit, and the prefatory materials include possible micro and macro course outlines incorporating the readings. We doubt that most teachers will want to assign more than about 20 readings a semester, but we believe different professors will select different sets of 20 readings.

At the beginning of each selection, we provide a brief discussion of the writer and his or her relevance to modern issues. We keep these short to leave more room for the selections, but we believe these introductions are useful to give a bit of context for the selection.

The Editing Process

A few notes about the editing process: This is a collection for beginning students, not for historians of thought. Thus we have left out many of the niceties, such as footnotes, and discussions of how different editions differ in content and word usage—discussions that would be *de rigueur* for a history of thought collection. Students should note that many of what look like incorrect spellings and grammar are not necessarily mistakes.

Appropriate grammar, spelling, and punctuation change over the years, and for the most part we have left the original spelling. These variations give the reader a flavor of the times in which each selection was written, as well as a brief sense of the individuality of each writer. However, where it seemed as if the different spelling would get in the way of understanding, as we believe it would have with John's Law's 18th Century English, we modernized it.

Another aspect of the writing that we left, which glares out to modern textbook writers, was the usage of "man" and "he" to refer to the human race. The reader should be clear that general concern about this usage came about only in the last 20 years. The selections are reflections of their times.

That's it for our introduction; this isn't our book. It belongs to the authors we selected, and we want to leave the talking to them.

INTRODUCTION

Introduction
Alfred Marshall: Economics   4
Adam Smith: Of the Principle Which Gives Occasion to the Division of Labour   6

Supply and Demand
R. A. Radford: The Price System in Microcosm: A P.O.W. Camp   9
Bertrand de Jouvenel: Rent Control: An Example of Price Fixing   18

Economic Systems
Karl Marx and Friedrich Engels: Selections from "Manifesto of the
      Communist Party"   20
F. A. Hayek: Individualism and Collectivism   24
Joseph Schumpeter: Can Capitalism Survive?   27

Economic Institutions
Arnold Toynbee: The Chief Features of the Industrial Revolution   31
Abba Lerner: The "Unproductive Middleman"   36
Adolph A. Berle: The American Political-Economic System   39

Alfred Marshall
(1842-1924)

It seems appropriate that we start off this set of readings with a brief introduction from Alfred Marshall's Principles Of Economics *because Marshall's* Principles *serves as a role model for the Colander* Economics *that this set of readings accompanies. Marshall saw economics not as being about abstract theory but, instead, about "mankind in the ordinary business of life." His* Principles, *first published in 1890, shied away from economic theory that was just for the sake of theory, and always tried to relate the argument to the real world.*

When Marshall started writing, there was a fight between the German historical school and the mathematical theoretical school. He tried to place himself right in the middle, arguing that both had important insights, and that what was at stake was to use one's common sense and one's power of observation. One should choose the approach that shed the most light on the matter. He argued that "economic doctrine is not a body of concrete truth, but an engine of discovery of concrete truth." Thus, in many ways it was Marshall who first focused modern economics on economic reasoning rather than on economic truths.

Marshall was born in England in 1842 and he died in 1924. He studied mathematics in college and started to teach mathematics at Cambridge University, but he soon decided that his true passion was for economics. He became a professor of economics at Cambridge, and in that position was important in establishing economics as a separate field of study.

This brief selection is from the 8th edition of his Principles of Economics. *It gives his definition of economics, and shows his view of economic laws.*

Alfred Marshall. 1890 (8th edition: 1920). *Principles of Economics*. London: MacMillan & Co., pp. 1-2, 31-33, 36.

Economics

Political economy or economics is a study of mankind in the ordinary business of life; it examines that part of individual and social action which is most closely connected with the attainment and with the use of the material requisites of well-being.

Thus it is on the one side a study of wealth; and on the other, and more important side, a part of the study of man. For man's character has been moulded by his every-day work, and the material resources which he thereby procures, more than by any other influence unless it be that of his religious ideals; and the two great forming agencies of the world's history have been the religious and the economic. Here and there the ardour of the military or the artistic spirit has been for a while predominant; but religious and economic influences have nowhere been displaced from the front rank even for a time; and they have nearly always been more important than all others put together. Religious motives are more intense than economic, but their direct action seldom extends over so large a part of life. For the business by which a person earns his livelihood generally fills his thoughts during by far the greater part of those hours in which his mind is at its best; during them his character is being formed by the way in which he uses his faculties in his work, by the thoughts and feelings which it suggests, and by his relations to his associates in work, his employers or his employees. (pp. 1-2). . . .

Let us then consider more closely the nature of economic laws, and their limitations. Every cause has a tendency to produce some definite result if nothing occurs to hinder it. Thus gravitation tends to make things fall to the ground. . . .

It is a very exact statement—so exact that mathematicians can calculate a National Almanac, which will show the moments at which each satellite of Jupiter will hide itself behind Jupiter. They make this calculation for many years beforehand; and navigators take it to sea, and use it in finding out where they are. Now there are no economic tendencies which act as steadily and can be measured as exactly as gravitation can; and consequently there are no laws of economics which can be compared for precision with the law of gravitation.

But let us look at a science less exact than astronomy. The science of the tides explains how the tide rises and falls twice a day under the action of the sun and the moon: how there are strong tides at new and full moon, and weak tides at the moon's first and third quarters; and how the tide running up into a closed channel . . . will be very high; and so on. Thus, having studied the lie of the land and the water all around the British Isles, people can calculate beforehand when the tide will *probably* be at its highest on any day at London Bridge or at Gloucester; and how high it will be there. They have to use the word *probably,* which the astronomers do not need to use when talking about the eclipses of Jupiter's satellites. For, though many forces act upon Jupiter and its satellites, each one of them acts in a definite manner which can be predicted beforehand: but no one knows enough about the weather to be able to say beforehand how it will act. A heavy downpour of rain in the upper Thames valley, or a strong northeast wind in the German Ocean, may make the tides at London Bridge differ a good deal from what had been expected.

The laws of economics are to be compared with the laws of the tides, rather than with the simple and exact law of gravitation. For the actions of men are so various and uncertain that the best statement of tendencies, which we can make in a science of human conduct, must needs be inexact and faulty. This might be urged as a reason against making any statement at all on the subject; but that would almost be to abandon life. Life is human conduct, and the thoughts and emotions that grow up around it. By the fundamental impulses of our nature we all—high and low, learned and unlearned—are in our several degrees constantly striving to understand the courses of human action, and to shape them for our purposes, whether selfish or unselfish, whether noble or ignoble. And since we must form to ourselves some notions of the tendencies of human action, our choice is between forming those notions carelessly and forming them carefully. The harder the task, the greater the need for steady patient inquiry; for turning to account the experience, that has been reaped by the more advanced physical sciences; and for framing as best we can well thought-out estimates, or provisional laws, of the tendencies of human action.

* * * *

Economic Laws, or *statements* of economic tendencies, are those social laws which relate to branches of conduct in which the strength of the motives chiefly concerned can be measured by a money price.

There is thus no hard and sharp line of division between those social laws which are, and those which are not, to be regarded also as economic laws. For there is a continuous gradation from social laws concerned almost exclusively with motives that can be measured by price, to social laws in which such motives have little place; and which are therefore generally as much less precise and exact than economic laws, as those are than the laws of the more exact physical sciences.

It is sometimes said that the laws of economics are "hypothetical." Of course, like every other science, it undertakes to study the effect which will be produced by certain causes, not absolutely, but subject to the condition that other things are equal, and that the causes are able to work out their effects undisturbed. Almost every scientific doctrine, when carefully and formally stated, will be found to contain some proviso to the effect that other things are equal: the action of the causes in question is supposed to be isolated; certain effects are attributed to them, but only on the hypothesis that no cause is permitted to enter except those distinctly allowed for. It is true, however, that the condition that time must be allowed for causes to produce their effects is a source of great difficulty in economics. For, meanwhile, the material on which they work, and perhaps even the causes themselves, may have changed; and the tendencies which are being described will not have a sufficiently "long run" in which to work themselves fully. . .

Adam Smith
(1723-1790)

The economist who is generally known as the founder of the classical school is Adam Smith. He was born in Britain and spent his life there. His Wealth of Nations *(1776) is seen as the beginning point from which classical economics ideas flowed, and his concept of "the invisible hand" still plays a central role today in economic thinking and teaching.*

Actually, Smith was more than simply an economist; he was a moral philosopher, and his Theory of Moral Sentiments, *written in 1759, seventeen years before* The Wealth of Nations, *set the context in which the invisible handshake and culture is seen as a backdrop for the workings of the market. This selection, from* The Wealth of Nations, *shows some of the best-known passages from that book. Because the book was written about 200 years ago, its punctuation, grammar, and some of its vocabulary may seem quaint today. Note that here "trucking" means the give-and-take of barter and trade; a "street porter" was a person who delivered merchandise by pushing it through the street on a kind of cart.*

In this selection Smith argues that humankind is different from all other creatures because of human beings' proclivity to trade, and that that proclivity allows the specialization upon which the wealth of nations depends.

Adam Smith. 1776 (6th edition: 1791). *An Enquiry into the Nature and Causes of the Wealth of Nations*. London: A. Strahan.

Of the Principle Which Gives Occasion to the Division of Labour

This division of labour, from which so many advantages are derived, is not originally the effect of any human wisdom, which foresees and intends that general opulence to which it gives occasion. It is the necessary, though very slow and gradual consequence of a certain propensity in human nature which has in view no such extensive utility; the propensity to truck, barter, and exchange one thing for another.

Whether this propensity be one of those original principles in human nature, of which no further account can be given; or whether, as seems more probable, it be the necessary consequence of the faculties of reason and speech, it belongs not to our present subject to enquire. It is common to all men, and to be found in no other race of animals, which seem to know neither this nor any other species of contracts. Two greyhounds, in running down the same hare, have sometimes the appearance of acting in some sort of concert. Each turns her towards his companion, or endeavours to intercept her when his companion turns her towards himself.

This, however, is not the effect of any contract, but of the accidental concurrence of their passions in the same object at that particular time. Nobody ever saw a dog make a fair and deliberate exchange of one bone for another with another dog. Nobody ever saw one animal by its gestures and natural cries signify to another, this is mine, that yours; I am willing to give this for that. When an animal wants to obtain something either of a man or of another animal, it has no other means of persuasion but to gain the favour of those whose service it requires. A puppy fawns upon its dam, and a spaniel endeavours by a thousand attractions to engage the attention of its master who is at dinner, when it wants to be fed by him. Man sometimes uses the same arts with his brethren, and when he has no other means of engaging them to act according to his inclinations, endeavours by every servile and fawning attention to obtain their good will. He has not time, however, to do this upon every occasion. In civilised society he stands at all times in need of the cooperation and assistance of great multitudes, while his whole life is scarce sufficient to gain the friendship of a few persons.

INTRODUCTION

In almost every other race of animals each individual, when it is grown up to maturity, is entirely independent, and in its natural state has occasion for the assistance of no other living creature. But man has almost constant occasion for the help of his brethren, and it is in vain for him to expect it from their benevolence only. He will be more likely to prevail if he can interest their self-love in his favour, and show them that it is for their own advantage to do for him what he requires of them. Whoever offers to another a bargain of any kind, proposes to do this. Give me that which I want, and you shall have this which you want, is the meaning of every such offer; and it is in this manner that we obtain from one another the far greater part of those good offices which we stand in need of. It is not from the benevolence of the butcher, the brewer, or the baker, that we expect our dinner, but from their regard to their own interest. We address ourselves, not to their humanity but to their self-love, and never talk to them of our own necessities but of their advantages. Nobody but a beggar chooses to depend chiefly upon the benevolence of his fellow-citizens. Even a beggar does not depend upon it entirely. The charity of well-disposed people, indeed, supplies him with the whole fund of his subsistence. But though this principle ultimately provides him with all the necessaries of life which he has occasion for, it neither does nor can provide him with them as he has occasion for them. The greater part of his occasional wants are supplied in the same manner as those of other people, by treaty, by barter, and by purchase. With the money which one man gives him he purchases food. The old clothes which another bestows upon him he exchanges for other old clothes which suit him better, or for lodging, or for food, or for money, with which he can buy either food, clothes, or lodging, as he has occasion.

As it is by treaty, by barter, and by purchase, that we obtain from one another the greater part of those mutual good offices which we stand in need of, so it is this same trucking disposition which originally gives occasion to the division of labour. In a tribe of hunters or shepherds a particular person makes bows and arrows, for example, with more readiness and dexterity than any other. He frequently exchanges them for cattle or for venison with his companions; and he finds at last that he can in this manner get more cattle and venison, than if he himself went to the field to catch them. From a regard to his own interest, therefore, the making of bows and arrows grows to be his chief business, and he becomes a sort of armourer. Another excels in making the frames and covers of their little huts or moveable houses. He is accustomed to be of use in this way to his neighbours, who reward him in the same manner with cattle and with venison, till at last he finds it his interest to dedicate himself entirely to this employment, and to become a sort of house-carpenter. In the same manner a third becomes a smith or a brazier, a fourth a tanner or dresser of hides or skins, the principal part of the clothing of savages. And thus the certainty of being able to exchange all that surplus part of the produce of his own labour, which is over and above his own consumption, for such parts of the produce of other men's labour as he may have occasion for, encourages every man to apply himself to a particular occupation, and to cultivate and bring to perfection whatever talent or genius he may possess for that particular species of business.

The difference of natural talents in different men is, in reality, much less than we are aware of; and the very different genius which appears to distinguish men of different professions, when grown up to maturity, is not upon many occasions so much the cause, as the effect of the division of labour. The difference between the most dissimilar characters, between a philosopher and a common street porter, for example, seems to arise not so much from nature, as from habit, custom, and education. When they came into the world, and for the first six or eight years of their existence, they were, perhaps, very much alike, and neither their parents nor play-fellows could perceive any remarkable difference. About that age, or soon after, they come to be employed in very different occupations. The difference of talents comes then to be taken notice of, and widens by degrees, till at last the vanity of the philosopher is willing to acknowledge scarce any resemblance. But without the disposition to truck, barter, and exchange, every man must have procured to himself every necessary and convenience of life which he wanted. All must have had the same duties to perform, and the same work to do, and there could have been no such difference of employment as could alone give occasion to any great difference of talents.

As it is this disposition which forms that difference of talents, so remarkable among men of different professions, so it is this same disposition which renders that difference useful. Many tribes of animals acknowledged to be all of the same species, derive from nature a much more remarkable distinction of genius, than what, antecedent to custom and education, appears to take place among men. By nature a philosopher is not in genius and disposition half so different from a street porter, as a mastiff is from a greyhound, or a greyhound from a spaniel, or this last from a shepherd's dog. Those different tribes of animals, however, though all of the same species, are of scarce any use to one another. The strength of the mastiff is not, in the least, supported either by the swiftness of the greyhound, or by the sagacity of the spaniel, or by the docility of the shepherd's dog. The effects of those different geniuses and talents, for want of the power or disposition to barter and exchange, cannot be brought into a common stock, and do not in the least contribute to the better accommodation and convenience of the species. Each animal is still obliged to support and defend itself, separately and independently, and derives no sort of advantage from that variety of talents with which nature has distinguished its fellows. Among men, on the contrary, the most dissimilar geniuses are of use to one another; the different produces of their respective talents, by the general disposition to truck, barter, and exchange, being brought, as it were, into a common stock, where every man may purchase whatever part of the produce of other men's talents he has occasion for.

R.A. Radford
(1919-)

Most of the selections in this book are from the works of famous economists. However, for every famous economist there are probably 5,000 not-so-famous, yet superb, economists. Among these, every so often, an economist has an experience, and writes an article about that experience, which in a unique way captures a number of elements of economic issues. R.A. Radford, an Englishman, is one such economist. Richard Radford's schooling at Cambridge was interrupted by World War II. He had the unlucky draw in life to be captured by the Germans in World War II and to spend time in one of their prisoner of war camps. After the war he returned to Cambridge and finished his degree in 1947. He then moved to the U.S. and worked as an economist at the International Monetary Fund until he retired in 1980.

Upon his return from war, he turned his unlucky imprisonment into a good fortune by analyzing the activities in the camp from an economist's perspective. What Radford found in a prison camp was an economy in miniature—one in which most of the laws of both microeconomics and macroeconomics were relevant. His account of the economics of a prisoner of war camp has rightly become a classic in the teaching of economics.

The article contains many words which would have been familiar to every English reader in the 1940s but may be unfamiliar today. Those most worth noting are "bully" (canned beef); "bungalow" (a kind of house); "Kam" (trade name of a canned English delicacy); "treacle" (called molasses in the United States); "relict" (a survivor); "clipped" (debased, as in clipping tiny amounts of metal from many coins until there is enough metal to counterfeit a new coin); "sweated" (another term for debased); "variety turns" (amateur performances such as singing or telling jokes); "bedlam" (chaos and uproar); "the Allies" (nations allied with England in World War II); "Sikhs" (members of an East Indian sect) and "Urdu" (the Sikhs' language); and Oflag and Stalag (types of prison camps). Also note: British paper money is called the pound and its symbol is £; for example, "50 pounds" is written "£50"; and "Reichmarks" were the German currency of the time.

R.A. Radford. 1945. "The Economic Organization of a P.O.W. Camp." *Economica*, XII, No. 48, New Series, pp. 189-201.

The Price System in Microcosm: A P.O.W. Camp

After allowance has been made for abnormal circumstances, the social institutions, ideas and habits of groups in the outside world are to be found reflected in a prisoner-of-war camp. It is an unusual but a vital society. Camp organization and politics are matters of real concern to the inmates, as affecting their present and perhaps their future existences. Nor does this indicate any loss of proportion. No one pretends that camp matters are of any but local importance or of more than transient interest, but their importance is great. . . .

One aspect of social organization is to be found in economic activity, and this, along with other manifestations of a group existence, is to be found in any P.O.W. camp. True, a prisoner is not dependent on his exertions for the provision of the necessaries, or even the luxuries of life, but through his economic activity, the exchange of goods and services, his standard of material comfort is considerably enhanced. . . .

Naturally, entertainment, academic and literary interests, games, and discussions of the "other world" bulk larger in everyday life than they do in the life of more normal societies. But it would be wrong to underestimate the importance of economic activity. Everyone receives a roughly equal share of essentials; it is by trade that individual preferences are given expression and comfort increased. All at some time, and most people regularly, make exchanges of one sort or another.

. . . But the essential interest lies in the universality and the spontaneity of this economic life; it came into existence not by conscious imitation but as a response to the immediate needs and circumstances. Any similarity between prison organization and outside organization arises from similar stimuli evoking similar responses.

The following is as brief an account of the essential data as may render the narrative intelligible. The camps of which the writer had experience were Oflags and consequently the economy was not complicated by payments for work by the detaining power. They consisted normally of between 1,200, and 2,500 people, housed in a number of separate but intercommunicating bungalows, one company of 200 or so to a building. Each company formed a group within the main organization and inside the company the room and the messing syndicate, a voluntary and spontaneous group who fed together, formed the constituent units.

Between individuals there was active trading in all consumer goods and in some services. Most trading was for food against cigarettes or other foodstuffs, but cigarettes rose from the status of a normal commodity to that of currency. Reichmarks existed but had no circulation save for gambling debts, as few articles could be purchased with them from the canteen.

Our supplies consisted of rations provided by the detaining power and (principally) the contents of Red Cross food parcels—tinned milk, jam, butter, biscuits, bully, chocolate, sugar, cigarettes, and so forth. So far the supplies to each person were equal and regular. Private parcels of clothing, toilet requisites and cigarettes were also received, and here equality ceased owing to the different numbers despatched and the vagaries of the post. All these articles were the subject of trade and exchange.

The Development and Organization of the Market

Very soon after capture people realized that it was both undesirable and unnecessary, in view of the limited size and the equality of supplies, to give away or to accept gifts of cigarettes or food. "Goodwill" developed into trading as a more equitable means of maximizing individual satisfaction.

We reached a transit camp in Italy about a fortnight after capture and received one-quarter of a Red Cross food parcel each a week later. At once exchanges, already established, multiplied in volume. Starting with simple direct barter, such as a nonsmoker giving a smoker friend his cigarette issue in exchange for a chocolate ration, more complex exchanges soon became an accepted custom. Stories circulated of a padre who started off round the camp with a tin of cheese and five cigarettes and returned to his bed with a complete parcel in addition to his original cheese and cigarettes; the market was not yet perfect. Within a week or two as the volume of trade grew, rough scales of exchange values came into existence. Sikhs, who had at first exchanged tinned beef for practically any other foodstuff, began to insist on jam and margarine. It was realized that a tin of jam was worth one-half pound of margarine plus something else; that a cigarette issue was worth several chocolate issues, and a tin of diced carrots was worth practically nothing.

In this camp we did not visit other bungalows very much and prices varied from place to place; hence the germ of truth in the story of the itinerant priest. By the end of a month, when we reached our permanent camp, there was a lively trade in all commodities and their relative values were well known, and expressed not in terms of one another—one didn't quote bully in terms of sugar—but in terms of cigarettes. The cigarette became the standard of value. In the permanent camp, people started by wandering through the bungalows calling their offers— "cheese for seven" (cigarettes)—and the hours after parcel issue were bedlam. The inconvenience of this system soon led to its replacement by an Exchange and Mart notice board in every bungalow, where under the headings "name," "room number," "wanted," and "offered" sales and wants were advertised. When a deal went through, it was crossed off the board. The public and semi-permanent records of transactions led to cigarette prices being well known and thus tending to equality throughout the camp, although there were always opportunities for an astute trader to make a profit from arbitrage. With this development everyone, including nonsmokers, was willing to sell for cigarettes, using them to buy at another time and place. Cigarettes became the normal currency, though, of course, barter was never extinguished.

The unity of the market and the prevalence of a single price varied directly with the general level of organization and comfort in the camp. A transit camp was always chaotic and uncomfortable: people were overcrowded, no one knew where anyone else was living, and few took the trouble to find out. Organization was too slender to include an Exchange and Mart board, and private advertisements were the most that appeared. Consequently a transit camp was not one market but many. The price of a tin of salmon is known to have varied by two cigarettes and twenty between one end of a hut and the other. Despite a high level of organization in Italy, the market was morcellated in this manner at the first transit camp we reached after our removal to Germany in the autumn of 1943. In this camp—Stalag VIIA at Moosburg in Bavaria—there were up to 50,000 prisoners of all nationalities. French, Russians, Italians, and Jugo-Slavs were free to move about within the camp: British and Americans were confined to their compounds, although a few cigarettes given to a sentry would always procure permission for one or two men to visit other compounds. The people who first visited the highly organized French trading center, with its stalls and known prices, found coffee extract—relatively cheap among the tea-drinking English —commanding a fancy price in biscuits or cigarettes, and some enterprising people made small fortunes that way. (Incidentally we found out later that much of the coffee went "over the wire" and sold for phenomenal prices at black market cafés in Munich: some of the French prisoners made substantial sums in R[eichmark]s. This was one of the few occasions on which our normally closed economy came into contact with other economic worlds.)

Eventually public opinion grew hostile to these monopoly profits—not everyone could make contact with the French—and trading with them was put on a regulated basis. Each group of beds was given a quota of articles to offer and the transaction was carried out by accredited representatives from the British compound, with monopoly rights. The same method was used for trading with sentries elsewhere, as in this trade secrecy and reasonable prices had a peculiar importance, but as is ever the case with regulated companies, the interloper proved too strong.

The permanent camps in Germany saw the highest level of commercial organization. In addition to the Exchange and Mart notice boards, a shop was organized as a public utility, controlled by representatives of the Senior British Officer, on a no profit basis. People left their surplus clothing, toilet requisites, and food there until they were sold at a fixed price in cigarettes. Only sales in cigarettes were accepted—there was no barter—and there was no haggling. For food, at least, there were standard prices: clothing is less homogeneous and the price was decided around a norm by the seller and the shop manager in agreement; shirts would average say 80, ranging from 60 to 120 according to quality and age. Of food, the shop carried small stocks for convenience; the capital was provided by a loan from the bulk store of Red Cross cigarettes and repaid by a small commission taken on the first transactions. Thus, the cigarette attained its fullest currency status, and the market was almost completely unified.

It is thus to be seen that a market came into existence without labor or production. The [Red Cross] may be considered as "Nature" of the textbook, and the articles of trade—food, clothing and cigarettes—as free gifts— land or manna. Despite this, and despite a roughly equal distribution of resources, a market came into spontaneous operation, and prices were fixed by the operation of supply and demand. It is difficult to reconcile this fact with the labor theory of value.

Actually there was an embryo labor market. Even when cigarettes were not scarce, there was usually some unlucky person willing to perform services for them. Laundrymen advertised at two cigarettes a garment. Battle-dress was scrubbed and pressed and a pair of trousers lent for the interim period for twelve. A good pastel portrait cost thirty or a tin of "Kam." Odd tailoring and other jobs similarly had their prices.

There were also entrepreneurial services. There was a coffee stall owner who sold tea, coffee, or cocoa at two cigarettes a cup, buying his raw materials at market prices and hiring labor to gather fuel and to stoke; he actually enjoyed the services of a chartered accountant at one stage. After a period of great prosperity he overreached himself and failed disastrously for several hundred cigarettes. Such large-scale private enterprise was rare but several middlemen or professional traders existed. The padre in Italy, or the men at Moosburg who opened trading relations with the French, are examples: the more subdivided the market, the less perfect the advertisement of prices, and the less stable the prices, the greater was the scope for these operators. One man capitalized his knowledge of Urdu by buying meat from the Sikhs and selling butter and jam in return: as his operations became better known more and more people entered this trade, prices in the Indian Wing approximated more nearly to those elsewhere, though to the end a "contact" among the Indians was valuable, as linguistic difficulties prevented the trade from being quite free. Some were specialists in the Indian trade, the food, clothing, or even the watch trade. Middlemen traded on their own account or on commission. Price rings and agreements were suspected and the traders certainly cooperated. Nor did they welcome newcomers. Unfortunately, the writer knows little of the workings of these people: public opinion was hostile and the professionals were usually of a retiring disposition.

One trader in food and cigarettes, operating in a period of dearth, enjoyed a high reputation. His capital, carefully saved, was originally about fifty cigarettes, with which he bought rations on issue days and held them until the price rose just before the next issue. He also picked up a little by arbitrage; several times a day he visited every Exchange or Mart notice board and took advantage of every discrepancy between prices of goods offered and wanted. His knowledge of prices, markets, and names of those who had received cigarette parcels was phenomenal. By these means he kept himself smoking steadily—his profits—while his capital remained intact.

Sugar was issued on Saturday. About Tuesday, two of us used to visit [a favorite trader] and make a deal; as old customers he would advance as much of the price as he could spare then, and entered the transaction in a book. On Saturday morning he left cocoa tins on our beds for the ration, and picked them up on Saturday afternoon. We were hoping for a calendar at Christmas, but [our trader] failed too. He was left holding a big black treacle issue when the price fell, and in this weakened state was unable to withstand an unexpected arrival of parcels and the consequent price fluctuations. He paid in full, but from his capital. The next Tuesday, when I paid my usual visit he was out of business.

Credit entered into many, perhaps into most transactions, in one form or another. [Our favorite trader] paid in advance as a rule for his purchases of future deliveries of sugar, but many buyers asked for credit, whether the commodity was sold spot or future. Naturally prices varied according to the terms of sale. A treacle ration might be advertised for four cigarettes now or five next week. And in the future market "bread now" was a vastly different thing from "bread Thursday." Bread was issued on Thursday and Monday, four and three days' rations respectively, and by Wednesday and Sunday night it had risen at least one cigarette per ration, from seven to eight, by suppertime. One man always saved a ration to sell then at the peak price: his offer of "bread now" stood out on the board among a number of "bread Monday's" fetching one or two less, or not selling at all—and he always smoked on Sunday night.

The Cigarette Currency

Although cigarettes as currency exhibited certain peculiarities, they performed all the functions of a metallic currency as a unit of account, as a measure of value and as a store of value, and shared most of its characteristics. They were homogeneous, reasonably durable, and of convenient size for the smallest or, in packets, for the largest transactions. Incidentally, they could be clipped or sweated by rolling them between the fingers so that tobacco fell out.

Cigarettes were also subject to the working of Gresham's Law. Certain brands were more popular than others as smokes, but for currency purposes a cigarette was a cigarette. Consequently buyers used the poorer qualities and the Shop rarely saw the more popular brands: cigarettes such as Churchman's No. 1 were rarely used for trading. At one time cigarettes hand-rolled from pipe tobacco began to circulate. Pipe tobacco was issued in lieu of cigarettes by the

Red Cross at a rate of twenty-five cigarettes to the ounce and this rate was standard in exchanges, but an ounce would produce thirty home-made cigarettes. Naturally, people with machine-made cigarettes broke them down and re-rolled the tobacco, and the real cigarette virtually disappeared from the market. Hand-rolled cigarettes were not homogeneous and prices could no longer be quoted in them with safety: each cigarette was examined before it was accepted and thin ones rejected, or extra demanded as a make-weight. For a time we suffered all the inconveniences of a debased currency.

Machine-made cigarettes were always universally acceptable, both for what they would buy and for themselves. It was this intrinsic value which gave rise to their principal disadvantage as currency, a disadvantage which exists, but to a far smaller extent, in the case of metallic currency—that is, a strong demand for nonmonetary purposes. Consequently our economy was repeatedly subject to deflation and to periods of monetary stringency. While the Red Cross issue of fifty or twenty-five cigarettes per man per week came in regularly, and while there were fair stocks held, the cigarette currency suited its purpose admirably. But when the issue was interrupted, stocks soon ran out, prices fell, trading declined in volume and became increasingly a matter of barter. This deflationary tendency was periodically offset by the sudden injection of new currency. Private cigarette parcels arrived in a trickle throughout the year, but the big numbers came in quarterly when the Red Cross received its allocation of transport. Several hundred thousand cigarettes might arrive in the space of a fortnight. Prices soared, and then began to fall, slowly at first but with increasing rapidity as stocks ran out, until the next big delivery. Most of our economic troubles could be attributed to this fundamental instability.

Price Movements

Many factors affected prices, the strongest and most noticeable being the periodical currency inflation and deflation described in the last paragraphs. The periodicity of this price cycle depended on cigarette and, to a far lesser extent, on food deliveries. At one time in the early days, before any private parcels had arrived and when there were no individual stocks, the weekly issue of cigarettes and food parcels occurred on a Monday. The nonmonetary demand for cigarettes was great, and less elastic than the demand for food: consequently prices fluctuated weekly, falling towards Sunday night and rising sharply on Monday morning. Later, when many people held reserves, the weekly issue had no such effect, being too small a proportion of the total available. Credit allowed people with no reserves to meet their nonmonetary demand over the week-end.

The general price level was affected by other factors. An influx of new prisoners, proverbially hungry, raised it. Heavy air raids in the vicinity of the camp probably increased the nonmonetary demand for cigarettes and accentuated deflation. Good and bad war news certainly had its effect, and the general waves of optimism and pessimism which swept the camp were reflected in prices. Before breakfast one morning in March of this year, a rumor of the arrival of parcels and cigarettes was circulated. Within ten minutes I sold a treacle ration for four cigarettes (hitherto offered in vain for three), and many similar deals went through. By ten o'clock the rumor was denied, and treacle that day found no more buyers even at two cigarettes.

More interesting than changes in the general price level were changes in the price structure. Changes in the supply of a commodity, in the German ration scale or in the make-up of Red Cross parcels, would raise the price of one commodity relative to others. Tins of oatmeal, once a rare and much sought after luxury in the parcels, became a commonplace in 1943, and the price fell. In hot weather the demand for cocoa fell, and that for soap rose. A new recipe would be reflected in the price level: the discovery that raisins and sugar could be turned into an alcohol liquor of remarkable potency reacted permanently on the dried fruit market. The invention of electric immersion heaters run off the power points made tea, a drug on the market in Italy, a certain seller in Germany.

In August, 1944, the supplies of parcels and cigarettes were both halved. Since both sides of the equation were changed in the same degree, changes in prices were not anticipated. But this was not the case: the nonmonetary demand for cigarettes was less elastic than the demand for food, and food prices fell a little. More important however were the changes in the price structure. German margarine and jam, hitherto valueless owing to adequate supplies of Canadian butter and marmalade, acquired a new value. Chocolate, popular and a certain seller, and sugar, fell. Bread rose; several standing contracts of bread for cigarettes were broken, especially when the bread ration was reduced a few weeks later.

In February, 1945, the German soldier who drove the ration wagon was found to be willing to exchange loaves of bread at the rate of one loaf for a bar of chocolate. Those in the know began selling bread and buying chocolate, by then almost unsalable in a period of serious deflation. Bread, at about forty, fell slightly; chocolate rose from fifteen; the supply of bread was not enough for the two commodities to reach parity, but the tendency was unmistakable.

The substitution of German margarine for Canadian butter when parcels were halved naturally affected their relative values, margarine appreciating at the expense of butter. Similarly, two brands of dried milk, hitherto differing in quality and therefore in price by five cigarettes a tin, came together in price as the wider substitution of the cheaper raised its relative value.

Enough has been cited to show that any change in conditions affected both the general price level and the price structure. It was this latter phenomenon which wrecked our planned economy.

Paper Currency—Bully Marks

Around D-Day, food and cigarettes were plentiful, business was brisk, and the camp in an optimistic mood. Consequently the Entertainments Committee felt the moment opportune to launch a restaurant, where food and hot drinks were sold while a band and variety turns performed. Earlier experiments, both public and private, had pointed the way, and the scheme was a great success. Food was bought at market prices to provide the meals and the small profits were devoted to a reserve fund and used to bribe Germans to provide grease-paints and other necessities for the camp theatre. Originally meals were sold for cigarettes but this meant that the whole scheme was vulnerable to the periodic deflationary waves, and furthermore heavy smokers were unlikely to attend much. The whole success of the scheme depended on an adequate amount of food being offered for sale in the normal manner. To increase and facilitate trade, and to stimulate supplies and customers therefore, and secondarily to avoid the worst effects of deflation when it should come, a paper currency was organized by the Restaurant and the Shop. The Shop bought food on behalf of the Restaurant with paper notes and the paper was accepted equally with the cigarettes in the Restaurant or Shop, and passed back to the Shop to purchase more food. The Shop acted as a bank of issue. The paper money was backed 100 per cent by food; hence its name, the Bully Mark. The BMk. was backed 100 per cent by food: there could be no over-issues, as is permissible with a normal bank of issue, since the eventual dispersal of the camp and consequent redemption of all BMk.s was anticipated in the near future.

Originally one BMk. was worth one cigarette and for a short time both circulated freely inside and outside the Restaurant. Prices were in BMk.s and cigarettes with equal freedom— and for a short time the BMk. showed signs of replacing the cigarette as currency. The BMk. was tied to food, but not to cigarettes: as it was issued against food, say forty-five for a tin of milk and so on, any reduction in the BMk. prices of food would have meant that there were unbacked BMk.s in circulation. But the price of both food and BMk.s could and did fluctuate with the supply of cigarettes.

While the Restaurant flourished, the scheme was a success: the Restaurant bought heavily, all foods were saleable and prices were stable.

In August parcels and cigarettes were halved and the camp was bombed. The Restaurant closed for a short while and sales of food became difficult. Even when the Restaurant reopened, the food and cigarette shortage became increasingly acute and people were unwilling to convert such valuable goods into paper and to hold them for luxuries like snacks and tea. Less of the right kinds of food for the Restaurant were sold, and the Shop became glutted with dried fruit, chocolate, sugar, and so forth, which the Restaurant could not buy. The price level and the price structure changed. The BMk. fell to four-fifths of a cigarette and eventually farther still, and it became unacceptable save in the Restaurant. There was a flight from the BMk., no longer convertible into cigarettes or popular foods. The cigarette re-established itself.

But the BMk. was sound! The Restaurant closed in the New Year with a progressive food shortage and the long evenings without lights due to intensified Allied air raids, and BMk.s could only be spent in the Coffee Bar—relict of the Restaurant—or on the few unpopular foods in the Shop, the owners of which were prepared to accept them. In the end all holders of BMk.s were paid in full, in cups of coffee or in prunes. People who had bought BMk.s for cigarettes or valuable jam or biscuits in their heyday were grieved that they should have stood the loss involved by their restricted choice, but they suffered no actual loss of market value.

Price Fixing

Along with this scheme came a determined attempt at a planned economy, at price fixing. The Medical Officer had long been anxious to control food sales, for fear of some people selling too much, to the detriment of their health. The deflationary waves and their effects on prices were inconvenient to all and would be dangerous to the Restaurant which had to carry stocks. Furthermore, unless the BMk. was convertible into cigarettes at about par it had little chance of gaining confidence and of succeeding as a currency. As has been explained, the BMk. was tied to food but could not be tied to cigarettes, which fluctuated in value. Hence, while BMk. prices of food were fixed for all time, cigarette prices of food and BMk.s varied.

The Shop, backed by the Senior British Officer, was now in a position to enforce price control both inside and outside its walls. Hitherto a standard price had been fixed for food left for sale in the Shop, and prices outside were roughly in conformity with this scale, which was recommended as a "guide" to sellers, but fluctuated a good deal around it. Sales in the Shop at recommended prices were apt to be slow though a good price might be obtained: sales outside could be made more quickly at lower prices. (If sales outside were to be at higher prices, goods were withdrawn from the Shop until the recommended price rose: but the recommended price was sluggish and could not follow the market closely by reason of its very purpose, which was stability.) The Exchange and Mart notice boards came under the control of the Shop: advertisements which exceeded a 5 per cent departure from the recommended scale were liable to be crossed out by authority: unauthorized sales were discouraged by authority and also by public opinion, strongly in favor of a just and stable price. (Recommended prices were fixed partly from market data, partly on the advice of the Medical Officer.)

At first the recommended scale was a success: the Restaurant, a big buyer, kept prices stable around this level: opinion and the 5 per cent tolerance helped. But when the price level fell with the August cuts and the price structure changed, the recommended scale was too rigid. Unchanged at first, as no deflation was expected, the scale was tardily lowered, but the prices of goods on the new scale remained in the same relation to one another, owing to the BMk., while on the market the price structure had changed. And the modifying influence of the Restaurant had gone. The scale was moved up and down several times, slowly following the inflationary and deflationary waves, but it was rarely adjusted to changes in the price structure. More and more advertisements were crossed off the board, and black market sales at unauthorized prices increased: eventually public opinion turned against the recommended scale and authority gave up the struggle. In the last few weeks, with unparalleled deflation, prices fell with alarming rapidity, no scales existed and supply and demand, alone and unmellowed, determined prices.

Public Opinion

Public opinion on the subject of trading was vocal if confused and changeable, and generalizations as to its direction are difficult and dangerous. A tiny minority held that all trading was undesirable as it engendered an unsavory atmosphere; occasional frauds and sharp practices were cited as proof. Certain forms of trading were more generally condemned; trade with the Germans was criticized by many. Red Cross toilet articles, which were in short supply and only issued in cases of actual need, were excluded from trade by law and opinion working in unshakable harmony. At one time, when there had been several cases of malnutrition reported among the more devoted smokers, no trade in German rations was permitted, as the victims became an additional burden on the depleted food reserves of the Hospital. But while certain activities were condemned as anti-social, trade itself was practiced, and its utility appreciated, by almost everyone in the camp.

More interesting was opinion on middlemen and prices. Taken as a whole, opinion was hostile to the middleman. His function, and his hard work in bringing buyer and seller together, were ignored; profits were not regarded as a reward for labor, but as the result of sharp practice. Despite the fact that his very existence was proof to the contrary, the middleman was held to be redundant in view of the existence of an official Shop and the Exchange and Mart. Appreciation only came his way when he was willing to advance the price of a sugar ration, or to buy goods spot and carry them against a future sale. In these cases the element of risk was obvious to all, and the convenience of the service was felt to merit some reward. Particularly unpopular was the middleman with an element of monopoly, the man who contacted the ration wagon driver, or the man who utilized his knowledge of Urdu. And middlemen as a group were blamed for reducing prices. Opinion notwithstanding, most people dealt with a middleman, whether consciously or unconsciously, at some time or another.

There was a strong feeling that everything had its "just price" in cigarettes. While the assessment of the just price, which incidentally varied between camps, was impossible of explanation, this price was nevertheless pretty closely known. It can best be defined as the price usually fetched by an article in good times when cigarettes were plentiful. The "just price" changed slowly; it was unaffected by short-term variations in supply, and while opinion might be resigned to departures from the "just price," a strong feeling of resentment persisted. A more satisfactory definition of the "just price" is impossible. Everyone knew what it was, though no one could explain why it should be so.

As soon as prices began to fall with a cigarette shortage, a clamor arose, particularly against those who held reserves and who bought at reduced prices. Sellers at cut prices were criticized and their activities referred to as the black market. In every period of dearth the explosive question of "should nonsmokers receive a cigarette ration?" was discussed to profitless length. Unfortunately, it was the nonsmoker, or the light smoker with his reserves, along with the hated middleman, who weathered the storm most easily.

The popularity of the price-fixing scheme, and such success as it enjoyed, were undoubtedly the result of this body of opinion. On several occasions the fall of prices was delayed by the general support given to the recommended scale. The onset of deflation was marked by a period of sluggish trade; prices stayed up but no one bought. Then prices fell on the black market, and the volume of trade revived in that quarter. Even when the recommended scale was revised, the volume of trade in the Shop would remain low. Opinion was always overruled by the hard facts of the market.

Curious arguments were advanced to justify price fixings. The recommended prices were in some way related to the calorific values of the foods offered: hence some were overvalued and never sold at these prices. One argument ran as follows: not everyone has private cigarette parcels: thus, when prices were high and trade good in the summer of 1944, only the lucky rich could buy. This was unfair to the man with few cigarettes. When prices fell in the following winter, prices should be pegged high so that the rich, who had enjoyed life in the summer, should put many cigarettes into circulation. The fact that those who sold to the rich in the summer had also enjoyed life then, and the fact that in the winter there was always someone willing to sell at low prices were ignored. Such arguments were hotly debated each night after the approach of Allied aircraft extinguished all lights at 8 p.m. But prices moved with the supply of cigarettes, and refused to stay fixed in accordance with a theory of ethics.

Conclusion

The economic organization described was both elaborate and smooth-working in the summer of 1944. Then came the August cuts and deflation. Prices fell, rallied with deliveries of cigarette parcels in September and December, and fell again. In January, 1945, supplies of Red Cross cigarettes ran out: and prices slumped still further: in February the supplies of food parcels were exhausted and the depression became a blizzard. Food, itself scarce, was almost given away in order to meet the nonmonetary demand for cigarettes. Laundries ceased to operate, or worked for £s or RMk.s: food and cigarettes sold for fancy prices in £s, hitherto unheard of. The Restaurant was a memory and the BMk. a joke. The Shop was empty and the Exchange Mart notices were full of unaccepted offers for cigarettes. Barter increased in volume, becoming a larger proportion of a small volume of trade. This, the first serious and prolonged food shortage in the writer's experience, caused the price structure to change again, partly because German rations were not easily divisible. A margarine ration gradually sank in value until it exchanged directly for a treacle ration. Sugar slumped sadly. Only bread retained its value. Several thousand cigarettes, the capital of the Shop, were distributed without any noticeable effect. A few fractional parcel and cigarette issues, such as one-sixth of a parcel and twelve cigarettes each, led to momentary price recoveries and feverish trade, especially when they coincided with good news from the Western Front, but the general position remained unaltered.

By April, 1945, chaos had replaced order in the economic sphere: sales were difficult, prices lacked stability. Economics has been defined as the science of distributing limited means among unlimited and competing ends. On April 12th, with the arrival of elements of the 30th U.S. Infantry Division, the ushering in of an age of plenty demonstrated the hypothesis that with infinite means economic organization and activity would be redundant, as every want could be satisfied without effort.

Bertrand de Jouvenel
(1903-1987)

Bertrand de Jouvenel was a French philosopher and economist who played a role in a variety of debates. Here, in another classic teaching article, he describes the effects of rent control in Paris. The money amounts, which are given in dollars rather than French francs, are 1948 dollars. If they were updated to current-day dollars, the prices would still be extremely low.

Bertrand de Jouvenel. 1948. "No Vacancies," in *The Reader's Digest Condensation*. Irvington-on-Hudson, New York: The Foundation for Economic Education, pp. 33-46.

Rent Control: An Example of Price Fixing

A dollar a month pays a wage-earner's rent in Paris; quarters adequate for a family of six cost $2 (equivalent to eleven packages of the cheapest cigarettes) Middle-class apartments of three or four main rooms frequently cost from $1.50 to $2.50 per month. Important officials or executives pay from $3.50 a month to $8 or $10 a month.

This may seem a desirable state of affairs, but there are drawbacks. There are no vacant lodgings; nor is anyone going to vacate, nor can the owners expel anyone. Young couples must live with in-laws. . . .

The only opportunity to get quarters is to watch for deaths. Tottering old people sunning themselves in public gardens are shadowed back to their flat by an eager young wife who strikes a bargain with the *concierge* to be first in at the death. Other apartment-chasers have an understanding with funeral parlors.

There are two ways of obtaining an apartment made available by death. Legally, if you fulfill certain conditions which give you priority, you may obtain an order of requisition, but usually you find that the same order for the same apartment has been given to two or three other applicants. The illegal method is the surest—an arrangement with the heir that some pieces of your furniture be carried in immediately upon death of the tenant. As soon as you are in, you are the king of the castle.

Buying one's way into an apartment will cost anything from $500 to $1,500 per room. Wage-earners might as well give up hope of setting up house; they have to stay with their families or live in miserable hotels.

Paris has 84,000 buildings for habitation, almost 90 per cent of them built before World War I. Even a very lenient officialdom estimates that 16,000 are in such disrepair that they should be pulled down. Nor are the others altogether satisfactory; 82 per cent of Parisians have no bath, more than half must go out of their lodgings to find a lavatory, and a fifth do not even have running water. Little more than one in six of the existing buildings is pronounced in good condition by the public inspectors.

Owners are not financially able to keep up their buildings, let alone improve them. To take an example of a very common situation, there is a woman who owns three buildings containing thirty-four apartments, all inhabited by middle-class families. Her net loss from the thirty-four apartments, after taxes and repairs, is $80 per year. Not only must her son take care of her, but he must also pay out the $80. She cannot sell; there are no buyers.

When the owner tries to milk a little net income from his property by cutting down the repairs, he runs great risks. One landlord postponed repairs on his roofs and rain filtering into an apartment spoiled a couple of armchairs. He was sued for damages and condemned to pay a sum amounting to three years of the tenant's paltry rent. Since 1914, rents at the most have multiplied 6.8 times, while taxes have multiplied 13.2 times, and repairs cost from 120 to 150 times the 1914 price!

INTRODUCTION

An outsider may be tempted to think that only an incredible amount of folly can have led us to this condition. But it is not so. We got there by easy, almost unnoticed stages, slipping down on the gentle slope of rent control. And this was not the work of the Reds but of succeeding governments, most of which were considered rather conservative.

The story starts with World War I. It then seemed humane and reasonable to stabilize housing costs while the boys were in the Army or working for victory. So existing rentals were frozen. It was also reasonable to avoid disturbances at the end of the war lest the veterans' homecoming be spoiled by evictions and rent increases. Thus prewar situations hardened into rights. The owner lost—"temporarily," of course—the disposition of his property.

When the situation was reviewed in 1926, retail prices had trebled, and it was plain that lifting controls would bring huge rent increases. The legislators shrunk from this crisis and decided to confirm the tenants' right to stay in possession but to raise rents slightly. A new owner-tenant relationship thus took shape. The owner was powerless either to evict the tenant or to discuss the rent with him. The State took care of the price, which rose slowly, while regulation was extended to bring in flats not previously regulated. Only buildings put up since 1915 were left unregulated, this to stimulate construction.

No systematic view inspired this policy. It just grew from the fear of a sudden return to liberty, which seemed ever more dangerous as prices stepped up. And, of course, if one must control the price of rent, one could not allow the owner to dismiss tenants, because in that case he might so easily have stipulated secretly with the new tenants.

As rent-control law making continued—no single subject has taken up so much of the time and energy of Parliament—the real income from buildings crumbled from year to year. Then came World War II. The return to liberty which had been devised for 1943 was, of course, abandoned, and all rents were frozen, including those of recent buildings, which had till then escaped.

Since the Liberation, new laws have provided for increases in rents, but retail prices increased much more. To put it briefly, owners of new buildings (built since 1914) have been allowed, in terms of real income, less than a tenth of what they got before World War II. Owners of old buildings, that is, nine-tenths of all buildings, have been allowed in terms of real income either 12 per cent of what they got in 1939 or a little less than 7 per cent of what they got in 1914—whichever is less.

If today a builder were to put up apartments, they would have to rent for prices from ten to thirteen times present rent ceilings, in order to break even. Thus, according to a report of the Economic Council, a wage-earner's apartment of three small rooms and a kitchen now renting for $13 to $16 a year (!) would have to be rented for $166 to $200 a year. Obviously, construction will not be undertaken.

Such is the spread between the legal and the economic price of lodgings that even the most fervent advocates of freedom shudder at the thought of its return; the thing, they say, has gone too far and the right to dismiss tenants, if restored, could not be executed. The whole nation of tenants would go on a sit-down strike.

* * * *

The French example may prove of some interest and use to our friends across the sea. It goes to show that rent control is self-perpetuating and culminates in both the physical ruin of housing and the legal dispossession of the owners. The havoc wrought in France is not the work of the enemy, but is the result of our own measures.

Karl Marx and Friedrich Engels

(Marx: 1818-1883)
(Engels: 1820-1895)

Karl Marx is probably the most famous critic of economics, and his legacy changed the course of history. Born in Germany, he moved to England because of political persecution and failure to find a job at home. He could not find a job in Britain either, but with the help of the industrialist Friedrich Engels (another German who was living in Britain), he managed to keep enough money coming in so he could continue his research and writing.

Friedrich Engels was a German who worked in England for his father's international textile business. He became interested in the condition of the working people of the 1840s and this led him to Marx. Engels collaborated with Marx on The Communist Manifesto *(as it is usually referred to) and on other writings—he finished Marx's* Das Kapital *(Capital), which was incomplete at Marx's death.*

In The Communist Manifesto, *Marx and Engels survey history, arguing that it is a history of class antagonisms. Then they argue that the proletariat—workers—will become the ruling class under a new economic system—communism. The selection below ends with one of the most famous cries in all literature: "The proletarians have nothing to lose but their chains. They have a world to win. Working men of all countries, unite!"*

This selection was written in German and translated into English in 1850. This accounts for any awkward grammar and syntax you may notice. One verb that is correctly used for 1848 but is rarely seen in this usage today is "to exercise" (in the first paragraph), meaning "to harass, vex, or worry."

Karl Marx and Friedrich Engels. 1848 (published in German in 1848; first English translation in 1850). *The Manifesto of the Communist Party.*

Selections from "Manifesto of the Communist Party"

A spectre is haunting Europe—the spectre of Communism. All the Powers of old Europe have centered into a Holy Alliance to exercise this spectre; Pope and Czar, Metternich and Guizot, French Radicals and German police-spies.

Where is the party in opposition that has not been decried as communistic by its opponents in power? Where the opposition that has not hurled back the branding reproach of Communism against the more advanced opposition parties, as well as against its reactionary adversaries?

Two things result from this fact.

I.   Communism is already acknowledged by all European Powers to be itself a Power.

II. It is high time that Communists should openly, in the face of the whole world, publish their views, their aims, their tendencies, and meet this nursery tale of the Spectre of Communism with a Manifesto of the party itself.

To this end, Communists of various nationalities have assembled in London and sketched the following Manifesto, to be published in the English, French, German, Italian, Flemish, and Danish languages.

INTRODUCTION

I. Bourgeois and Proletarians

The history of all hitherto existing society is the history of class struggles.

Freeman and slave, patrician and plebeian, lord and serf, guild-master and journeyman, in a word, oppressor and oppressed, stood in constant opposition to one another, carried on uninterrupted, now hidden, now open fight, a fight that each time ended, either in a revolutionary reconstitution of society at large, or in the common ruin of the contending classes.

In the earlier epochs of history we find almost everywhere a complicated arrangement of society into various orders, a manifold gradation of social rank. In ancient Rome we have patricians, knights, plebeians, slaves; in the middle ages, feudal lords, vassals, guild-masters, journeymen, apprentices, serfs; in almost all of these classes, again, subordinate gradations.

The modern bourgeois society that has sprouted from the ruins of feudal society has not done away with class antagonisms. It has but established new classes, new conditions of oppression, new forms of struggle in place of the old ones.

Our epoch, the epoch of the bourgeoisie, possesses, however, this distinctive feature; it has simplified the class antagonisms. Society as a whole is more and more splitting up into two great hostile camps, into two great classes directly facing each other: Bourgeoisie and Proletariat.

From the serfs of the Middle Ages sprang the chartered burghers of the earliest towns. From these burgesses the first elements of the bourgeoisie were developed.

The discovery of America, the rounding of the Cape, opened up fresh ground for the rising bourgeoisie. The East Indian and Chinese markets, the colonization of America, trade with the colonies, the increase in the means of exchange and in commodities generally, gave to commerce, to navigation, to industry, an impulse never before known, and thereby, to the revolutionary element in the tottering feudal society, a rapid development.

The feudal system of industry, under which industrial production was monopolized by close guilds, now no longer sufficed for the growing wants of the new market. The manufacturing system took its place. The guild-masters were pushed on one side by the manufacturing middle class; division of labor between the different corporate guilds vanished in the face of division of labor in each single workshop.

Meantime the markets kept ever growing, the demand ever rising. Even manufacture no longer sufficed. Thereupon, steam and machinery revolutionized industrial production. The place of manufacture was taken by the giant Modern Industry, the place of the industrial middle class, by industrial millionaires, the leaders of whole industrial armies, the modern bourgeois.

Modern industry has established the world-market, for which the discovery of America paved the way. This market has given an immense development to commerce, to nagivation, to communication by land. This development has, in its turn, reacted on the extension of industry; and in proportion as industry, commerce, navigation, railways extended, in the same proportion the bourgeoisie developed, increased its capital, and pushed into the background every class handed down from the Middle Ages.

We see, therefore, how the modern bourgeoisie is itself the product of a long course of development, of a series of revolutions in the modes of production and of exchange. . . .

The charges against Communism made from a religious, a philosophical, and generally, from an ideological standpoint, are not deserving of serious examination.

Does it require deep intuition to comprehend that man's ideas, views, and conceptions, in one word, man's consciousness, changes with every change in the conditions of his material existence, in his social relations, and in his social life?

What else does the history of ideas prove than that intellectual production changes in character in proportion as material production is changed? The ruling ideas of each age have ever been the ideas of its ruling class.

When people speak of ideas that revolutionize society they do but express the fact that within the old society the elements of a new one have been created, and that the dissolution of the old ideas keeps even pace with the dissolution of the old conditions of existence.

When the ancient world was in its last throes the ancient religions were overcome by Christianity. When Christian ideas succumbed in the eighteenth century to rationalist ideas, feudal society fought its death-battle with the then revolutionary bourgeoisie. The ideas of religious liberty and freedom of conscience merely gave expression to the sway of free competition within the domain of knowledge.

"Undoubtedly," it will be said, "religious, moral, philosophical, and judicial ideas have been modified in the course of historical development. But religion, morality, philosophy, political science, and law, constantly survived this change."

"There are, besides, eternal truths, such as Freedom, Justice, and so forth, that are common to all states of society. But Communism abolishes eternal truth, it abolishes all religion and all morality, instead of constituting them on a new basis; it therefore acts in contradiction to all past historical experience."

What does this accusation reduce itself to? The history of all past society has consisted in the development of class antagonisms, antagonisms that assumed different forms at different epochs.

But whatever form they may have taken, one fact is common to all past ages—namely, the exploitation of one part of society by the other. No wonder, then, that the social consciousness of past ages, despite all the multiplicity and variety it displays, moves within certain common forms, or general ideas, which cannot completely vanish except with the total disappearance of class antagonisms.

The Communist revolution is the most radical rupture with traditional property-relations; no wonder that its development involves the most radical rupture with traditional ideas.

But let us have done with the bourgeois objections to Communism.

We have seen above that the first step in the revolution by the working class is to raise the proletariat to the position of ruling class, to win the battle of democracy.

The proletariat will use its political supremacy to wrest, by degrees, all capital from the bourgeoisie, to centralize all instruments of production in the hands of the state,—that is, of the proletariat organized as a ruling class; and to increase the total productive forces as rapidly as possible.

Of course, in the beginning, this cannot be effected except by means of despotic inroads on the rights of property, and on the conditions of bourgeois production; by means of measures, therefore, which appear economically insufficient and untenable, but which in the course of movement outstrip themselves, necessitate further inroads upon the old social order, and are unavoidable as a means of entirely revolutionizing the mode of production.

These measures will of course be different in different countries.

Nevertheless in the most advanced countries the following will be pretty generally applicable:

1. Abolition of property in land and application of all rents of land to public purposes.
2. A heavy progressive or graduated income tax.
3. Abolition of all right of inheritance.
4. Confiscation of the property of all emigrants and rebels.
5. Centralization of credit in the hands of the state, by means of a national bank with state capital and an exclusive monopoly.
6. Centralization of the means of communication and transport in the hands of the state.
7. Extension of factories and instruments of production owned by the state; the bringing into cultivation of waste lands, and the improvement of the soil generally in accordance with a common plan.
8. Equal liability of all to labor. Establishment of industrial armies, especially for agriculture.

9. Combination of agriculture with manufacturing industries; gradual abolition of the distinction between town and country by a more equable distribution of the population over the country.
10. Free education for all children in public schools. Abolition of children's factory labor in its present form. Combination of education with industrial production, and so forth.

When, in the course of development, class distinctions have disappeared, and all production has been concentrated in the hands of a vast association of the whole nation, the public power will lose its political character. Political power, properly so called, is merely the organization power of one class for oppressing another. If the proletariat during its contest with the bourgeoisie is compelled, by the force of circumstances, to organize itself as a class, if, by means of a revolution, it makes itself the ruling class, and, as such, sweeps away by force the old conditions of production, then it will, along with these conditions, have swept away the conditions for the existence of class antagonisms, and of classes generally, and will thereby have abolished its own supremacy as a class.

In place of the old bourgeois society, with its classes and class antagonisms, we shall have an association in which the free development of each is the condition for the free development of all. . . .

In short, the Communists everywhere support every revolutionary movement against the existing social and political order of things.

In all these movements they bring to the front, as the leading question in each, the property question, no matter what its degree of development at the time.

Finally, they labor everywhere for the union and agreement of the democratic parties of all countries.

The Communists disdain to conceal their views and aims. They openly declare that their ends can be attained only by the forcible overthrow of all existing social conditions. Let the ruling classes tremble at a Communistic revolution. The proletarians have nothing to lose but their chains. They have a world to win.

Working men of all countries, unite!

F. A. Hayek
(1898-1992)

F. A. Hayek is probably the most well known member of the "Austrian" school of economics. He was born in Austria but spent much of his life in England, where he taught at the London School of Economics for nearly twenty years, and in the United States, where he became a professor of economics at the University of Chicago in 1950. In 1974 he, together with Gunnar Myrdal of Sweden, won the Nobel Prize in economics.

Hayek played central roles in a variety of debates, including those focusing on socialism and planning and on Keynesian economics. His Road to Serfdom *(1944) became a classic as soon as it was written, although it was a forgotten classic for a number of years after that. In the 1970s Hayek's ideas made a comeback and attracted a large following among the Austrian school of economists.*

With the fall of communism in Eastern Europe, the demand for Hayek's Road to Serfdom *increased enormously, and in the early 1990s it was often considered the most-desired book in Eastern Europe. Although Hayek has often been viewed by the popular press as an ultraconservative and a pure laissez-faire economist, he is far more complicated than that. His work emphasizes the role of law and legal structures—what we call the invisible handshake—as central to the operation of an economy. He contends that markets, as well as a respect for tradition and laws, are absolutely essential to keep the political power of the state from becoming too large.*

This selection from The Road to Serfdom *gives one a good sense of his views on economic problems, on the role of the individual, and on the need for markets in an economy. In it, he argues that the debate between "planners" and liberals such as himself is not about planning, but instead is about the type of planning. Liberals want a guiding plan that makes use of the economic forces and competition. Unfortunately, he argues, planning cannot be done in small measures, and once one has started down that road, one is on the road to serfdom.*

F. A. Hayek. 1944. *The Road to Serfdom*. Chicago: University of Chicago Press, pp. 34-38, 41-42.

Individualism and Collectivism

The socialists believe in two things which are absolutely different and perhaps even contradictory: freedom and organization.—Élie Halévy.

* * * *

"Planning" owes its popularity largely to the fact that everybody desires, of course, that we should handle our common problems as rationally as possible and that, in so doing, we should use as much foresight as we can command. In this sense everybody who is not a complete fatalist is a planner, every political act is (or ought to be) an act of planning, and there can be differences only between good and bad, between wise and foresighted and foolish and short-sighted planning. An economist, whose whole task is the study of how men actually do and how they might plan their affairs, is the last person who could object to planning in this general sense. But it is not in this sense that our enthusiasts for a planned society now employ this term, nor merely in this sense that we must plan if we want the distribution of income or wealth to conform to some particular standard. According to the modern planners, and for their purposes, it is not sufficient to design the most rational permanent framework within which the various activities would be conducted by different persons according to their individual plans. This liberal plan, according to them, is no plan—and it is, indeed, not a plan designed to satisfy particular views about who should have what. What our planners demand is a central direction of all economic activity according to a single plan, laying down how the resources of society should be "consciously directed" to serve particular ends in a definite way.

The dispute between the modern planners and their opponents is, therefore, *not* a dispute on whether we ought to choose intelligently between the various possible organizations of society; it is not a dispute on whether we ought to employ foresight and systematic thinking in planning our common affairs. It is a dispute about what is the best way of so doing. The question is whether for this purpose it is better that the holder of coercive power should confine himself in general to creating conditions under which the knowledge and initiative of individuals are given the best scope so that *they* can plan most successfully; or whether a rational utilization of our resources requires *central* direction and organization of all our activities according to some consciously constructed "blueprint." The socialists of all parties have appropriated the term "planning" for planning of the latter type, and it is now generally accepted in this sense. But though this is meant to suggest that this is the only rational way of handling our affairs, it does not, of course, prove this. It remains the point on which the planners and the liberals disagree.

It is important not to confuse opposition against this kind of planning with a dogmatic laissez faire attitude. The liberal argument is in favor of making the best possible use of the forces of competition as a means of co-ordinating human efforts, not an argument for leaving things just as they are. It is based on the conviction that, where effective competition can be created, it is a better way of guiding individual efforts than any other. It does not deny, but even emphasizes, that, in order that competition should work beneficially, a carefully thought-out legal framework is required and that neither the existing nor the past legal rules are free from grave defects. Nor does it deny that, where it is impossible to create the conditions necessary to make competition effective, we must resort to other methods of guiding economic activity. Economic liberalism is opposed, however, to competition's being supplanted by inferior methods of co-ordinating individual efforts. And it regards competition as superior not only because it is in most circumstances the most efficient method known but even more because it is the only method by which our activities can be adjusted to each other without coercive or arbitrary intervention of authority. Indeed, one of the main arguments in favor of competition is that it dispenses with the need for "conscious social control" and that it gives the individuals a chance to decide whether the prospects of a particular occupation are sufficient to compensate for the disadvantages and risks connected with it.

The successful use of competition as the principle of social organization precludes certain types of coercive interference with economic life, but it admits of others which sometimes may very considerably assist its work and even requires certain kinds of government action. But there is good reason why the negative requirements, the points where coercion must not be used, have been particularly stressed. It is necessary in the first instance that the parties in the market should be free to sell and buy at any price at which they can find a partner to the transaction and that anybody should be free to produce, sell, and buy anything that may be produced or sold at all. And it is essential that the entry into the different trades should be open to all on equal terms and that the law should not tolerate any attempts by individuals or groups to restrict this entry by open or concealed force. Any attempt to control prices or quantities of particular commodities deprives competition of its power of bringing about an effective co-ordination of individual efforts, because price changes then cease to register all the relevant changes in circumstances and no longer provide a reliable guide for the individual's actions.

This is not necessarily true, however, of measures merely restricting the allowed methods of production, so long as these restrictions affect all potential producers equally and are not used as an indirect way of controlling prices and quantities. Though all such controls of the methods or production impose extra costs (i.e., make it necessary to use more resources to produce a given output), they may be well worth while. To prohibit the use of certain poisonous substances or to require special precautions in their use, to limit working hours or to require certain sanitary arrangements, is fully compatible with the preservation of competition. The only question here is whether in the particular instance the advantages gained are greater than the social costs which they impose. Nor is the preservation of competition incompatible with an extensive system of social services—so long as the organization of these services is not designed in such a way as to make competition ineffective over wide fields.

It is regrettable, though not difficult to explain, that in the past much less attention has been given to the positive requirements of a successful working of the competitive system than to these negative points. The functioning of a competition not only requires adequate organization of certain institutions like money, markets, and channels of information—some of which can never be adequately provided by private enterprise but it depends, above all, on the existence of an appropriate legal system, a legal system designed both to preserve competition and to make it operate as beneficially as possible. It is by no means sufficient that the law should recognize the principle of private property and freedom of contract; much depends on the precise definition of the right of property as applied to different things. The systematic study of the forms of legal institutions which will make the competitive system work efficiently has been sadly neglected; and strong arguments can be advanced that serious shortcomings here, particularly with regard to the law of corporations and of patents, not only have made competition work much less effectively than it might have done but have even led to the destruction of competition in many spheres.

* * * *

The idea of complete centralization of the direction of economic activity still appalls most people, not only because of the stupendous difficulty of the task, but even more because of the horror inspired by the idea of everything being directed from a single center. If we are, nevertheless, rapidly moving toward such a state, this is largely because most people still believe that it is must be possible to find some middle way between "atomistic" competition and central direction. Nothing, indeed, seems at first more plausible, or is more likely to appeal to reasonable people, than the idea that our goal must be neither the extreme decentralization of free competition nor the complete centralization of a single plan but some judicious mixture of the two methods. Yet mere common sense proves a treacherous guide in this field. Although competition can bear some admixture of regulation, it cannot be combined with planning to any extent we like without ceasing to operate as an effective guide to production. Nor is "planning" a medicine which, taken in small doses, can produce the effects for which one might hope from its thoroughgoing application. Both competition and central direction become poor and inefficient tools if they are incomplete; they are alternative principles used to solve the same problem, and a mixture of the two means that neither will really work and that the result will be worse than if either system had been consistently relied upon. Or, to express it differently, planning and competition can be combined only by planning for competition but not by planning against competition.

It is of the utmost importance to the argument of this book for the reader to keep in mind that the planning against which all our criticism is directed is solely the planning against competition—the planning which is to be substituted for competition. This is the more important, as we cannot, within the scope of this book, enter into a discussion of the very necessary planning which is required to make competition as effective and beneficial as possible. But as in current usage "planning" has become almost synonymous with the former kind of planning, it will sometimes be inevitable for the sake of brevity to refer to it simply as planning, even though this means leaving to our opponents a very good word meriting a better fate.

Joseph Schumpeter

(1883-1950)

Joseph Schumpeter was a wide-ranging economist who wrote with a broad brush about economic systems. He was born in Czechoslovakia but spent much of his life in the United States. Except for the period 1919-20 when he was Austria's minister of finance, he was a professor of economics, teaching at various universities, including Harvard from 1932 until the end of his life.

A scholar whose interests encompassed many fields, not just economics, he once said that he was the best of his time in two of the following three categories: horseman, economist, lover. In which two of the three was he the best? He always left this decision to his audience.

His Capitalism, Socialism, and Democracy, *first published in 1942, is one of the most popular economics books. In this selection he argues that capitalism, by its own success, will undermine its dynamic—entrepreneurship—and that the true "pacemakers of socialism were not the intellectuals or agitators who preached it but the [giant industrialists] Vanderbilts, Carnegies and Rockefellers."*

Joseph Schumpeter. 1942 (3rd edition: 1950). *Capitalism, Socialism, and Democracy.* New York: Harper Torchbooks, Harper and Row Publishers, pp. 132-34, 141-42, 150-51, 417-18.

Can Capitalism Survive?

We have seen that the function of entrepreneurs is to reform or revolutionize the pattern of production by exploiting an invention or, more generally, an untried technological possibility for producing a new commodity or producing an old one in a new way, by opening up a new source of supply of materials or a new outlet for products, by reorganizing an industry and so on. Railroad construction in its earlier stages, electrical power production before the First World War, steam and steel, the motorcar, colonial ventures afford spectacular instances of a large genus which comprises innumerable humbler ones —down to such things as making a success of a particular kind of sausage or toothbrush. This kind of activity is primarily responsible for the recurrent "prosperities" that revolutionize the economic organism and the recurrent "recessions" that are due to the disequilibrating impact of the new products or methods. To undertake such new things is difficult and constitutes a distinct economic function, first, because they lie outside of the routine tasks which everybody understands and, secondly, because the environment resists in many ways that vary, according to social conditions, from simple refusal either to finance or to buy a new thing, to physical attack on the man who tries to produce it. To act with confidence beyond the range of familiar beacons and to overcome that resistance requires aptitudes that are present in only a small fraction of the population and that define the entrepreneurial type as well as the entrepreneurial function. This function does not essentially consist in either inventing anything or otherwise creating the conditions which the enterprise exploits. It consists in getting things done.

This social function is already losing importance and is bound to lose it at an accelerating rate in the future even if the economic process itself of which entrepreneurship was the prime mover went on unabated. For, on the one hand, it is much easier now than it has been in the past to do things that lie outside familiar routine—innovation itself is being reduced to routine. Technological progress is increasingly becoming the business of teams of trained specialists who turn out what is required and make it work in predictable ways. The romance of earlier commercial adventure is rapidly wearing away, because so many more things can be strictly calculated that had of old to be visualized in a flash of genius.

On the other hand, personality and will power must count for less in environments which have become accustomed to economic change—best instanced by an incessant stream of new consumers' and producers' goods—and which, instead of resisting, accept it as a matter of course. The resistance which comes from interests threatened by an innovation in the productive process is not likely to die out as long as the capitalist order persists. It is, for instance, the great obstacle on the road toward mass production of cheap housing which presupposes radical mechanization and wholesale elimination of inefficient methods of work on the plot. But every other kind of resistance—the resistance, in particular, of consumers and producers to a new kind of thing because it is new—has well-nigh vanished already.

Thus, economic progress tends to become depersonalized and automatized. Bureau and committee work tends to replace individual action. . . . [R]eference to the military analogy will help to bring out the essential point.

Of old, roughly up to and including the Napoleonic Wars [1803-1815], generalship meant leadership and success meant the personal success of the man in command who earned corresponding "profits" in terms of social prestige. The technique of warfare and the structure of armies being what they were, the individual decision and driving power of the leading man—even his actual presence on a showy horse—were essential elements in the strategical and tactical situations. Napoleon's presence was, and had to be, actually felt on his battlefields. This is no longer so. Rationalized and specialized office work will eventually blot out personality, the calculable result, the "vision." The leading man no longer has the opportunity to fling himself into the fray. He is becoming just another office worker—and one who is not always difficult to replace.

Or take another military analogy. Warfare in the Middle Ages was a very personal affair. The armored knights practiced an art that required lifelong training and every one of them counted individually by virtue of personal skill and prowess. It is easy to understand why this craft should have become the basis of a social class in the fullest and richest sense of that term. But social and technological change undermined and eventually destroyed both the function and the position of that class. Warfare itself did not cease on that account. It simply became more and more mechanized—eventually so much so that success in what now is a mere profession no longer carries that connotation of individual achievement which would raise not only the man but also his group into a durable position of social leadership.

Now a similar social process—in the last analysis the same social process—undermines the role and, along with the role, the social position of the capitalist entrepreneur. His role, though less glamorous than that of medieval warlords, great or small, also is or was just another form of individual leadership acting by virtue of personal force and personal responsibility for success. His position, like that of warrior classes, is threatened as soon as this function in the social process loses its importance, and no less if this is due to the cessation of the social needs it served than if those needs are being served by other, more impersonal, methods.

But this affects the position of the entire bourgeois stratum. Although entrepreneurs are not necessarily or even typically elements of that stratum from the outset, they nevertheless enter it in case of success. Thus, though entrepreneurs do not *per se* form a social class, the bourgeois class absorbs them and their families and connections, thereby recruiting and revitalizing itself currently while at the same time the families that sever their active relation to "business" drop out of it after a generation or two. Between, there is the bulk of what we refer to as industrialists, merchants, financiers and bankers; they are in the intermediate stage between entrepreneurial venture and mere current administration of an inherited domain. The returns on which the class lives are produced by, and the social position of the class rests on, the success of this more or less active sector—which of course may, as it does in this country, form over 90 per cent of the bourgeois stratum—and of the individuals who are in the act of rising into that class. Economically and sociologically, directly and indirectly, the bourgeoisie therefore depends on the entrepreneur and, as a class, lives and will die with him, though a more or less prolonged transitional stage—eventually a stage in which it may feel equally unable to die and to live—is quite likely to occur, as in fact it did occur in the case of the feudal civilization.

To sum up this part of our argument: if capitalist evolution—"progress"—either ceases or becomes completely automatic, the economic basis of the industrial bourgeoisie will be reduced eventually to wages such as are paid for current administrative work excepting remnants of quasi-rents and monopoloid gains that may be expected to linger on for some time. Since capitalist enterprise, by its very achievements, tends to automatize progress, we conclude that it tends to make itself superfluous—to break to pieces under the pressure of its own success. The perfectly bureaucratized giant industrial unit not only ousts the small or medium-sized firm and "expropriates" its owners, but in the end it also ousts the entrepreneur and expropriates the bourgeoisie as a class which in the process stands to lose not only its income but also what is infinitely more important, its function. The true pacemakers of socialism were not the intellectuals or agitators who preached it but the Vanderbilts, Carnegies and Rockefellers. This result may not in every respect be to the taste of Marxian socialists, still less to the taste of socialists of a more popular (Marx would have said, vulgar) description. But so far as prognosis goes, it does not differ from theirs. . .

Thus the capitalist process pushes into the background all those institutions, the institutions of property and free contracting in particular, that expressed the needs and ways of the truly "private" economic activity. Where it does not abolish them, as it already has abolished free contracting in the labor market, it attains the same end by shifting the relative importance of existing legal forms—the legal forms pertaining to corporate business for instance as against those pertaining to the partnership or individual firm—or by changing their contents or meanings. The capitalist process, by substituting a mere parcel of shares for the walls of, and the machines in, a factory, takes the life out of the idea of property. It loosens the grip that once was so strong—the grip in the sense of the legal right and the actual ability to do as one pleases with one's own; the grip also in the sense that the holder of the title loses the will to fight, economically, physically, politically, for "his" factory and his control over it, to die if necessary on its steps. And this evaporation of what we may term the material substance of property—its visible and touchable reality—affects not only the attitude of holders but also that of the workmen and of the public in general. Dematerialized, defunctionalized and absentee ownership does not impress and call forth moral allegiance as the vital form of property did. Eventually there will be *nobody* left who really cares to stand for it—nobody within and nobody without the precincts of the big concerns [companies].

The reasons for believing that the capitalist order tends to destroy itself and that centralist socialism is . . . a likely heir apparent I have explained elsewhere. Briefly and superficially, these reasons may be summed up under four heads. First, the very success of the business class in developing the productive powers of this country and the very fact that this success has created a new standard of life for all classes has paradoxically undermined the social and political position of the same business class whose economic function, though not obsolete, tends to become obsolescent and amenable to bureaucratization. Second, capitalist activity, being essentially "rational," tends to spread rational habits of mind and to destroy those loyalties and those habits of super- and subordination that are nevertheless essential for the efficient working of the institutionalized leadership of the producing plant: no social system can work which is based exclusively upon a network of free contracts between (legally) equal contracting parties and in which everyone is supposed to be guided by nothing except his own (short-run) utilitarian ends. Third, the concentration of the business class on the tasks of the factory and the office was instrumental in creating a political system and an intellectual class, the structure and interests of which developed an attitude of independence from, and eventually of hostility to, the interests of large-scale business. The latter is becoming increasingly incapable of defending itself against raids that are, in the short run, highly profitable to other classes. Fourth, in consequence of all this, the scheme of values of capitalist society, though causally related to its economic success, is losing its hold not only upon the public mind but also upon the "capitalist" stratum itself. Little time, though more than I have, would be needed to show how modern drives for security, equality, and regulation (economic engineering) may be explained on these lines.

The best method of satisfying ourselves as to how far this process of disintegration of capitalist society has gone is to observe the extent to which its implications are being taken for granted both by the business class itself and by the large number of economists who feel themselves to be opposed to (one hundred per cent) socialism and are in the habit of denying the existence of any tendency toward it. To speak of the latter only, they accept not only unquestioningly but also approvingly: (1) the various stabilization policies which are to prevent recessions or at least depressions, that is, a large amount of public management of business situations even if not the principle of full employment; (2) the "desirability of greater equality of incomes," rarely defining how far short of absolute equality they are prepared to go, and in connection with this the principle of redistributive taxation; (3) a rich assortment of regulative measures, frequently rationalized by antitrust slogans, as regards prices; (4) public control, though within a wide range of variation, over the labor and the money market; (5) indefinite extension of the sphere of wants that are, now or eventually, to be satisfied by public enterprise, either gratis or on some post-office principle; and (6) of course all types of security legislation. I believe that there is a mountain in Switzerland on which congresses of economists have been held which express disapproval of all or most of these things. But these anathemata have not even provoked attack.

Arnold Toynbee
(1852-1883)

Arnold Toynbee was an important British economic historian, philosopher, and reformer. He lived only thirty-one years but was still an important influence in the application of historical analysis to economics. He is credited with coining the term "Industrial Revolution" to describe the dramatic changes which took place in Western Europe in the late 1700s and early 1800s.

In this selection Toynbee reviews early classical writing on economics and then provides a discussion of the facts of the Industrial Revolution, a revolution that changed the face of our society. He argues that the agrarian revolution played as large a part in the Industrial Revolution as did the manufacturing revolution. He further argues that the changes led to changes in income distribution and that those changes have caused a need to modify the role of the state. Specifically, he writes: "The effects of the Industrial Revolution prove that free competition may produce wealth without producing well being."

In this selection, when he discusses "manufactures" he refers to several inventions, such as the water-frame and the self-acting mule. All these inventions were machines used in the textile industry. Also in his discussion of the textile industry he mentions merchants who "gave out the warp themselves." This refers to the end of the weaving industry as conducted in countless private houses (the cottage industry) and the institution, instead, of weaving factories.

Arnold Toynbee. 1884 (published after Toynbee's death). *Lectures on the Industrial Revolution in England: Popular Addresses, Notes and other Fragments*. London: Rivingtons, pp. 85-93.

The Chief Features of the Industrial Revolution

The essence of the Industrial Revolution is the substitution of competition for the mediæval regulations which had previously controlled the production and distribution of wealth. On this account it is not only one of the most important facts of English history, but Europe owes to it the growth of two great systems of thought—Economic Science, and its antithesis, Socialism. The development of Economic Science in England has four chief landmarks, each connected with the name of one of the four great English economists. The first is the publication of Adam Smith's *Wealth of Nations* in 1776, in which he investigated the causes of wealth and aimed at the substitution of industrial freedom for a system of restriction. The production of wealth, not the welfare of man, was what Adam Smith had primarily before his mind's eye; in his own words, "the great object of the Political economy of every country is to increase the riches and power of that country." His great book appeared on the eve of the Industrial Revolution. A second stage in the growth of the science is marked by Malthus's *Essay on Population*, published in 1798, which may be considered the product of that revolution, then already in full swing. Adam Smith had concentrated all his attention on a large production; Malthus directed his inquiries, not to the causes of wealth but to the causes of poverty, and found them in his theory of population. A third stage is marked by Ricardo's *Principles of Political Economy and Taxation*, which appeared in 1817, and in which Ricardo sought to ascertain the laws of the distribution of wealth. Adam Smith had shown how wealth could be produced under a system of industrial freedom, Ricardo showed how wealth is distributed under such a system, a problem which could not have occurred to any one before his time. The fourth stage is marked by John Stuart Mill's *Principles of Political Economy*, published in 1848. Mill himself asserted that "the chief merit of his treatise" was the distinction drawn between the laws of production and those of distribution, and the problem he tried to solve was, how wealth *ought to be* distributed. A great advance was made by Mill's attempt to show what was and what was not inevitable under a system of free competition. In it we see the influence which the rival system of Socialism was already beginning to exercise upon the economists. The whole spirit of Mill's book is quite different from that of any economic works which had up to his time been written in England. Though a re-statement of Ricardo's system, it contained the admission that the distribution of wealth is the result of "particular social arrangements," and it recognized that competition alone is not a satisfactory basis of society.

Competition, heralded by Adam Smith, and taken for granted by Ricardo and Mill, is still the dominant idea of our time; though since the publication of the *Origin of Species*, we hear more of it under the name of the "struggle for existence." I wish here to notice the fallacies involved in the current arguments on this subject. In the first place it is assumed that all competition is a competition for existence. This is not true. There is a great difference between a struggle for mere existence and a struggle for a particular kind of existence. For instance, twelve men are struggling for employment in a trade where there is only room for eight; four are driven out of that trade, but they are not trampled out of existence. A good deal of competition merely decides what kind of work a man is to do; though of course when a man can only do one kind of work, it may easily become a struggle for bare life. It is next assumed that this struggle for existence is a law of nature, and that therefore all human interference with it is wrong. To that I answer that the whole meaning of civilization is interference with this brute struggle. We intend to modify the violence of the fight, and to prevent the weak being trampled under foot.

Competition, no doubt, has its uses. Without competition no progress would be possible, for progress comes chiefly from without; it is external pressure which forces men to exert themselves. Socialists, however, maintain that this advantage is gained at the expense of an enormous waste of human life and labour, which might be avoided by regulation. But here we must distinguish between competition in production and competition in distribution, a difference recognized in modern legislation, which has widened the sphere of contract in the one direction, while it has narrowed it in the other. For the struggle of men to outvie one another in production is beneficial to the community; their struggle over the division of the joint produce is not. The stronger side will dictate its own terms; and as a matter of fact, in the early days of competition the capitalists used all their power to oppress the labourers, and drove down wages to starvation point. This kind of competition has to be checked; there is no historical instance of its having lasted long without being modified either by combination or legislation, or both. In England both remedies are in operation, the former through Trades-Unions, the latter through factory legislation. In the past other remedies were applied. It is this desire to prevent the evils of competition that affords the true explanation of the fixing of wages by Justices of the Peace, which seemed to Ricardo a remnant of the old system of tyranny in the interests of the strong. Competition, we have now learnt, is neither good nor evil in itself; it is a force which has to be studied and controlled; it may be compared to a stream whose strength and direction have to be observed, that embankments may be thrown up within which it may do its work harmlessly and beneficially. But at the period we are considering it came to be believed in as a gospel, and, the idea of necessity being superadded, economic laws deduced from the assumption of universal unrestricted competition were converted into practical precepts, from which it was regarded as little short of immoral to depart.

Coming to the facts of the Industrial Revolution, the first thing that strikes us is the far greater rapidity which marks the growth of population. Before 1751 the largest decennial increase, so far as we can calculate from our imperfect materials, was 3 per cent. For each of the next three decennial periods the increase was 6 per cent.; then between 1781 and 1791 it was 9 per cent.; between 1791 and 1801, 11 per cent.; between 1801 and 1811, 14 per cent.; between 1811 and 1821, 18 per cent. This is the highest figure ever reached in England, for since 1815 a vast emigration has been always tending to moderate it; between 1815 and 1880 over eight millions (including Irish) have left our shores. But for this our normal rate of increase would be 16 or 18 instead of 12 per cent. in every decade.

Next we notice the relative and positive decline in the agricultural population. In 1811 it constituted 35 per cent of the whole population of Great Britain; in 1821, 33 per cent; in 1831, 28 per cent. And at the same time its actual members have decreased. In 1831 there were 1,243,057 adult males employed in agriculture in Great Britain; in 1841 there were 1,207,989. In 1851 the whole number of persons engaged in agriculture in England was 2,084,153; in 1861 it was 2,010,454, and in 1871 it was 1,657,138. Contemporaneously with this change, the centre of density of population has shifted from the Midlands to the North; there are at the present day 458 persons to the square mile in the counties north of the Trent, as against 312 south of the Trent. And we have lastly to remark the change in the relative population of England and Ireland. Of the total population of the three kingdoms, Ireland had in 1821, 32 per cent, in 1881 only 14.6 per cent.

An agrarian revolution plays as large part in the great industrial change of the end of the eighteenth century as does the revolution in manufacturing industries, to which attention is more usually directed. Our next inquiry must therefore be: What were the agricultural changes which led to this noticeable decrease in the rural population? The three most effective causes were: the destruction of the common-field system of cultivation; the enclosure, on a large scale, of commons and waste lands; and the consolidation of small farms into large. We have already seen that while between 1710 and 1760 some 300,000 acres were enclosed, between 1760 and 1843 nearly 7,000,000 underwent the same process. Closely connected with the enclosure system was the substitution of large for small farms. In the first half of the century Laurence, though approving of consolidation from an economic point of view, had thought that the odium attaching to an evicting landlord would operate as a strong check upon it. But these scruples had now disappeared. Eden in 1795 notices how constantly the change was effected, often accompanied by the conversion of arable to pasture; and relates how in a certain Dorsetshire village he found two farms where twenty years ago there had been thirty. The process went on uninterruptedly into the present century. Cobbett, writing in 1826, says: "In the parish of Burghclere one single farmer holds, under Lord Carnarvon, as one farm, the lands that those now living remember to have formed fourteen farms, bringing up in a respectable way fourteen families." The consolidation of farms reduced the number of farmers, while the enclosures drove the labourers off the land, as it became impossible for them to exist without their rights of pasturage for sheep and geese on common lands.

Severely, however, as these changes bore upon the rural population, they wrought, without doubt, distinct improvement from an agricultural point of view. They meant the substitution of scientific for unscientific culture. "It has been found," says Laurence, "by long experience, that common or open fields are great hindrances to the public good, and to the honest improvement which every one might make of his own." Enclosures brought an extension of arable cultivation and the tillage of inferior soils; and in small farms of 40 to 100 acres, where the land was exhausted by repeated corn crops, the farm buildings of clay and mud walls and three-fourths of the estate often saturated with water, consolidation into farms of 100 to 500 acres meant rotation of crops, leases of nineteen years, and good farm buildings. The period was one of great agricultural advance; the breed of cattle was improved, rotation of crops was generally introduced, the steam-plough was invented, agricultural societies were instituted. In one respect alone the change was injurious. In consequence of the high prices of corn which prevailed during the French war, some of the finest permanent pastures were broken up. Still, in spite of this, it was said in 1813 that during the previous ten years agricultural produce had increased by one-fourth, and this was an increase upon a great increase in the preceding generation.

Passing to manufactures, we find here the all-prominent fact to be the substitution of the factory for the domestic system, the consequence of the mechanical discoveries of the time. Four great inventions altered the character of the cotton manufacture; the spinning-jenny, patented by Hargreaves in 1770; the water-frame, invented by Arkwright the year before; Crompton's mule introduced in 1779, and the self-acting mule, first invented by Kelly in 1792, but not brought into use till Roberts improved it in 1825. None of these by themselves would have revolutionized the industry. But in 1769—the year in which Napoleon and Wellington were born—James Watt took out his patent for the steam-engine. Sixteen years later it was applied to the cotton manufacture. In 1785 Boulton and Watt made an engine for a cotton-mill at Papplewick in Notts, and in the same year Arkwright's patent expired. These two facts taken together mark the introduction of the factory system. But the most famous invention of all, and the most fatal to domestic industry, the power-loom, though also patented by Cartwright in 1785, did not come into use for several years, and till the power-loom was introduced the workman was hardly injured. At first, in fact, machinery raised the wages of spinners and weavers owing to the great prosperity it brought to the trade. In fifteen years the cotton trade trebled itself; from 1788 to 1803 has been called "its golden age;" for, before the power-loom but after the introduction of the mule and other mechanical improvements by which for the first time yarn sufficiently fine for muslin and a variety of other fabrics was spun, the demand became such that "old barns, cart-houses, outbuildings of all descriptions were repaired, windows broke through the old blank walls, and all fitted up for loom-shops; new weavers' cottages with loom-shops arose in every direction, every family bringing home weekly from 40 to 120 shillings per week." At a later date, the condition of the workman was very different. Meanwhile, the iron industry had been equally revolutionized by the invention of smelting by pit-coal brought into use between 1740 and 1750, and by the application in 1788 of the steam-engine to blast furnaces. In the eight years which followed this latter date, the amount of iron manufactured nearly doubled itself.

A further growth of the factory system took place independent of machinery, and owed its origin to the expansion of trade, an expansion which was itself due to the great advance made at this time in the means of communication. The canal system was being rapidly developed throughout the country. In 1777 the Grand Trunk canal, 96 miles in length, connecting the Trent and Mersey, was finished; Hull and Liverpool were connected by one canal while another connected them both with Bristol; and in 1792, the Grand Junction canal, 90 miles in length, made a waterway from London through Oxford to the chief midland towns. Some years afterwards, the roads were greatly improved under Telford and Macadam; between 1818 and 1829 more than a thousand additional miles of turnpike road were constructed; and the next year, 1830, saw the opening of the first railroad. These improved means of communication caused an extraordinary increase in commerce, and to secure a sufficient supply of goods it became the interest of the merchants to collect weavers around them in great numbers, to get looms together in a workshop, and to give out the warp themselves to the workpeople. To these latter this system meant a change from independence to dependence; at the beginning of the century the report of a committee asserts that the essential difference between the domestic and the factory system is, that in the latter the work is done "by persons who have no property in the goods they manufacture." Another direct consequence of this expansion of trade was the regular recurrence of periods of over-production and of depression, a phenomenon quite unknown under the old system, and due to this new form of production on a large scale for a distant market.

These altered conditions in the production of wealth necessarily involved an equal revolution in its distribution. In agriculture the prominent fact is an enormous rise in rents. Up to 1795, though they had risen in some places, in others they had been stationary since the Revolution [1688, when the English deposed King James II and brought in King William III] But between 1790 and 1833, according to Porter, they at least doubled. In Scotland, the rental of land, which in 1795 had amounted to £2,000,000, had risen in 1815 to £5,278,685. A farm in Essex, which before 1793 had been rented at 10s. an acre, was let in 1812 at 50s., though six years after, this had fallen again to 35s. In Berks and Wilts, farms which in 1790 were let at 14s., were let in 1810 at 70s., and in 1820 at 50s. Much of this rise, doubtless, was due to money invested in improvements—the first Lord Leicester is said to have expended £400,000 on his property—but it was far more largely the effect of the enclosure system, of the consolidation of farms, and of the high price of corn during the French war. Whatever may have been its causes, however, it represented a great social revolution, a change in the balance of political power and in the relative position of classes. The farmers shared in the prosperity of the landlords; for many of them held their farms under beneficial leases, and made large profits by them. In consequence, their character completely changed; they ceased to work and live with their labourers, and became a distinct class. The high prices of the war time thoroughly demoralized them, for their wealth then increased so fast, that they were at a loss what to do with it. Cobbett has described the change in their habits, the new food and furniture, the luxury and drinking, which were the consequences of more money coming into their hands than they knew how to spend. Meanwhile, the effect of all these agrarian changes upon the condition of the labourer was an exactly opposite and most disastrous one. He felt all the burden of high prices, while his wages were steadily falling, and he had lost his common-rights. It is from this period, the beginning of the [20th] century, that the alienation between farmer and labourer may be dated.

Exactly analogous phenomena appeared in the manufacturing world. The new class of great capitalist employers made enormous fortunes, they took little or no part personally in the work of their factories, their hundreds of workmen were individually unknown to them; and as a consequence, the old relations between masters and men disappeared, and a "cash nexus" was substituted for the human tie. The workmen on their side resorted to combination, and Trades-Unions began a fight which looked as if it were between mortal enemies rather than joint producers. The misery which came upon large sections of the working people at this epoch was often, though not always, due to a fall in wages, for, as I said above, in some industries they rose. But they suffered likewise from the conditions of labour under the factory system, from the rise of prices, especially from the high price of bread before the repeal of the corn-laws, and from those sudden fluctuations of trade, which, ever since production has been on a large scale, have exposed them to recurrent periods of bitter distress. The effects of the Industrial Revolution prove that free competition may produce wealth without producing wellbeing. We all know the horrors that ensued in England before it was restrained by legislation and combination.

Abba Lerner

(1903-1982)

Abba Lerner was another of the colorful economists of the mid-20th century. He was born in Poland but moved to England at the age of nine. In 1938 he moved again, this time to the United States when he received a fellowship. He resided in the United States the rest of his life, except for a period in the 1950s when he lived in Israel and was an adviser to the government there.

When he was a student of Hayek at the London School of Economics in the 1930s, he heard about the Keynesian revolution and went up to Cambridge to correct such confused thinking. He did not; instead he was converted to Keynesianism. Thus he brings to his economics writing a strange combination of Hayekian liberalism and favoring of the market, a socialist leaning from his earlier background, and a Keynesian view.

His exceptionally clear writing makes his work beautiful for teaching introductory economics. It is often said that his graduate seminar lectures sounded very much like introductory economics lectures because they were so clear, and upon attending them, graduate students learned what they had missed as introductory students: a deeper sense of the workings of the market. Like another critic, Thorstein Veblen, whom we will read below, he was rather unconventional. He was Jewish at a time when the number of Jews at universities, both as students and faculty, was limited by quotas the schools established. This, combined with his Keynesian views, made it difficult, if not impossible, for him to get a permanent job at a top school until late in his career. Nonetheless, he played an important role in the neoclassical graphical revolution that forms the basis of the microeconomics you learn and of Keynesian macroeconomics. He is one of the originators of many of the concepts that we now take as givens. He was considered likely to receive a Nobel prize, but his unconventional views precluded that.

This selection was written in the late 1940s, soon after the close of World War II in 1945. His reference to "recent gray markets" in steel reflects the fact that during that war, almost all steel was officially devoted to military production. In this selection he argues that traders—middlemen—are central to the economy and that one should not think of production as the production of goods alone, but also as the production of useful services.

A.P. Lerner. 1949. "The Myth of the Parasitic Middleman." *Commentary,* July 1949, pp. 45-46, 49-50.

The "Unproductive Middleman"

The charge is well known: the middleman is nothing but a go-between. He is a trader who does not produce anything. He buys goods from the producer and sells them to the consumer at a profit; he is therefore an excrescence on the body economic, the profiteer, the "exploiter" *par excellence.*

The charge rests on a distinction between the "productiveness" of work and the "unproductiveness" of trade. But on what is this distinction based—apart from confused thinking?

Consider, for example, the question of the so-called "gray market," which was recently blamed for encouraging inflation. A moment's thought will serve to make one realize that the "gray marketeers" performed a useful social function; they broke through monopolistic practices and supplied vital materials like steel, sorely needed to keep vital productive processes going, which could not be obtained by any other means. Is it not perhaps because we are uneasily aware of this fact that we changed the color from black to gray?

Yet even the middlemen themselves plead guilty: often they are the first to deprecate their own social usefulness, to admit that they are parasites who not merely fail to do their fair share of work but are actually engaged in socially harmful activities.

* * * *

This apologetic attitude is quite uncalled for. Viewed from a fundamental standpoint, the work of the middleman or trader has more than the ordinary usefulness: it consists in facilitating a socially desirable movement of things from one place to another. The trader buys something in one place for less than he can sell it for in another. That the commodity is dearer in the second place simply indicates that it is needed there more. The middleman, therefore, moves things from where they are needed less to where they are needed more.

* * * *

Now it is common for people to understand and accept the foregoing analysis and then, nevertheless, repeat the old accusation: the middleman does not "produce" anything. He "merely" moves from one place to another.

Those who persist in making this statement have overlooked something both obvious and startling. For what we have defined as the peculiarity of the middleman—that his activity consists in moving things from one place to another—is actually true of all economic activity. *All* the "real" or "direct" production with which the middleman's activity is unfavorably contrasted boils down to exactly the same thing.

Workers cannot create material things; they can only manipulate materials that already exist. A worker moves coal from the face of the mine to the truck which takes it away; he moves it on the truck from the mine face to the mine shaft, from below ground to above ground, from the coal-producing area to the homes and factories where it is needed. The farmer moves small pieces of earth with spade or plow; he moves fertilizer to where it is needed; he moves seeds from his bins to his fields; and, finally, he moves the ripe crops from the field to the barn. The automobile worker moves one piece of metal to join it to another piece and moves the screws so that they hold tight. The textile worker draws cotton or wool into threads, or arranges the threads so that they are entangled with each other to form cloth or joined with other pieces of thread to form suits and dresses and shirts.

Thus, since all work can be reduced to "shifting dirt from one place to another," there can be no *physical* way of distinguishing between productive and unproductive occupations. Only one significant test exists: whether the results are *useful*—how much they contribute to the needs and desires of human beings.

* * * *

Nowhere is the special usefulness of the middleman seen more clearly than in Russia, where his activities are prohibited by law. The trader who buys screws or nails or other small items in one Russian town and sells them in another at a profit has to brave severe punishment for "speculation." Yet his work is probably as productive as that of any worker in Russia. Many a huge Russian factory has had to curtail its work because it could not get some small items; and for these [items] to be obtained by the regular bureaucratic methods would take an unconscionably long time. The trader who illegally transports these small but essential items is performing a service of the highest importance in keeping the wheels of industry turning. Nevertheless, his critics claim that he is "exploiting" the workers when he makes a profit.

The condemnation of such useful trading as "speculation" rests on a confusion between two different kinds of activity which unfortunately have been given the same name—speculation. The kind of trading discussed above may be called *competitive* speculation, to distinguish it from *monopolistic* speculation. Monopolistic speculation consists in *creating* scarcities and thus causing prices to rise to the speculator's profit. Sometimes this is done by *destroying* goods in order to sell the remainder at higher prices. But much more important even than this destruction, since it occurs more frequently and on a larger scale, is the harm done in creating scarcity simply by limiting production. The greater part of the evil done by the monopolistic speculator thus lies not in what he takes out of the social product for himself, but in the part he destroys (mainly by preventing its production) in order to be able to take a larger share of what remains. As a result, the rest of society is doubly impoverished—first by what the monopolist takes for himself and again by the reduction in the total output.

This kind of speculation cannot be carried on by the ordinary middleman. It involves an extensive control over productive resources, for without this control it is impossible to bring about artificial scarcity and the concomitant higher prices. The competitive speculator—the middleman—has no such powers. He cannot influence prices, for he is too small in relation to the total market; on the contrary, he must accept the prevailing prices. His activity can therefore only be the moving of goods from where he finds them cheap to where he finds them dear, to the net benefit of society.

It is true, of course, that the economy could not live if everybody were a middleman and nobody engaged in direct production. But neither could the economy live if everybody became a coal miner or if everybody became a farmer.

It is also true that if there were a very good distribution of goods and services between different places and between different dates, and if this were brought about by a social authority without the use of middlemen, then there would not be much for middlemen to do. But this does not mean that middlemen should be discouraged or restricted. It means only that the authorities should try to bring about such a perfect distribution that the middlemen would be unnecessary. A perfect distribution would show itself in balanced prices throughout the economy. The middleman would then not be able to find any places where goods were relatively plentiful and cheap or where they were relatively scarce and dear. To have such a perfect distribution of goods would of course be a good thing, quite apart from its effects in diminishing the need for middlemen and setting them free for other useful activities. But so long as middlemen can make a living by competitive speculation, this stands as proof of an insufficiently perfect distribution, and shows that they have not been rendered unnecessary.

The fact that middlemen would not be needed if distribution were perfect is no more significant than the fact that plumbers would not be needed if pipes never leaked. In actuality our water and gas pipes are not perfect and we do suffer from leaks. Yet no one supposes that the plumbing situation would be improved by decrying the usefulness of plumbers and imposing restrictions on their activity in repairing the leaks that do occur. If we don't want plumbers and middlemen, then let us improve the quality of piping and the efficiency of goods distribution so that plumbers and middlemen will find little to do and will be available for other jobs. The manhours needed for all sorts of operations are continually being reduced by increased efficiency and technological advances, and they would be reduced still further by the abolition of "feather-bedding" practices. The ultimate in mechanization is presumably the complete elimination of the need for work, altogether. Yet nobody has argued that this proves that workers are useless members of society.

* * * *

The middleman's function is to bring together the producer and the consumer. Those who do not understand his usefulness sometimes conceive of him as *separating* producers from consumers rather than joining them together, much as one might say that the mortar in a wall separates the bricks rather than joining them to each other. Actually, of course, what makes the wall stand is the way the mortar holds the bricks together. . . .

Adolph A. Berle
(1895-1971)

Adolph Berle was an American lawyer, teacher, economist, diplomat, and public official. He entered public life in 1933 as an adviser to President Franklin Roosevelt. In 1934-1937 he was a planner for both the Federal government and the city of New York; he laid the groundwork for the federal Securities and Exchange Act and for the government of New York City under Mayor Fiorello LaGuardia. As a diplomat, he was Assistant Secretary of State for Latin Affairs in 1938-1944 and implemented the "good neighbor" policy; he was U.S. Ambassador to Brazil in 1945-1946; and in the early 1960s he was a special adviser on Latin affairs to President John Kennedy.

In this selection, written in 1963, Berle argues that an economic system is a means to an end, not an end in itself, and that life has many more dimensions than the economic dimension. He says that one must carefully consider the moral, social, and esthetic, as well as economic, implications of economic systems.

Adolph A. Berle. 1963. *The American Economic Republic*. New York: Harcourt, Brace and World, Inc., pp. 3-7.

The American Political-Economic System

The American political-economic system, judged by its total achievement, is the most successful in the present-day world. By the same standard of judgment, it is more successful than any in recorded history—though there were civilizations like that of the Inca and the Maya of which we have no adequate record. Its outstanding success has been, first, a level of production never attained by any other large population, and, second, distribution to a point at which only a fraction of the American people have any fear of catastrophic want. Most of them have no acquaintance with poverty, in the sense that poverty exists over great areas of the earth.

This does not mean the system is ideal. Its shortcomings are many and obvious. Its problems and injustices properly engage the attention of many Americans and incite the criticism of students. Yet, I must add, no ideal system has anywhere been proposed, let alone achieved, partly because no two philosophers have ever agreed even on the basic goals or outline of such a system. If today such agreement were had, the sights would be lifted by the next wave of thought. Any perfection conceived by this generation would be overpassed and restated by the ideas of the next.

No adequate description of the American political and economic system as it presently operates is now extant. Only the superb statistical material gathered and collated by the government of the United States and by institutions like the National Bureau of Economic Research and other academic institutions tells the tale. These statistical services give a reasonably fair picture of what has happened. They rarely, if ever, attempt to tell how and, especially, why the results occurred. Most commentators who do make the attempt assume motives and describe processes as these were assumed or thought to have existed many years ago. Their assumptions are chiefly those worked out at the end of the nineteenth century or in the first decade of the twentieth, from which most of our current political-economic thinking is drawn. Their relevance to the processes of today is increasingly limited.

There are, fortunately, an increasing number of studies of specific parts or functions of the American system not thus limited. These are the product of observers who attempted to note and state what the system was doing in their particular areas of study. That is, they dealt with facts and left theorists to harmonize their conclusions and evolve a general theory. No such theorist has arisen in the past generation. The great economic theorist at the close of the nineteenth century, Professor Alfred Marshall, remained virtually supreme in his field until in

1935 the late John Maynard Keynes wrote his book *The General Theory of Employment, Interest, and Money*. Accepting most of the premises of Marshallian economics, Keynes introduced a set of new conceptions. Most of these were based on his cold observation of the way the British and allied European systems operated after the close of World War I. Keynes was—and still is—a controversial figure. Controversy is supposed to rage around his monetary theories. But I suspect the reason for continuing attack on him lies deeper. Keynes challenged the comfortable nineteenth-century *laissez-faire* men who condemned any attempt by the political state to interfere with results of unhindered economic operations by businessmen. In doing so, he challenged a power group—challenged it so effectively, in fact, that no economy in the civilized world is now left merely to financiers or businessmen. Academic economic controversy dies down. Changes in power structure, on the other hand, are never forgiven as long as they live by those whose power is diminished.

Obviously Keynes did not do this all by himself. It is arguable indeed that the processes he described and the emergence of planned or guided economy were under way before he wrote. But he, more than any other in the Western World, rationalized and gave basis for the doctrine that an organized state—possibly a group of states—could stabilize, stimulate, and direct the course of its economy *without* resorting to dictatorship, and *without* superseding a system based on property by a system based on naked power, as the Russians have done. In doing so, he recreated the conception that economics and politics are indissolubly united. This is the practice of the entire modern world today. It is also the reason why in this volume we shall call the American system a system of political economy—not merely an economic system.

We must here demolish a rarely stated, but prevalent, notion. A system of political economy is only an instrument—a means to an end. It is not an end in itself. Nor is it a "civilization," though its processes powerfully affect civilization as we understand it. Primarily, its function is to supply the jobs, materials, goods, and services from which a civilization is built. Secondarily, its task is to establish these jobs, create these materials, and offer these services under conditions and on terms which offer the greatest opportunity for civilization and development, as the evolving morals, perceptions, and dreams of the population may conceive civilization, and thereby give outlet for human endeavor. A political-economic system does not by itself create either a good life or a good society. It can offer the materials from which men can realize and expand their individual conception of the good life. And, because human life (good or, indeed, bad) can only be lived in the framework of the organization we call "society," it must be the instrument for meeting the material needs of that organization as it attempts to realize the "good society."

Part, perhaps, of the current confusion about the American system lies in failure to understand this distinction. The habit of thinking that life is primarily economic is an old one. Probably it rises from the fact that when there is not enough to go around, when want is chronic, when most of a population asks "Can I live another year?," men do live chiefly on the economic plane. That condition of chronic want was certainly the case throughout the entire world until well into the twentieth century. It is the situation in Asia, Africa, and considerable parts of South America today. Professor J. Kenneth Galbraith pays pungent tribute to the fact in his book *The Affluent Society*. He notes that nineteenth-century theorists not only assumed the fact, but also, thanks to Malthus, demonstrated that it must always be the fact. Malthus had explained that population must always outrun production—which led Scrooge in *The Christmas Carol* to reject a request for charity because, if the proposed objects of it starved, it would help reduce the surplus population.

Worse yet, the reformers, the humanitarians, the justly angry men of the nineteenth century accepted the premise that man's whole problem was economic—though in their case it was perhaps excusable. The Socialist and Communist movements, as indeed most of the welfare movements not based on socialist doctrine, took this view. When all human beings were reasonably provided for, were reasonably housed, their problems would be over. Then civilization on a newer, happier, more human pattern would result. What else might be involved could be left to that time.

INTRODUCTION

It remained for the Communist experiment to teach a bitter lesson. An economic system does set up the conditions under which men work and produce and distribute. It does powerfully affect the lives of the individuals composing it. It is thus a formative influence of great power. But it remained for Lenin and Stalin to prove to the twentieth-century world a terrible thesis. When the economic instrument is primarily used to form life, the compulsions, the cruelties, the limitations, physical and moral, the injustices, the resulting personal agonies transcend any oppression yet known. Statistically, it kills, imprisons, exiles, and otherwise torments more of its population than any existing modern system. This is why, for example, the number of prisoners in concentration camps in the Soviet Union has steadily been greater than the entire number of men and women unemployed in the United States save perhaps for one brief period during the Great Depression. The correlation is not accidental.

The important point is, therefore, that a political and economic system is a means to a greater end—an entirely good society. That goal (it will never be reached until the human mind stops developing) is not, as we shall see later, determined primarily by economic considerations. When the attempt is made by economic means alone to reach the good society, the economy falters, and may break down. This fact is outstanding. It is perhaps the greatest single difference between the operation of the American political-economic system of today and the nineteenth-century systems whose shadows still obscure the understanding of the remarkable economic and social achievements (even after allowing for all defects and failures) attained in the United States.

It also explains the problems, moral, social, and esthetic, and some of the economic shortcomings evident on the American scene. As an instrument, our system is obviously capable of doing anything the American public consensus really wishes it to do. It provided both guns and butter for America and a number of other nations during World War II—perhaps the greatest war in history. It could—and one day will—build cities as splendid in beauty as they are now in strength. It has not done so—but this is not the fault of the economic instrument. When the American value system demands stateliness, beauty, and repose as well as consumer goods, fast transportation, and great armament, the instrument can and will provide them, and that within a relatively short time.

${\rm \large M}$ACROECONOMICS

The Question of Full Employment
    Lord William Beveridge: Full Employment in a Free Society   43
    Robert Lekachman: The Specter of Full Employment   47
    Henry Hazlitt: "Full Employment" as the Goal   50
    Robert E. Lucas, Jr.: Unemployment Policy   55
    U.S. Congress: The Full Employment and Balanced Growth Act of 1976   59

Keynesian Theory
    John Maynard Keynes: Preface and First Chapter to *The General Theory*   63
    John Kenneth Galbraith: How Keynes Came to America   65
    John Maynard Keynes: Magneto Trouble   69
    Alvin H. Hansen: The American Economy on the March   72
    Henry Hazlitt: The Multiplier   75
    Abba Lerner: The Economic Steering Wheel: The Story of the People's New Clothes   78
    Milton Friedman: Fiscal Policy   81

Money and Monetary Policy
    John Law: The Importance of Money   84
    Walter Bagehot: Why Lombard Street is Often Very Dull and Sometimes
        Extremely Excited   86
    Irvin Fisher: 100 Per Cent Reserves   89
    Henry C. Simons: Rules Versus Authorities in Monetary Policy   95

Inflation and the Phillips Curve
    John Maynard Keynes: Inflation and Deflation   100
    Paul Samuelson and Robert Solow: Policy Implications of the Phillips Curve   101
    Milton Friedman: The Stages of the Phillips Curve   104

The Keynesian Policy Legacy
    James M. Buchanan and Richard E. Wagner: The Consequences of
        Mr. Keynes   109
    William H. Hutt: The Keynesian Episode   113
    Franco Modigliani: The Monetarist Controversy, or Should We Forsake
        Stabilization Policy?   117
    John Maynard Keynes: Concluding Notes on the Social Philosophy Towards
        Which the General Theory Might Lead   124

Lord William Beveridge
(1879-1963)

One of the ongoing debates in macroeconomics has concerned the meaning of full employment and of unemployment. The next five readings give you some sense of that debate. This first selection comes from Lord William Beveridge.

The role of many economists has been in policy, not in theory, and Beveridge will maintain a place among key economists for his part in The Beveridge Report of 1942, *which was the blueprint for the British Labor government's social legislation after 1945—that is, after the end of World War II. His was the culmination of efforts begun by Beatrice and Sidney Webb with the founding, in 1895, of the London School of Economics (LSE) using money designed to promote socialism throughout the Western world. In this selection we see what Beveridge meant by "full employment." Notice as you read it that without some other pressure holding down wages, his concept of full employment would lead to accelerating inflation. As we will see, this will play a significant role in later debates.*

Note that he refers to "the Essential Work Order" and to "ration coupons." The Work Order was a British wartime regulation limiting the right of certain workers to change jobs; and ration coupons were distributed to everyone, allowing them to buy only so much of commodities that were in short supply, like sugar and meat.

William Beveridge. 1944. *Full Employment in a Free Society: A Report by Lord Beveridge.* New York: W.W. Norton, pp. 18-23.

Full Employment in a Free Society

What is meant by "full employment," and what is not meant by it? Full employment does not mean literally no unemployment; that is to say, it does not mean that every man and woman in the country who is fit and free for work is employed productively on every day of his or her working life. In every country with a variable climate there will be seasons when particular forms of work are impossible or difficult. In every progressive society there will be changes in the demand for labour, qualitatively if not quantitatively; that is to say, there will be periods during which particular individuals can no longer be advantageously employed in their former occupations and may be unemployed till they find and fit themselves for fresh occupations. Some frictional unemployment there will be in a progressive society however high the demand for labour. Full employment means that unemployment is reduced to short intervals of standing by, with the certainty that very soon one will be wanted in one's old job again or will be wanted in a new job that is within one's powers.

Full employment is sometimes defined as "a state of affairs in which the number of unfilled vacancies is not appreciably below the number of unemployed persons, so that unemployment at any time is due to the normal lag between a person losing one job and finding another." Full employment in this Report means more than that in two ways. It means having always more vacant jobs than unemployed men, not slightly fewer jobs. It means that the jobs are at fair wages, of such a kind, and so located that the unemployed men can reasonably be expected to take them; it means, by consequence, that the normal lag between losing one job and finding another will be very short.

The proposition that there should always be more vacant jobs than unemployed men means that the labour market should always be a seller's market rather than a buyer's market. For this, on the view of society underlying this Report—that society exists for the individual—there is a decisive reason of principle. The reason is that difficulty in selling labour has consequences of a different order of harmfulness from those associated with difficulty in buying labour. A person who has difficulty in buying the labour that he wants suffers inconvenience or reduction of profits. A person who cannot sell his labour is in effect told that he is of no use. The first difficulty causes annoyance or loss. The other is a personal catastrophe. This difference remains even if an adequate income is provided, by insurance or otherwise, during unemployment; idleness even on an income corrupts; the feeling of not being wanted demoralizes. The difference remains even if most people are unemployed only for relatively short periods. As long as there is any long-term unemployment not obviously due to personal deficiency, anybody who loses his job fears that he may be one of the unlucky ones who will not get another job quickly. The short-term unemployed do not know that they are short-term unemployed till their unemployment is over.

The human difference between failing to buy and failing to sell labour is the decisive reason for aiming to make the labour market a seller's rather than a buyer's market. There are other reasons, only slightly less important. One reason is that only if there is work for all is it fair to expect workpeople, individually and collectively in trade unions, to co-operate in making the most of all productive resources, including labour, and to forgo restrictionist practices. Another reason, related to this, is that the character and duration of individual unemployment caused by structural and technical change in industry will depend on the strength of the demand for labour in the new forms required after the change. The greater the pace of the economic machine, the more rapidly will structural unemployment disappear, the less resistance of every kind will there be to progress. Yet another reason is the stimulus to technical advance that is given by shortage of labour. Where men are few, machines are used to save men for what men alone can do. Where labour is cheap it is often wasted in brainless, unassisted toil. The new lands empty of men are the homes of invention and business adventure in peace. Stimulus to labour saving of all kinds is one of the by-products of full employment in war.

The full employment that is the aim of this Report means more vacant jobs than unemployed men. It means something else as well. If there were 2 million chronically unemployed men in Britain and 2-1/4 million vacant jobs which they could not or would not fill, there would be more vacant jobs than unemployed men, but to call this state of affairs "full employment" would be mockery. It is not enough to say that there must be more vacant jobs than idle men—more or about as many. It is also necessary to be sure that the number unemployed, or rather the duration of unemployment in the individual case, is not excessive. Full employment, in any real sense, means that unemployment in the individual case need not last for a length of time exceeding that which can be covered by unemployment insurance without risk of demoralization. Those who lose jobs must be able to find new jobs at fair wages within their capacity, without delay. This means that the demand for labour and the supply of labour are related qualitatively as well as quantitatively. The demand must be adjusted to the kind of men available or the men must be capable of adjusting themselves to the demand. In the light of the facts of unemployment . . . it is clear that the qualitative and local adjustment of demand for labour and supply of labour has to be approached from both ends, that of demand and that of supply. The demands must not only be sufficient in total but must be directed with regard to the quality and the location of the labour that is available. The labour supply must be capable of following the changes of demand that are inseparable from technical advance.

The Purpose of Employment

Idleness is not the same as Want, but a separate evil, which men do not escape by having an income. They must also have the chance of rendering useful service and of feeling that they are doing so. This means that employment is not wanted for the sake of employment, irrespective of what it produces. The material end of all human activity is consumption. Employment is wanted as a means to more consumption or more leisure, as a means to a higher standard of life. Employment which is merely time-wasting, equivalent to digging holes and filling them again, or merely destructive, like war and preparing for war, will not serve that purpose. Nor will it be felt worth while. It must be productive and progressive. The proposals of this Report are designed to preserve all the essential springs of material progress in the community, to leave to special efforts its rewards, to leave scope for change, invention, competition and initiative.

In so far as room is left for change and for freedom of movement from job to job, room is left for some unemployment. The aim of this Report . . . expressed in numerical terms [is] a reduction of unemployment to not more than 3 per cent, as compared with the 10 to 22 per cent experienced in Britain between the wars. But though the Report assumes the continuance of some unemployment and suggests a figure of 3 per cent, it is the essence of the proposals made in the Report that this 3 per cent should be unemployed only because there is industrial friction, and not because there are no vacant jobs. For men to have value and a sense of value there must always be useful things waiting to be done, with money to pay for doing them. Jobs, rather than men, should wait.

Preservation of Essential Liberties

The labour market in the past has invariably, or all but invariably, been a buyer's market rather than a seller's market, with more unemployed men—generally many more unemployed men—than unfilled jobs. To reverse this and make the labour market always a seller's rather than a buyer's market, to remove not only unemployment but the fear of unemployment, would affect the working of many existing institutions. It would change and is meant to change fundamentally the conditions of living and working in Britain, to make Britain again a land of opportunity for all. There are some things in Britain which neither full employment nor the means of achieving it should be allowed to change.

The Report, as its title indicates, is not concerned simply with the problem of full employment. It is concerned with the necessity, possibility and methods of achieving full employment in a free society, that is to say, subject to the proviso that all essential citizen liberties are preserved. The precise effect of the proviso depends on the list of essential citizen liberties. For the purpose of this Report they are taken as freedom of worship, speech, writing, study and teaching; freedom of assembly and of association for political and other purposes, including the bringing about of a peaceful change of the governing authority; freedom in choice of occupation; and freedom in the management of a personal income. The proviso excludes the totalitarian solution of full employment in a society completely planned and regimented by an irremovable dictator. [This] makes the problem of full employment more complex in many ways, of which four call for special notice.

First, in a free society the governing authority is liable to be changed at short intervals by peaceful methods of political organization and voting. There must be reasonable continuity of economic policy in spite of such changes of government. The machinery of government, while responsive to general changes of opinion, must be resistant to "lobbies"—that is to say, organized sectional pressures.

Second, freedom of association for industrial purposes raises the issue of wage determination. Under conditions of full employment, can a rising spiral of wages and prices be prevented if collective bargaining, with the right to strike, remains absolutely free? Can the right to strike be limited generally in a free society in peace-time?

Third, freedom in choice of occupations makes it harder to ensure that all men at all times are occupied productively. It makes it impossible to retain men forcibly in particular work or to direct them to it with the threat of imprisonment if they refuse to go. One assumption underlying this Report is that neither the Essential Work Order nor the powers of industrial direction which have been found necessary in war should be continued when the war is over. In Britain at peace the supply of labour cannot be adjusted by decree to the demand for labour; it can only be guided by economic motives. From another angle, freedom in choice of occupation raises also the issue of industrial discipline. Under conditions of full employment, if men are free to move from one employment to another and do not fear dismissal, may not some of them at least become so irregular and undisciplined in their behaviour, as to lower appreciably the efficiency of industry?

Fourth, freedom in the management of a personal income complicates the problem of full employment from another side. If men cannot be forced to buy just what has been produced, this means that the demands for labour and its products cannot be fitted forcibly to the supply. There may be continual changes in the kinds of things on which consumers want to spend their money, that is to say, in the quality of consumers' outlay. There may be changes also in its quantity. For freedom in the management of a personal income includes freedom to decide between spending now and saving so as to have the power of spending later. A totalitarian regime, even if it used money and price and wage differentials to stimulate and guide individual activity, might abolish freedom of saving. It might retain from the national income of each year that portion which it needed for investment, i.e. for the sustenance of persons engaged in making instruments and materials of further production, and might issue to consumers money which, like ration coupons, could not be saved for spending later. In a free society individuals must be allowed to plan their spending over their lives as a whole. . . .

None of these freedoms can be exercised irresponsibly. Perpetual instability of economic or social policy would make full employment and any other social reforms futile or impossible. Bargaining for wages must be responsible, looking not to the snatching of short sectional advantages, but to the permanent good of the community. Choice of occupation means freedom in choosing between occupations which are available; it is not possible for an individual to choose to be an Archbishop of Canterbury, if that post is already filled by another. Work means doing what is wanted, not doing just what pleases one. All liberties carry their responsibilities. This does not mean that the liberties themselves must be surrendered. They must be retained.

In all the respects named, and possibly in some others, the problem of maintaining full employment is more complicated in a free society than it would be under a totalitarian regime. From one complication of some historic importance the problem, as posed here, is free. The list of essential liberties given above does not include liberty of a private citizen to own means of production and to employ other citizens in operating them at a wage. Whether private ownership of means of production to be operated by others is a good economic device or not, it must be judged as a device. It is not an essential citizen liberty in Britain, because it is not and never has been enjoyed by more than a very small proportion of the British people. It cannot even be suggested that any considerable proportion of the people have any lively hope of gaining such ownership later.

On the view taken in this Report, full employment is in fact attainable while leaving the conduct of industry in the main to private enterprise, and the proposals made in the Report are based on this view. But if, contrary to this view, it should be shown by experience or by argument that abolition of private property in the means of production was necessary for full employment, this abolition would have to be undertaken.

Robert Lekachman
(1920-1989)

Robert Lekachman was a professor of economics at Lehman College, City University of New York, and a well-known critic of mainstream economic thinking. He published numerous books—including The Age of Keynes *(1966),* The Permanent Problem of Boom and Bust *(1973), and* Economist at Bay *(1976). He was also a columnist for* Dissent, *a publication that disseminated Keynesian ideas.*

In this selection Lekachman argues that the reason we accept high rates of unemployment is the brutal fact that "unemployment at 'moderate' rates confers a good many benefits upon the prosperous and the truly affluent. ... [For them] there are far worse phenomena than unemployment."

Note that Leonard Woodcock, to whom Lekachman refers, was, at the time, a powerful union leader and president of the United Auto Workers of America. Also, when he talks about the problems of full employment he mentions Russell Long, who was a prominent U.S. Senator at the time, and Lutèce, which was, and still is, a very expensive French restaurant in New York City.

Robert Lekachman. 1977. "The Specter of Full Employment." *Harper's Magazine*, February, pp 35-40.

The Specter of Full Employment

Men and women want to work. Work, private and public, is there to be done. How come, a wandering rationalist might ask, the work and the workers are not happily married? Well, as the radicals of my youth were wont to intone, it is no accident that we tolerate as a nation years of 7, 8, even 9 percent general unemployment and horrifying rates of teen-age joblessness which among urban blacks exceed, by some estimates, 50 percent.

The brutal fact is that unemployment at "moderate" rates confers a good many benefits upon the prosperous and the truly affluent. If everyone could be employed, extraordinarily high wages would have to be paid to toilers in restaurant kitchens, laundries, filling stations, and other humble positions. Whenever decent jobs at living wages are plentiful, it is exceedingly difficult to coax young men and women into our volunteer army. Without a volunteer army, how can the children of the middle and upper classes be spared the rigors of the draft?

Unemployment calms the unions and moderates their wage demands. Business periodicals have been noting with unconcealed gratification that last year's contract settlements between major unions and large corporations were considerably less expensive for employers than those of 1975, even though union members were steadily losing ground to inflation. When people are scared about losing their jobs, they work harder and gripe less. In more dignified language, absenteeism declines and productivity ascends.

Better still, factory and office workers, alert to potential layoffs and plant shutdowns, are unlikely to nag unions and employers to make work more interesting, and less menacing to health and personal safety. It cannot be mere coincidence that in Sweden, where job enrichment and plant democracy have had their greatest success, unemployment is practically zero and astute management of their economy protected Swedes even from the worldwide economic crisis of 1973-75. The new government, elected on the fortuitous issue of nuclear safety, has promised to extend even further the social benefits for which Sweden has become celebrated. American employers preserve themselves from Swedish experiments in good part by keeping the industrial reserve army plentifully manned.

Nor is this quite the end of the tale. The hunger of communities and regions for jobs and tax revenues has allowed large corporations to extort an endless assortment of valuable concessions from local and state governments, either as blackmail to keep existing installations or bribes to lure new ones. Few major corporations pay their fair share of property taxes. Propaganda by oil, steel, chemical, and paper industries has noticeably slowed the pace of regulation to protect the environment. Leonard Woodcock, who knows better, has allied himself with the major auto companies in seeking to postpone the application of the next wave of auto standards, entirely out of concern for the jobs of his UAW constituents.

By contrast, full employment on a sustained and assured basis (the system can stand a spell of full employment so long as all parties understand that it is temporary) presents an embarrassment to the movers and shapers of American plutocracy. To begin with, full employment is the most efficient agent of equitable income redistribution which is at all politically feasible in the United States. Full employment sucks into the labor force men and women who now struggle on welfare, food stamps, Social Security, and unemployment compensation. It pushes up the wages of low-paid people whose position is scarcely less precarious than that of the unemployed. It is an especial boon to blacks, Hispanics, teen-agers, and women—last hired and first fired in expansion and recession alike. A long spell of full employment would substantially narrow existing wide differentials between the earnings of these groups and those of white males. In a time of layoff and business contraction, affirmative action is a mockery, but when there is full employment the cry for justice is heard more sympathetically by members of a majority whose own security is not threatened.

These repercussions are severe enough to alarm gentlemen in their clubs and boardrooms. The threat, I suspect, is still more grave. For men of property the charm of the 1970s lies in the way economic adversity has cooled the campuses and shoved American politics, already the most conservative in the developed world, still further right; one only has to look at Gerald Ford of all people, after Watergate and the Nixon pardon, and in the middle of a messed-up economy, very nearly winning the Presidential election. This could not have happened without general apprehension and dampened expectations of the efficacy of action by any national administration. As one comedian commented upon the stock-market decline which preceded the election, investors were selling out of deadly fear that one of the candidates would win. Lift the burdens of apprehension and apathy from the psyches of ordinary folk and—who knows?—they might entertain radical thoughts of inviting the rich to share rather more of their capital gains and inheritances.

It goes without saying that it is scarcely respectable for the rich and their mercenaries, lawyers, economists, politicians, public-relations types, and so on, to openly proclaim their affection for unemployment, although among friends they tend to be more candid. One requires a respectable rationale, a convenient theory that combines apparent concern about the sufferings of the unemployed with actual capacity to avoid any action realistically calculated to alter their status.

My colleagues (I am an economist, but I am confessing, not boasting) have risen to the challenge. As their apologetic runs, we can't proceed sensibly toward universal job guarantees, even in the cautious, timid shape of the Humphrey-Hawkins Full Employment Bill, a revival of the 1945 [Full Employment Bill, the] original effort to write a serious job guarantee into law, because of the horrifying menace of more inflation. That menace is among economists embodied in a marvelous constriction interred in the textbooks under the rubric of the Phillips curve.

The provenance of this notion that democratic societies must choose between inflation and unemployment deserves a paragraph. The late A. W. Phillips, a British economist who taught for much of his career in Australia, published in 1958 an article catchily entitled "The Relationship between Unemployment and the Rate of Change in Money Wage Rates in the United Kingdom, 1862-1957." Phillips's data appeared to demonstrate that, as unemployment rose, wages increased less and less rapidly. The man said nothing at all about prices, price inflation, or the manner in which rising wages might or might not be translated into commensurate increases in the cost of living. Nevertheless, his findings were rapidly extended in statements like this typical textbook pronouncement: "Low rates of unemployment tend to be associated with high rates of inflation and, conversely, price stability or low rates of inflation tend to be associated with high rates of unemployment." Triumphant conclusion: "There seems to be a trade-off between employment and the price level."

Economists shifted from Phillips's cautious conclusions about unemployment and wage rates to the words just cited very simply. After all, wages and salaries, including those of executives and other overpriced folk, amount to about 70 percent of business costs. Wherever competition reigns, employers have no choice except to pass along plumper labor costs to their customers in the shape of higher prices. The line of causation is direct: low unemployment stimulates wage demands, higher wages enlarge business costs, and these in turn lead to higher prices. It's an indisputable pity, but if we are to restrain demand inflation, we simply must operate the economy at what an MIT economist, Robert Hall, has recently labeled the "natural" rate of unemployment. A bit hard on those selected to serve their country by losing their jobs, but their patriotic sacrifice is nothing less than a valuable public service.

* * * *

Does the political will to shape a national full employment policy exist? It is difficult to answer yes to that question. Last year full employment struck a Democratic Congress as sufficiently radical to bury Humphrey-Hawkins. For, as has been noted, full employment means diminishing long-standing inequalities of income, wealth, and power; inviting the black, brown, young, and female to the American celebration; and controlling the rapacity of doctors, lawyers, giant corporations, and other reputable extortionists. After full employment who will iron Russell Long's shirts, clean up after the Lutèce diners, and do the world's dirty work? Settle the job issue once and for all, and even American unions will begin to entertain dangerous thoughts about job redesign, codetermination, and similarly radical Swedish and German nonsense.

The fine men whom the good Lord has placed in the seats of authority and the halls of the mighty know that there are far worse phenomena than unemployment. One of them is full employment.

* * * *

Until a credible left rises in the United States, unemployment will be a little higher when the Republicans are in the White House, a little lower when the Democrats take their turn. Genuine full employment, decent jobs at decent wages for every man, woman, and youth interested in working, has been a myth, is a myth, and will stay a myth so long as every four years voters choose between one party minimally to the right of dead center and a second minimally to the left.

Henry Hazlitt
(1894-1993)

In this selection we get a quite different view of the unemployment problem, written by Henry Hazlitt. Hazlitt was a great popularizer of economic principles. He wrote in a classical tradition and said he owed his greatest intellectual debt to Frédéric Bastiat, Phillip Wicksteed and Ludwig von Mises. Hazlitt's Economics in One Lesson *is still considered a classic in popular economics.*

Hazlitt's argument of what determines the degree of unemployment is different from William Beveridge's, both empirically and logically. He challenges "Sir William's" definition of full employment, calling it, instead, overemployment. He then goes further and argues that the unemployment goals set by Keynesians are neither attainable nor desirable.

Note that Paul Douglas, to whom Hazlitt refers, was an economist at the University of Chicago who was elected to the U.S. Senate and served there for many years. Lionel Robbins, also mentioned in the selection, was a prominent British economist.

Henry Hazlitt. 1959. *The Failure of the "New Economics."* Princeton, NJ: Van Nostrand, Chapter XXVI, pp. 399-408.

"Full Employment" as the Goal

The "contribution" of Keynes that his disciples most often insist upon as valid and "permanent" is the substitution of "full employment" as the goal of economic activity rather than the "maximum production" of the classical economists.

We shall ask here three main questions about "full employment." 1. Is it definable? 2. Is it attainable? 3. Is it—at all times and under all conditions—even desirable?

1. Is It Definable?

Let us begin with the question of definition. The man in the street has few misgivings about this. "Full employment" means that "everybody" has a job. It means "jobs for all the people all the time."

This naive conception runs into immediate difficulties. Early in 1958, for example, the population of the United States was about 173 million. But there were only some 62 million employed. Therefore there must have been 111 million "unemployed"! Yet the official estimate was that there were at that time only 5 million unemployed.

For the government statisticians, the "unemployed" consist only of those in the "labor force" who are not employed. But just how was the line drawn between the 67.5 million who were counted as part of the labor force and the 105.5 million who were not? Here is how the U. S. Bureau of the Census described how it decided:

> Monthly estimates of the population of working age [14 years and over] showing the total number employed, the total unemployed, and the number not in the labor force are obtained from a scientifically selected sample of about 35,000 interviewed households in 330 areas throughout the country.

So the estimate of unemployed was in large part based on a sample of only one in every 1,400 households in the country.

My purpose here, however, is not to emphasize the probable error in such estimates, but to call attention to the necessarily arbitrary and in some cases purely subjective standards by which "unemployment" is officially determined.

The Bureau of the Census's explanation continues: "The unemployed total includes all jobless who were looking for work." How is the number of such persons estimated? From replies to the interviews. What constitutes realistically looking for work? The interviewers must rely in large part upon the realism of the replies. The labor force is not even a constant percentage of the total ("non-institutional") population. In July of 1957 it was 60.6 per cent; but in December only 58.1 per cent.

Some paradoxical results emerge. The monthly report for March of 1958, for example, opened as follows: "Employment rose by 300,000 between February and March . . . while unemployment was unchanged." How could that happen? The layman would naturally expect that if employment rose 300,000 in March unemployment would have dropped that much. The government statisticians' answer is that the "labor force" increased by that much.

The "labor force" increases partly by census estimates of the population reaching working age, etc., but also partly by changes in people's *decisions*. Suppose a man has a good job, with a wife at home and a son and daughter in college. He loses his job, where upon not only he, but his wife, his son, and his daughter start looking for work. Because one person has lost his job, four persons are now "unemployed." So "unemployment" goes up faster than employment goes down.

Let's turn now to the explanations of the Department of Labor:

> Effective January 1957, persons on layoff with definite instructions to return to work within 30 days of layoff and persons waiting to start new wage and salary jobs within the following 30 days, are classified as unemployed. Such persons had previously been classified as employed. . . . The combined total of the groups changing classification has averaged about 200,000 to 300,000 a month in recent years.

So the "unemployed" increased about a quarter of a million simply by a change of definition!

We get into the same kind of problems and arbitrary decisions when we come to the matter of working hours. Obviously there cannot be jobs for "all the people all the time." We must deduct time for eating, sleeping, rest, and leisure. But how much time? It is customary to think of men being "partly unemployed" when they are laid off for two working days a week. But obviously they are as much unemployed if they work every day for correspondingly reduced hours. In the United States today, the standard full working week is forty hours, or five eight-hour days. This is shorter than the standard working week used to be, and in future it may be shorter still. Obviously the length of the working week that constitutes "full employment" is also a matter of arbitrary and conventional definition.

Let us see whether we can get some help from the academic economists, and first of all, of course, Keynes.

In the *General Theory,* Keynes gives us *two* definitions, neither of which seems to have much relation to the other. On page 15 he gives an involved definition of "involuntary" unemployment which, as I have already tried to show (p. 30), is invalid. From this he postulates a state of affairs in the absence of "involuntary" unemployment: "This state of affairs we shall describe as 'full' employment, both 'frictional' and 'voluntary' unemployment being consistent with 'full' employment thus defined" (p. 16). In other words, "full" employment is a state in which there can be both "frictional" and "voluntary" unemployment! Full employment is not full.

Let's start again, this time with the definition on page 303:

> We have full employment when output has risen to a level at which the marginal return from a representative unit of the factors of production has fallen to the minimum figure at which a quantity of the factors sufficient to produce this output is available.

I confess I find it difficult to follow this jabberwocky; but I assume it implies that some sort of equilibrium has been reached. One is tempted to ask irreverently: Does this mean that Uncle Oscar has a job?

Let us turn to A. C. Pigou. Professor Pigou is aware of some of the difficulties we encounter when we try to define unemployment:

> A man is only unemployed when he is *both* not employed and *also* desires to be employed. Moreover, the notion of desiring to be employed must be interpreted in relation to established facts as regards (1) hours of work per day, (2) rates of wage, and (3) a man's state of health.

This definition reveals that many subjective and arbitrary elements enter into the concept of "unemployment." But we shall see presently that there are many more difficulties than even Pigou's definition allows for.

After considerable discussion Pigou ends up with the conclusion that "The quantity of unemployment prevailing at any time is equal to the number of would-be wage-earners *minus* the quantity of labor demanded *plus* the number of unfilled vacancies."

It is important to notice here that the "number of *would-be* wage-earners" is not only largely a *subjective* rather than an *objective* quantity, but that "the quantity of labor demanded" and "the number of unfilled vacancies" are also largely subjective, rather than objective, because they depend on the changing intentions of employers. If I could get a man to mow my lawn at a certain hourly rate, there would be an "unfilled vacancy" at that rate, but if the professional gardeners available all demand more, I may decide either to mow my lawn myself, or to let it grow.

This principle applies throughout industry. Whether there are "unfilled vacancies" in a given firm may depend not only on the wage-rate at which the vacancies could be filled but whether employees with certain special qualities could be obtained.

In another place Pigou writes:

> A contrast is often drawn between situations in which there are more men available for jobs than jobs available for men and situations in which there are more jobs than men. In the former class of situation we have less than full employment, that is unemployment, in the latter more than full employment, that is over-full or, more briefly, over-employment.

All this looks extremely simple. But the difficulty of statistical quantification, of deciding precisely what the numerical relationship is of "men available" to "jobs available," is precisely the difficulty of defining not only what is meant by "men *available*," but what is meant by a "job," particularly when it is "unfilled."

Let us try Sir William Beveridge. In his *Full Employment in a Free Society,* he defines full employment in his opening pages as "having always more vacant jobs than unemployed men. . . . The labor market should always be a seller's market rather than a buyer's market."

But this is obviously defining full employment as *over*employment. (Incidentally, Sir William's demand that there must always be more vacant jobs than unemployed men is a demand that labor should be always *underpaid*. For this condition could only exist if the marginal product of labor were higher than its wage-rate, and labor, though "fully employed," would therefore be getting less than its full potential income.)

One of the most realistic discussions of the difficulties in the concept of full employment is that of Edwin G. Nourse, formerly Chairman of the President's Council of Economic Advisers. Commenting upon the declaration of policy in the American Employment Act of 1946, he writes:

> The phrase, "those able, willing, and seeking to work," does not define a labor force for whose optimum utilization the federal government can, in good

economic conscience, pledge itself to "utilize all its plans, functions, and resources." In the absence of objective criteria, the word "able" becomes practically meaningless. Whether a given person is, in a commercial or industrial sense, able to work is a decidedly relative matter. Able to work steadily or only intermittently? At the kinds of work for which demand presently exists, only with other skills, or without any particular skill, aptitude, or even teachability? Able to work as determined by a doctor's certificate or by a foreman's report? Under standard shop or office conditions or only with special facilities or treatment? Equally rich in ambiguity is the companion term "willing." It was inserted as a gesture of reassurance to those who feared the camel of authoritarianism might be getting his nose under the tent of free enterprise. But does it mean willing to work at such jobs as are available or only at the job of one's dreams? Willing to work on a time schedule dictated by employers' needs or by workers' convenience? Seeking is, of necessity, the criterion relied on by the Census Bureau in giving us a monthly estimate of involuntary unemployment. But "wanting" would be a more apt term for our purpose since it is a commonplace in the experience of all who have dealt with the unemployed to find not a few persons who want work—may even need it desperately—and who yet are not actively seeking a job because they have become convinced that the search is hopeless.

The plain fact is that the size of our labor force is statistically determinate only within the limits of quite categorical definitions.

When we speak of full employment, therefore, we would do better to use the term not as the Keynesian zealots use it, and not with any effort at an unattainable mathematical precision, but in a loose, common-sense way to mean merely the absence of substantial or abnormal unemployment.

If it be objected that this is not in fact a definition of *full* employment (and it is certainly not *brimful* employment), then I suggest that the term might be dropped entirely, and the term *optimum* employment used instead. This would have, among other advantages, that of reminding the user as well as his audience that employment is rather a means than an end, and that its optimum size is relative to other conditions or goals.

2. Is It Attainable?

Is "full employment" attainable? Here even those who favor the goal begin to waver. Alvin Hansen, in his definition of full employment in *Economic Policy and Full Employment*, declares that: "In an economy as large as that of the United States, it is probable that at 'full employment' there would be at any one time between 2 and 3 million temporarily unemployed." (About 4.5 per cent of the civilian labor force of 1945-47.)

Paul Douglas, commenting on Beveridge's use of a 3 per cent margin for seasonal and transitional unemployment, declared that such a criterion would be "fatal" in the United States: "To use deficit financing to drive unemployment down below 6 per cent is very dangerous. It will tend to do far more harm through inflation than the good it will do by absorbing those who are unemployed from seasonal and transitional causes."

3. Is It Unconditionally Desirable?

So when "full employment" is seriously discussed, it turns out to be less than full employment. And the desirability of "full employment at whatever cost" is gravely questioned.

Lionel Robbins, quoting the Beveridge definition of full employment as "having always more vacant jobs than unemployed men," points out that: "A state of affairs in which, at current rates of wages, the demand for labor is continually greater than the supply, must be a state of affairs in which, in the absence of special restraints, the level of wage rates, and hence the level of prices, is tending continually to rise." He goes on to point out that even a full employment policy that tried to guarantee a mere *equality* of jobs and applicants would have to guarantee the trade unions that *"whatever [wage] rates they succeeded in getting, unemployment would not be permitted to emerge."* Professor Robbins concludes that Beveridgian full employment "tends to inflation, reduced adaptability, external disequilibrium and a most drastic curtailment of individual liberty."

Edwin Nourse, in the article from which I have previously quoted, declares that: "Ideally full employment would be such as promotes continuous maximization of production and real purchasing power for the people." But this definition recognizes that full employment is desirable, not as an end in itself, but only as a means to much broader ends.

Even the "maximization of production" must be understood, not in the sense of the mere piling up of physical things, but in the sense of the maximization of consumer satisfactions. And this includes also, for example, the "production" (or "consumption"?) of more leisure at the cost of less desired (physical) things.

If we are talking not of unavoidable means but of desired ends, then we must recognize that the economic objective of mankind is not more work but less. I hope I may be forgiven for quoting what I have written in another place:

> The economic goal of any nation, as of any individual, is to get the greatest results with the least effort. The whole economic progress of mankind has consisted in getting more production with the same labor. It is for this reason that men began putting burdens on the backs of mules instead of on their own; that they went on to invent the wheel and the wagon, the railroad and the motor truck. It is for this reason that men used their ingenuity to develop a hundred thousand labor-saving inventions.

> All this is so elementary that one would blush to state it if it were not being constantly forgotten by those who coin and circulate the new slogans. Translated into national terms, this first principle means that our real objective is to maximize production. In doing this, full employment—that is, the absence of involuntary idleness—becomes a necessary by-product. But production is the end, employment merely the means. We cannot continuously have the fullest production without full employment. But we can very easily have full employment without full production.

> Primitive tribes are naked, and wretchedly fed and housed, but they do not suffer from unemployment. China and India are incomparably poorer than ourselves, but the main trouble from which they suffer is primitive production methods (which are both a cause and a consequence of a shortage of capital) and not unemployment. Nothing is easier to achieve than full employment, once it is divorced from the goal of full production and taken as an end in itself. Hitler provided full employment with a huge armament program. The war provided full employment for every nation involved. The slave labor in Russia had full employment. Prisons and chain gangs have full employment. Coercion can always provide full employment. . . .

> The progress of civilization has meant the reduction of employment, not its increase. It is because we have become increasingly wealthy as a nation that we have been able virtually to eliminate child labor, to remove the necessity of work for many of the aged and to make it unnecessary for millions of women to take jobs. (*Economics in One Lesson*. 1946. New York: Harper, pp. 68-70.)

Robert E. Lucas, Jr.

(1937-)

Robert Lucas, Jr., is a leading modern macroeconomist. He has played a key role in revital-
izing the classical school of economics and has inherited the Chicago mantle of monetarism
from Milton Friedman. He is a superb theoretician and most of his work is highly technical and
extremely complicated. His theoretical work, with Leonard Rapping, on the foundation of the
Phillips curve was instrumental in converting economists from Keynesian economics to New
Classical economics, and he is probably the foremost rational expectations theorist today.

This article demonstrates his ability to derive meaningful implications from his theoretical
work. In it he argues that the distinction between voluntary and involuntary unemployment
cannot be made and that one "cannot, even conceptually, arrive at a usable definition of full
employment as a state in which no involuntary unemployment exists." He then goes on to argue
that normative macroeconomics should be practiced without a construct of full employment.

Robert Lucas. 1978. "Unemployment Policy." *American Economic Review*, May, pp. 353-357.

Unemployment Policy

The U.S. unemployment rate was certainly too high in 1975, and most economists would agree that it is too high today (1978). It will also be agreed that this observation poses a problem for public policy (in a sense that the observation that winters in Chicago are "too cold" does not). But what exactly is meant by the statement that unemployment is "too high," and what is the nature of the policy problem it poses? This question can be answered in more than one way, and the answer one chooses matters a great deal.

One common answer to this question is that there exists a rate of unemployment—call it "full employment"—which can and should serve as a "target" for economic policy. Unemployment above this rate is regarded as being of a different character from the "frictional" unemployment required to match workers and jobs efficiently, and is treated from a welfare point of view as waste, or deadweight loss. Elimination of this waste is an objective of monetary, fiscal, and perhaps other policies. In the first part of this [article] I will argue that this way of posing the issue does not lead to an operational basis for unemployment policy, mainly on the ground that economists have no coherent idea as to what full employment means or how it can be measured.

An alternative view, prevalent prior to the Great Depression and enjoying something of a revival today, treats *fluctuations* in unemployment and other variables as posing a policy problem. On this view, the average (or natural, or equilibrium) rate of unemployment is viewed as raising policy issues only insofar as it can be shown to be "distorted" in an undesirable way by taxes, external effects, and so on. Nine percent unemployment is then viewed as too high in the same sense that 2 percent is viewed as "too low": both are symptoms of costly and preventable instability in general economic activity. In the concluding part of this [article] I will sketch the approaches to unemployment policy which are suggested by this alternative view and some which are not.

I. Full Employment: Definition and Measurement

The idea that policy can and should be directed at the attainment of a particular, specifiable *level* of the measured rate of unemployment (as opposed to mitigating *fluctuations* in unemployment) owes its wide acceptance to John Maynard Keynes' *General Theory*. It is there derived from the prior hypothesis that measured unemployment can be decomposed into two distinct components: "voluntary" (or frictional) and "involuntary," with full employment then identified as the level prevailing when involuntary unemployment equals zero. It seems appropriate, then, to begin by reviewing Keynes' reasons for introducing this distinction in the first place.

Keynes (ch. 2, p. 7) classifies the factors affecting equilibrium employment in a real general equilibrium theory: the mechanics of matching workers to jobs, household labor-leisure preferences, technology, and the composition of product demand. Is it the case, he asks, that spontaneous shifts in any of these four real factors can account for employment fluctuations of the magnitude we observe? Evidently, the answer is negative. It follows that two kinds of theory must be needed to account for observed unemployment movements: granted that real general equilibrium theory may account for a relatively constant, positive component, *some other theory* is needed for the rest.

Accepting the necessity of a distinction between explanations for normal and cyclical unemployment does not, however, compel one to identify the first as voluntary and the second as involuntary, as Keynes goes on to do. This terminology suggests that the key to the distinction lies in some difference in the way two different types of unemployment are *perceived by workers*. Now in the first place, the distinction we are after concerns *sources* of unemployment, not differentiated types. One may, for example, seek very different theoretical explanations for the average price of a commodity and for its day-to-day fluctuations, without postulating two types of price for the same good. Similarly, one may classify motives for holding money without imagining that anyone can subdivide his own cash holdings into "transactions balances," "precautionary balances," and so forth. The recognition that one needs to distinguish among sources of unemployment does not in any way imply that one needs to distinguish among types.

Nor is there any evident reason why one would *want* to draw this distinction. Certainly the more one thinks about the decision problem facing individual workers and firms the less sense this distinction makes. The worker who loses a good job in prosperous times does not *volunteer* to be in this situation: he has suffered a capital loss. Similarly, the firm which loses an experienced employee in depressed times suffers an undesired capital loss. Nevertheless the unemployed worker at any time can always find *some* job at once, and a firm can always fill a vacancy instantaneously. That neither typically does so *by choice* is not difficult to understand given the quality of the jobs and the employees which are easiest to find. Thus there is an involuntary element in *all* unemployment, in the sense that no one chooses bad luck over good; there is also a voluntary element in all unemployment, in the sense that however miserable one's current work options, one can always choose to accept them.

Keynes, in chapter 2, deals with the situation facing an *individual* unemployed worker by evasion and wordplay only. Sentences like "more labor would, as a rule, be forthcoming at the existing money wage if it were demanded" are used again and again as though, from the, point of view of a jobless worker, it is unambiguous what is meant by *"the* existing money wage." Unless we define an individual's wage rate as the price someone else is willing to pay him for his labor (in which case Keynes' assertion above *is defined* to be false), what *is* it? The wage at which he would *like* to work more hours? Then it is true by definition and equally empty. The fact is, I think, that Keynes wanted to get labor markets out of the way in chapter 2 so that he could get on to the demand theory which really interested him. This is surely understandable, but what is the excuse for letting his carelessly drawn distinction between voluntary and involuntary unemployment dominate aggregative thinking on labor markets for the forty years following?

It is, to be sure, possible to write down theoretical models in which households are faced with an "hours constraint" limiting the hours they can supply at "the" prevailing wage, and in which, therefore, there is a clear distinction between the hours one can supply and the hours one would like to supply. Such an exercise is frequently motivated as an attempt to "explain involuntary (or Keynesian) unemployment." This misses the point: involuntary unemployment is not a fact or a phenomenon which it is the task of theorists to explain. It is, on the contrary, a theoretical construct which Keynes introduced in the hope that it would be helpful in discovering a correct explanation for a genuine phenomenon: large-scale fluctuations in measured, total unemployment. Is it the task of modern theoretical economics to "explain" the theoretical constructs of our predecessors, whether or not they have proved fruitful? I hope not, for a surer route to sterility could scarcely be imagined.

In summary, it does not appear possible, even in principle, to classify individual unemployed people as either voluntarily or involuntarily unemployed depending on the characteristics of the decision problems they face. One cannot, even conceptually, arrive at a usable definition of full employment as a state in which no involuntary unemployment exists.

* * * *

II. Beyond Full-Employment Policy

Abandoning the constraint that any discussion of unemployment must begin first by drawing the voluntary-involuntary distinction and then thinking in separate ways about these two types of unemployment will, I think, benefit both positive and normative analysis. Practicing social science is hard enough without crippling oneself with dogmatic constraints. A terminology which precludes asking the question: "Why do people choose to take the actions we see them taking, instead of other actions they might take instead?" precludes any serious thinking about behavior at all.

Whether or not the body of work stemming from the Edmund Phelps volume, and earlier work of George Stigler, John McCall and others, has produced all the right answers about the determinants of employment and unemployment, it has at least begun to pose some of the right questions. By treating all unemployment as voluntary, this work has led to the examination of alternative arrangements which firms and employees might choose to adopt for dealing with fluctuations in product demand, and their reasons for choosing to react to such fluctuations in the way we observe them doing. Pursuit of this question has indicated both how very difficult it is, and even more so how much economics was swept under the rug by "explaining involuntary unemployment" by incompetent auctioneers or purely mechanical wage and price equations.

Practicing normative macroeconomics without the construct of full employment does take some getting used to. One finds oneself slipping into such sentences as: "There is no such thing as full employment, but I can tell you how it can be attained." But there are some immediate benefits. First, one dispenses with that entire meaningless vocabulary associated with full employment, phrases like potential output, full capacity, slack, and so on, which suggested that there was some *technical* reason why we couldn't all return to the 1890 workweek and produce half again the *GNP* we now produce. Second, one finds to one's relief that creating unemployment as a voluntary response to an unwelcome situation does not commit oneself to normative nonsense like blaming depressions on lazy workers.

The effect it does have on normative discussion is twofold. First, it focuses discussion of monetary and fiscal policy on *stabilization,* on the pursuit of price stability and on minimizing the disruptive effects of erratic policy changes. Some average unemployment rate would, of course, emerge from such a policy but as a by-product, not as a preselected target. Second, by thinking of this natural rate as an equilibrium emerging from voluntary exchange in the usual sense, one can subject it to the scrutiny of modern methods of public finance.

To take one example, as the level of unemployment compensation is varied, an entire range of average unemployment rates, all equally "natural," is available to society. At one extreme, severe penalties to declaring oneself unemployed could reduce unemployment rates to any desired level. Such a policy would result in serious real output losses, as workers retain poor jobs too long and accept poor jobs too readily. An output-maximizing unemployment compensation scheme would, with risk-averse workers, involve a subsidy to being unemployed, else workers retain a poor but relatively sure current wage in preference to the riskier but, on average, more productive return to seeking a new job. In view of the private market's inability to provide sufficient insurance against unemployment risk, still further gains in expected utility could be expected by still higher unemployment compensation, resulting in a deliberate sacrifice in real output in exchange for a preferred arrangement for allocating risk. Notice that as one traces out tradeoffs of this sort, the issue of slack or waste does not arise. Different policies result in different levels of real output, but output increases are necessarily obtained at the expense of something else. Whether any particular level of unemployment compensation is too high or too low is a difficult issue in practice, but it is one that cannot be resolved simply by observing that other, unemployment reducing, compensation levels are *feasible*.

The policy problem of reducing business cycle risk is a very real and important one, and one which I believe monetary and fiscal policies directed at price stability would go a long way toward achieving. The problem of finding arrangements for allocating unemployment risks over individuals in a satisfactory way is also important, and can be analyzed by the methods of modern welfare economics. The pursuit of a full-employment target which no one can measure or even define conceptually cannot be expected to contribute to the solution of either problem.

U.S. Congress

All the grand talk and arguments of economists doesn't mean a whole lot unless it is some-how translated into law. In 1946 the government made a commitment to maintaining high employment by enacting the "Employment Act of 1946" ("Full" was removed from the title after significant debate). However, because of contradictory goals, the commitment was unenforceable.

In the 1970s a group in Congress again tried to build a commitment to full employment into U.S. law. The result was the "Full Employment and Balanced Growth Act of 1976" summarized here. As you read it, try to figure out what mandates it places on government and how it might make, or fail to make, the achievement of full employment more likely.

U.S. Congress, Committee on Education and Labor, Hearings on Equal Opportunities, 94th Congress. Washington, D.C. GPO, 1976.

Full Employment and Balanced Growth Act of 1976

The Full Employment and Balanced Growth Act of 1976 establishes the right of all adult Americans able, willing, and seeking to work to opportunities for useful paid employment at fair rates of compensation. To support that right, the act commits the U. S. Government to fundamental reform in the management of the economy so that full employment and balanced economic growth are achieved and sustained. This includes the creation of a permanent institutional framework within which the President, the Federal Reserve Board, and the Congress are systematically encouraged to develop and establish the economic goals and policies necessary to provide productive employment for all adult Americans, as well as the mandating of specific employment programs to achieve the goal of 3 percent unemployment as promptly as possible, but within not more than 4 years after the date of the enactment of this act.

Section-by-Section Analysis

SECTIONS 1 AND 2. These sections include the title, table of contents, and general findings. Among the most important general findings are: (1) the high social and economic costs of unemployment; (2) the need for explicit economic goals and a coordinated economic policy among the President, the Federal Reserve and Congress; (3) that inflation is often aggravated by high unemployment; and (4) that there must be direct employment and anti-inflation policies to supplement aggregate monetary and fiscal policies to achieve and maintain full employment and balanced growth.

TITLE I—ESTABLISHMENT OF GOALS, PLANNING AND GENERAL ECONOMIC POLICIES

SEC. 101.—STATEMENT OF PURPOSE. The purpose of this title is to declare the general policies of the act, to provide an open process under which annual economic goals are proposed, reviewed, and established; to provide for the development of a long-range Full Employment and Balanced Growth Plan, to provide for economy in government measures, to insure that monetary, fiscal, anti-inflation and general economic policies are used to achieve the annual economic goals to support the long-range goals and priorities of the Full Employment and Balanced Growth Plan, and generally to strengthen and supplement the purposes of the Employment Act of 1946.

SEC. 102—DECLARATION OF POLICY. The Employment Act of 1946 is amended to declare that all adult Americans able, willing, and seeking work have the right to useful paid employment at fair rates of compensation. Moreover, the Congress further declares that the Federal Government use all practical means, including improved anti-inflation polices, to promote full employment, production and purchasing power.

SEC. 103—ECONOMIC GOALS AND THE ECONOMIC REPORT OF THE PRESIDENT. The Employment Act of 1946 is amended to require the President in each annual Economic Report to recommend numerical goals for employment, production, and purchasing power, as well as policies to support these goals and achieve balanced growth and full employment of the Nation's human and capital resources as promptly as possible.

SEC. 104—FULL EMPLOYMENT AND BALANCED GROWTH PLAN. The Employment Act of 1946 is amended to establish a process of long-range economic planning, through the Council of Economic Advisers, to analyze developing economic conditions, to recommend long-term goals for full employment, production, and purchasing power, and to propose priority policies and programs to achieve such goals and to meet national needs. A long-term full employment goal is set at 3 percent adult unemployment, to be attained as promptly as possible, but within not more than 4 years after the date of the enactment of this act.

SEC. 105—ECONOMY IN GOVERNMENT. This section establishes policies and procedures to improve the effectiveness of the Federal Government through the comprehensive planning framework established under this act. In conjunction with the submission of each Full Employment and Balanced Growth Plan, the President shall submit proposals for improving the efficiency and economy of the Federal Government, including, but not limited to, a review of existing Government rules and regulations to determine if they still serve a purpose, and an annual evaluation of 20 percent of the dollar volume of existing Federal programs.

SEC. 106—FISCAL AND MONETARY POLICIES. The Employment Act of 1946 is amended to require that monetary and fiscal policies be utilized in the optimum manner necessary to achieve full employment and balanced growth, including the requirement that the President determine the extent to which fiscal policy can be relied upon to achieve our economic goals and priorities, so that it becomes possible to estimate what supplementary job creation and anti-inflation policies must be utilized to achieve the objectives of this act.

This section also requires the Federal Reserve Board to make an independent report to the President and Congress, in conjunction with each Economic Report, identifying the extent to which the Federal Reserve will support the economic goals recommended in the President's Economic Report and, if the Federal Reserve Board does not support such goals, to provide a full justification of why and to what extent its policies will differ from those recommended by the President. If the President determines that the Board's policies are inconsistent with proposed economic goals and priorities, the President shall make recommendations to the Board and Congress to insure closer conformity with the purposes of this act.

SEC. 107—ANTI-INFLATION POLICIES. The Employment Act of 1946 is amended to require that each Economic Report contain a comprehensive set of anti-inflation policies to supplement monetary and fiscal policy, including, but not limited to, analyzing inflationary trends in individual economic sectors; actions to increase the supply of goods, services, labor, and capital in tight markets, particularly food and energy; provision for an export-licensing mechanism for critical materials in short supply; recommendations to increase productivity in the private sector; recommendations to strengthen and enforce the antitrust laws, and recommendations for administrative and legislative actions to promote reasonable price stability if situations develop that seriously threaten national price stability.

SEC. 108—COUNCIL OF ECONOMIC ADVISERS. The Employment Act of 1946 is amended to require the Council of Economic Advisers to prepare the Full Employment and Balanced Growth Plan, to consult with the Advisory Committee, and to meet other requirements under this act.

SEC. 109—ADVISORY COMMITTEE ON FULL EMPLOYMENT AND BALANCED GROWTH. The Employment Act of 1946 is amended to establish a 12-member private Advisory Committee on Full Employment and Balanced Growth to advise and assist the Council of Economic Advisers on matters relating to the Economic Report and this act. The members of the committee shall be appointed proportionately by the President, the Speaker of the House of Representatives, and the President pro tempore of the Senate in a manner broadly representative of the Public.

TITLE II—COUNTERCYCLICAL, STRUCTURAL AND YOUTH EMPLOYMENT POLICIES

SEC. 201—STATEMENT OF PURPOSE. This title establishes supplementary employment policies to close the employment gap, if one should exist, between the levels of employment achieved through aggregate monetary and fiscal policy and the employment goals established in sections 103 and 104. Accordingly, this title establishes a system of comprehensive and flexible employment policies to create jobs in both the private and public sectors of the economy. These supplementary employment policies shall vary according to economic conditions and the other actions taken under this act, but focus broadly upon reducing cyclical, structural, regional, youth unemployment, and unemployment due to discrimination. This title also establishes a Full Employment Office within the Department of Labor to use special means for training, assisting, and providing employment for those people who are otherwise unable to find employment. Finally, this title mandates improved integration of income-maintenance programs and full employment policies.

SEC. 202—COUNTERCYCLICAL EMPLOYMENT POLICIES. This section requires the development and submission by the President, within 90 days of the enactment of this act, of a coherent and flexible countercyclical program to reduce high unemployment arising from cyclical movements in the economy. This comprehensive program shall include, as appropriate, public service employment, standby public works, antirecession grants for State and local governments, skill training in both the public and private sectors, and other programs. Moreover, this program shall be automatically implemented during periods of high unemployment, allocate employment assistance to areas of highest unemployment, provide for a well-balanced combination of job creation and related activities in both the private and public sectors, and incorporate transitional mechanisms to aid individuals in returning to regular employment as the economy recovers.

SEC. 203—COORDINATION WITH STATE AND LOCAL GOVERNMENTS AND PRIVATE SECTOR ECONOMIC ACTIVITY. This section requires the development of policies that facilitate harmonious economic action between the Federal Government, regions, States, localities and the private sector. As a primary effort to achieve these ends, the President is required to submit legislation, within 90 days of the enactment of this act, creating a permanent, countercyclical grant program that will serve to stabilize State and local budgets during periods of recession and high unemployment. This program shall be automatically implemented when the national unemployment exceeds a specified level and distribute its funds to those areas of most serious unemployment.

SEC. 204—REGIONAL AND STRUCTURAL EMPLOYMENT POLICIES. This section requires the establishment of comprehensive employment policies designed to reduce the chronic underutilization of human and capital resources in certain areas of the country and in specific groups within the labor force. As a primary effort to reduce unemployment in chronically depressed areas, the President is required within 180 days after the date of enactment of this act to submit legislation providing an institutional means to make credit available: (1) for public and private investment in economically depressed regions, inner cities, and economic sectors; and (2) to provide an alternative source of capital funds for local and State governments to finance public facilities.

SEC. 205—YOUTH EMPLOYMENT POLICIES. This section requires the development and submission by the President, within 90 days of the enactment of this act, of a comprehensive youth employment program to: (1) foster a smoother transition from school to work; (2) prepare disadvantaged youths with employment handicaps for self-sustaining unemployment through education, training, medical services, counseling and other support activities; (3) develop methods for combining training with work, including apprenticeship and on-the job training in the private sector; and (4) provide job opportunities in a variety of tasks including conservation, public service activities, inner-city cleanup and rehabilitation
and other jobs of value to States, local communities, and the Nation.

SEC. 206—FULL EMPLOYMENT OFFICE AND JOB RESERVOIRS. To insure that full employment is achieved under this act, the President, through the Secretary of Labor, shall develop policies and programs to provide job opportunities to adult Americans who, despite a serious effort to obtain employment, are unable to do so in the general economic environment, or through any of the other provisions of this act. There is established within the Department of Labor a Full Employment Office to assist the Secretary of Labor in providing such job opportunities through counseling, training, and referral to job opportunities in the private sector and in positions drawn from sections 202, 204, and 205 of this act. Additional job opportunities will be provided, subject to regulations on job need and eligibility, through reservoirs of federally operated or approved employment projects, to be phased in by the President in conjunction with the annual employment recommendations required under section 3 of the Employment Act of 1946, and to achieve 3 percent unemployment within 4 years of enactment of this act.

SEC. 207—INCOME MAINTENANCE AND FULL EMPLOYMENT POLICIES. This section requires that full employment policies: (1) provide quality jobs that strengthen income and eliminate substandard earnings; (2) integrate existing income maintenance policies with the full employment policies established by this act; and (3) substitute work for income maintenance to the maximum extent feasible.

John Maynard Keynes

(1883-1946)

This selection is from John Maynard Keynes, to whom you have been introduced in the textbook. It comes from the preface and first chapter of his famous book, The General Theory of Employment Interest and Money *(1936), and it describes the evolution of his thinking—away from the quantity theory of money of the classical economists and toward a theory of output as a whole in which aggregate supply and aggregate demand are interdependent.*

Our selection includes the preface (written in December, 1935) and the entire first chapter of The General Theory—*at less than one page, it is the shortest chapter in the history of economic literature. He devotes his first chapter to emphasizing that his new theory is a general theory of which the classical theory is a special case.*

John Maynard Keynes. 1936. *The General Theory of Employment Interest and Money.* London: Macmillan, pp. v-viii, 3.

The General Theory

Preface

This book is chiefly addressed to my fellow economists. I hope that it will be intelligible to others. But its main purpose is to deal with difficult questions of theory, and only in the second place with the applications of this theory to practice. For if orthodox economics is at fault, the error is to be found not in the superstructure, which has been erected with great care for logical consistency, but in a lack of clearness and of generality in the premises. Thus I cannot achieve my object of persuading economists to re-examine critically certain of their basic assumptions except by a highly abstract argument and also by much controversy. I wish there could have been less of the latter. But I have thought it important, not only to explain my own point of view, but also to show in what respects it departs from the prevailing theory. Those, who are strongly wedded to what I shall call "the classical theory", will fluctuate, I expect between a belief that I am quite wrong and a belief that I am saying nothing new. It is for others to determine if either of these or the third alternative is right. My controversial passages are aimed at providing some material for an answer; and I must ask forgiveness if, in the pursuit of sharp distinctions, my controversy is itself too keen. I myself held with conviction for many years the theories which I now attack, and I am not, I think, ignorant of their strong points.

The matters at issue are of an importance which cannot be exaggerated. But, if my explanations are right, it is my fellow economists, not the general public, whom I must first convince. At this stage of the argument the general public, though welcome at the debate, are only eavesdroppers at an attempt by an economist to bring to an issue the deep divergences of opinion between fellow economists which have for the time being almost destroyed the practical influence of economic theory, and will, until they are resolved, continue to do so.

The relation between this book and my *Treatise on Money,* which I published five years ago, is probably clearer to myself than it will be to others; and what in my own mind is a natural evolution in a line of thought which I have been pursuing for several years, may sometimes strike the reader as a confusing change of view. This difficulty is not made less by certain changes in terminology which I have felt compelled to make. These changes of language I have pointed out in the course of the following pages; but the general relationship between the two books can be expressed briefly as follows. When I began to write my *Treatise on Money* I was still moving along the traditional lines of regarding the influence of money as something so to speak separate from the general theory of supply and demand. When I finished it, I had made some progress towards pushing monetary theory back to becoming a theory of output as a whole. But my lack of emancipation from preconceived ideas showed itself in what now seems to me to be the outstanding fault of the theoretical parts of that work (namely, Books III and IV), that I failed to deal thoroughly with the effects of *changes* in the level of output. My so called "fundamental equations" were an instantaneous picture taken on the assumption of a given output. They attempted to show how, assuming the given output, forces could develop which involved a profit-disequilibrium, and thus required a change in the level of output. But the dynamic development, as distinct from the instantaneous picture, was left incomplete and extremely confused. This book, on the other hand, has evolved into what is primarily a study of the forces which determine changes in the scale of output and employment as a whole; and, whilst it is found that money enters into the economic scheme in an essential and peculiar manner, technical monetary detail falls into the background. A monetary economy we shall find, is essentially one in which changing views about the future are capable of influencing the quantity of employment and not merely its direction. But our method of analysing the economic behaviour of the present under the influence of changing ideas about the future is one which depends on the interaction of supply and demand, and is in this way linked up with our fundamental theory of value. We are thus led to a more general theory, which includes the classical theory with which we are familiar, as a special case.

* * * *

The composition of this book has been for the author a long struggle of escape, and so must the reading of it be for most readers if the author's assault upon them is to be successful,—a struggle of escape from habitual modes of thought and expression. The ideas which are here expressed so laboriously are extremely simple and should be obvious. The difficulty lies, not in the new ideas, but in escaping from the old ones, which ramify, for those brought up as most of us have been, into every corner of our minds.

Chapter 1

I have called this book the *General Theory of Employment Interest and Money,* placing the emphasis on the prefix *general.* The object of such a title is to contrast the character of my arguments and conclusions with those of the *classical* theory of the subject, upon which I was brought up and which dominates the economic thought, both practical and theoretical, of the governing and academic classes of this generation, as it has for a hundred years past. I shall argue that the postulates of the classical theory are applicable to a special case only and not to the general case, the situation which it assumes being a limiting point of the possible positions—of equilibrium. Moreover, the characteristics of the special case assumed by the classical theory happen not to be those of the economic society in which we actually live, with the result that its teaching is misleading and disastrous if we attempt to apply it to the facts of experience.

John Kenneth Galbraith
(1908-)

Few economists have the range of John Kenneth Galbraith, whose work became well known to most people in the United States as well as to economists. In this selection, Galbraith discusses how Keynesian ideas came to the United States. In doing so, he introduces a number of the authors of our other macro section selections. Galbraith consistently expanded the domain of economics to include broader social issues and his New Industrial State *and* The Affluent Society *are considered classics in popular economic literature.*

John Kenneth Galbraith. 1971. *Economics, Peace and Laughter*. Boston: Houghton Mifflin, pp. 43-50.

How Keynes Came to America

I believe myself to be writing a book on economic theory which will largely revolutionize—not, I suppose, at once but in the course of the next ten years—the way the world thinks about economic problems.

Letter from John Maynard Keynes to George Bernard Shaw,
New Year's Day, 1935.

The most influential book on economic and social policy so far in this century, *The General Theory of Employment Interest and Money* by John Maynard Keynes, was published in 1936 in both Britain and the United States. A paperback edition became available in America for the first time not long ago and quite a few people who took advantage of this bargain must have been puzzled at the reason for the book's influence. Though comfortably aware of their own intelligence, they could not read it. They must have wondered, accordingly, how it persuaded so many other people—not all of whom, certainly, were more penetrating or diligent. This was only one of the remarkable things about this book and the revolution it precipitated.

By common, if not yet quite universal, agreement, the Keynesian revolution was one of the great modern accomplishments in social design. It brought Marxism in the advanced countries to a total halt. It led to a level of economic performance that inspired bitter-end conservatives to panegyrics of unexampled banality. Yet those responsible have had no honors and some opprobrium. For a long while, to be known as an active Keynesian was to invite the wrath of those who equate social advance with subversion. Those concerned developed a habit of reticence. As a further consequence, the history of the revolution is, perhaps, the worst told story of our era.

It is time that we knew better this part of our history and those who made it, and this is a little of the story. Much of it turns on the almost unique unreadability of *The General Theory* and hence the need for people to translate and propagate its ideas to government officials, students and the public at large. As Messiahs go, Keynes was deeply dependent on his prophets.

The General Theory appeared in the sixth year of the Great Depression and the fifty-third of Keynes's life. At the time Keynes, like his great contemporary Churchill, was regarded as too candid and inconvenient to be trusted. Public officials are not always admiring of men who say what the right policy should be. Their frequent need, especially in foreign affairs, is for men who will find persuasive reasons for the wrong policy. Keynes had foreseen grave difficulty from the reparations clauses of the Versailles Treaty and had voiced them in *The Economic Consequences of the Peace,* a brilliantly polemical volume, which may well have overstated his case and which certainly was unjust to Woodrow Wilson but which nonetheless provided what proved to be a clearer view of the postwar economic disasters than the men of more stately view wished anyone to expect.

65

Later in the twenties, in another book, he was equally untactful toward those who invited massive unemployment in Britain in order to return sterling to the gold standard of its prewar parity with the dollar. The man immediately responsible for this effort, a highly orthodox voice in economic matters at the time, was the then Chancellor of the Exchequer, Winston Churchill, and that book was called *The Economic Consequences of Mr. Churchill.*

From 1920 to 1940, Keynes was sought out by students and intellectuals in Cambridge and London; was well known in London theater and artistic circles; directed an insurance company; made, and on occasion lost, quite a bit of money; and was an influential journalist. But he wasn't really trusted on public questions. The great trade union which identifies trustworthiness with conformity kept him outside. Then came the Depression. There was much unemployment, much suffering. Even respectable men went broke. It was necessary, however unpleasant, to listen to the candid men who had something to say by way of remedy. This listening is the terrible punishment the gods reserve for fair weather statesmen.

It is a measure of how far the Keynesian revolution has proceeded that the central thesis of *The General Theory* now sounds rather commonplace. Until it appeared, economists, in the classical (or nonsocialist) tradition, had assumed that the economy, if left to itself, would find its equilibrium at full employment. Increases or decreases in wages and in interest rates would occur as necessary to bring about this pleasant result. If men were unemployed, their wages would fall in relation to prices. With lower wages and wider margins, it would be profitable to employ those from whose toil an adequate return could not previously have been made. It followed that steps to keep wages at artificially high levels, such as might result from (as it was said) the ill-considered efforts by unions, would cause unemployment. Such efforts were deemed to be the principal cause of unemployment.

Movements in interest rates played a complementary role by ensuring that all income would ultimately be spent. Thus, were people to decide for some reason to increase their savings, the interest rates on the now more abundant supply of loanable funds would fall. This, in turn, would lead to increased investment. The added outlays for investment goods would offset the diminished outlays by the more frugal consumers. In this fashion, changes in consumer spending or in investment decisions were kept from causing any change in total spending that would lead to unemployment.

Keynes argued that neither wage movements nor changes in the rate of interest had, necessarily, any such benign effect. He focused attention on the total of purchasing power in the economy—what freshmen are now taught to call aggregate demand. Wage reductions might not increase employment; in conjunction with other changes, they might merely reduce this aggregate demand. And he held that interest was not the price that was paid to people to save but the price they got for exchanging holdings of cash, or its equivalent, their normal preference in assets, for less liquid forms of investment. And it was difficult to reduce interest beyond a certain level. Accordingly, if people sought to save more, this wouldn't necessarily mean lower interest rates and a resulting increase in investment. Instead, the total demand for goods might fall, along with employment and also investment, until savings were brought back into line with investment by the pressure of hardship which had reduced saving in favor of consumption. The economy would find its equilibrium not at full employment but with an unspecified amount of unemployment.

Out of this diagnosis came the remedy. It was to bring aggregate demand back up to the level where all willing workers were employed; and this could be accomplished by supplementing private expenditure with public expenditure. This should be the policy wherever intentions to save exceeded intentions to invest. Since public spending would not perform this offsetting role if there were compensating taxation (which is a form of saving), the public spending should be financed by borrowing—by incurring a deficit. So far as Keynes can be condensed into two paragraphs, this is it. *The General Theory* is more difficult. There are nearly 400 pages, some of them of fascinating obscurity.

Before the publication of *The General Theory,* Keynes had urged his ideas directly on President Roosevelt, most notably in a famous letter to the *New York Times* on December 31,

1933: "I lay overwhelming emphasis on the increase of national purchasing power resulting from government expenditure which is financed by loans." And he visited FDR in the summer of 1934 to press his case, although the session was no great success; each, during the meeting, developed some doubts about the general good sense of the other.

In the meantime, two key Washington officials, Marriner Eccles, the exceptionally able Utah banker who was to become head of the Federal Reserve Board, and Lauchlin Currie, a recent Harvard instructor who was its assistant director of research and later an economic aide to Roosevelt (and later still a prominent victim of McCarthyite persecution), had on their own account reached conclusions similar to those of Keynes as to the proper course of fiscal policy. When *The General Theory* arrived, they took it as confirmation of the course they had previously been urging. Currie, a brilliant economist and teacher, was also a skilled and influential interpreter of the ideas in the Washington community. Not often have important new ideas on economics entered a government by way of its central bank. Nor should anyone be disturbed. There is not the slightest indication that it will ever happen again.

Paralleling the work of Keynes in the thirties and rivaling it in importance, though not in fame, was that of Simon Kuznets and a group of young economists and statisticians at the University of Pennsylvania, the National Bureau of Economic Research and the United States Department of Commerce. They developed from earlier beginnings the now familiar concepts of National Income and Gross National Product and their components, and made estimates of their amount. Included among the components of National Income and Gross National Product were the saving, investment, aggregate of disposable income and the other magnitudes of which Keynes was talking. As a result, those who were translating Keynes's ideas into action could now know not only what needed to be done but how much. And many who would never have been persuaded by the Keynesian abstractions were compelled to belief by the concrete figures from Kuznets and his inventive colleagues.

However, the trumpet—if the metaphor is permissible for this particular book—that was sounded in Cambridge, England, was heard most clearly in Cambridge, Massachusetts. Harvard was the principal avenue by which Keynes's ideas passed to the United States. Conservatives worry about universities being centers of disquieting innovation. Their worries may be exaggerated but it has occurred.

In the late thirties, Harvard had a large community of young economists, most of them held there by the shortage of jobs that Keynes sought to cure. They had the normal confidence of their years in their ability to remake the world and, unlike less fortunate generations, the opportunity. They also had occupational indication of the need. Massive unemployment persisted year after year. It was degrading to have to continue telling the young that this was merely a temporary departure from the full employment norm, and that one need only obtain the needed wage reductions.

Paul Samuelson, who subsequently taught economics to an entire generation and who almost from the outset was the acknowledged leader of the younger Keynesian community, has compared the excitement of the young economists, on the arrival of Keynes's book, to that of Keats on first looking into Chapman's Homer. Some will wonder if economists are capable of such refined emotion, but the effect was certainly great. Here was a remedy for the despair that could be seen just beyond the [Harvard] Yard. It did not overthrow the system but saved it. To the nonrevolutionary, it seemed too good to be true. To the occasional revolutionary, it was. The old economics was still taught by day. But in the evening and almost every evening from 1936 on, almost everyone in the Harvard community discussed Keynes.

This might, conceivably, have remained a rather academic discussion. As with the Bible and Marx, obscurity stimulated abstract debate. But in 1938, the practical instincts that economists sometimes suppress with success were catalyzed by the arrival in Cambridge from Minnesota of Alvin H. Hansen. He was then about fifty, an effective teacher and a popular colleague. But, most of all, he was a man for whom economic ideas had no standing apart from their use. . . .

He proceeded to expound the ideas in books, articles and lectures and to apply them to the American scene. He persuaded his students and younger colleagues that they should not only understand the ideas but win understanding in others and then go on to get action. Without ever seeking to do so or being quite aware of the fact, he became the leader of a crusade. In the late thirties Hansen's seminar in the new Graduate School of Public Administration was regularly visited by the Washington policy-makers. Often the students overflowed into the hall. One felt that it was the most important thing currently happening in the country and this could have been the case.

The officials took Hansen's ideas, and perhaps even more his sense of conviction, back to Washington.

John Maynard Keynes
(1883-1946)

By now you should be quite familiar with John Maynard Keynes, the father of macroeconomics, so here we will provide only a brief introduction. This piece was written in the 1920s and was included in his Essays in Persuasion *(1931) in an essay entitled, "Inflation and Deflation." In the preface to that book Keynes called himself a "Cassandra who could never influence the course of events in time." Notice that this essay contains many of the ideas of the Keynesian economics of* The General Theory *even though it was published long before* The General Theory *was published. That's because there was a continuity in Keynes' thinking even though the model through which he conveyed his ideas changed. Thus, the ideas should be seen as an evolution, not as a revolution, in Keynes' thinking.*

John Maynard Keynes. 1931. Excerpt from "Inflation and Deflation," in *Essays in Persuasion*. New York: W.W. Norton, pp. 140-47.

Magneto Trouble

We have magneto trouble. How, then, can we start up again? Let us trace events backwards:

1. Why are workers and plant unemployed? Because industrialists do not expect to be able to sell without loss what would be produced if they were employed.
2. Why cannot industrialists expect to sell without loss? Because prices have fallen more than costs have fallen—indeed, costs have fallen very little.
3. How can it be that prices have fallen more than costs? For costs are what a business man pays out for the production of his commodity, and prices determine what he gets back when he sells it. It is easy to understand how for an individual business or an individual commodity these can be unequal. But surely for the community as a whole the business men get back the same amount as they pay out, since what the business men pay out in the course of production constitutes the incomes of the public which they pay back to the business men in exchange for the products of the latter? For this is what we understand by the normal circle of production, exchange, and consumption.
4. No! Unfortunately this is not so; and here is the root of the trouble. It is not true that what the business men pay out as costs of production necessarily comes back to them as the sale-proceeds of what they produce. It is the characteristic of a boom that their sale-proceeds exceed their costs; and it is the characteristic of a slump that their costs exceed their sale-proceeds. Moreover, it is a delusion to suppose that they can necessarily restore equilibrium by reducing their total costs, whether it be by restricting their output or cutting rates of remuneration; for the reduction of their outgoings may, by reducing the purchasing power of the earners who are also their customers, diminish their sale-proceeds by a nearly equal amount.
5. How, then, can it be that the total costs of production for the world's business as a whole can be unequal to the total sale-proceeds? Upon what does the inequality depend? I think that I know the answer. But it is too complicated and unfamiliar for me to expound it here satisfactorily. (Elsewhere I have tried to expound it accurately.) So I must be somewhat perfunctory.

Let us take, first of all, the consumption-goods which come on to the market for sale. Upon what do the profits (or losses) of the producers of such goods depend? The total costs of production, which are the same thing as the community's total earnings looked at from another point of view, are divided in a certain proportion between the cost of consumption-goods and the cost of capital-goods. The incomes of the public, which are again the same thing as the community's total earnings, are also divided in a certain proportion between expenditure on the purchase of consumption-goods and savings. Now if the first proportion is larger than the second, producers of consumption-goods will *lose* money; for their sale proceeds, which are equal to the expenditure of the public on consumption-goods, will be less (as a little thought will show) than what these goods have cost them to produce. If, on the other hand, the second proportion is larger than the first, then the producers of consumption-goods will make exceptional gains. It follows that the profits of the producers of consumption-goods can only be restored, either by the public spending a larger proportion of their incomes on such goods (which means saving less), or by a larger proportion of production taking the form of capital-goods (since this means a smaller proportionate output of consumption-goods).

But capital-goods will not be produced on a larger scale unless the producers of such goods are making a profit. So we come to our second question—upon what do the profits of the producers of capital-goods depend? They depend on whether the public prefer to keep their savings liquid in the shape of money or its equivalent or to use them to buy capital-goods or the equivalent. If the public are reluctant to buy the latter, then the producers of capital-goods will make a loss; consequently less capital-goods will be produced; with the result that, for the reasons given above, producers of consumption-goods will also make a loss. In other words, all classes of producers will tend to make a loss; and general unemployment will ensue. By this time a vicious circle will be set up, and, as the result of a series of actions and reactions, matters will get worse and worse until something happens to turn the tide.

This is an unduly simplified picture of a complicated phenomenon. But I believe that it contains the essential truth. Many variations and fugal embroideries and orchestrations can be superimposed; but this is the tune.

If, then, I am right, the fundamental cause of the trouble is the lack of new enterprise due to an unsatisfactory market for capital investment. Since trade is international, an insufficient output of new capital-goods in the world as a whole affects the prices of commodities everywhere and hence the profits of producers in all countries alike.

Why is there an insufficient output of new capital-goods in the world as a whole? It is due, in my opinion, to a conjunction of several causes. In the first instance, it was due to the attitude of lenders—for new capital-goods are produced to a large extent with borrowed money. Now it is due to the attitude of borrowers, just as much as to that of lenders.

For several reasons lenders were, and are, asking higher terms for loans than new enterprise can afford. First, the fact, that enterprise could afford high rates for some time after the war whilst war wastage was being made good, accustomed lenders to expect much higher rates than before the war. Second, the existence of political borrowers to meet Treaty obligations, of banking borrowers to support newly restored gold standards, of speculative borrowers to take part in Stock Exchange booms, and latterly, of distress borrowers to meet the losses which they have incurred through the fall of prices, all of whom were ready if necessary to pay almost any terms, have hitherto enabled lenders to secure from these various classes of borrowers higher rates than it is possible for genuine new enterprise to support. Third, the unsettled state of the world and national investment habits have restricted the countries in which many lenders are prepared to invest on any reasonable terms at all. A large proportion of the globe is, for one reason or another, distrusted by lenders, so that they exact a premium for risk so great as to strangle new enterprise altogether. For the last two years, two out of the three principal creditor nations of the world, namely, France and the United States, have largely withdrawn their resources from the international market for long-term loans.

Meanwhile, the reluctant attitude of lenders has become matched by a hardly less reluctant attitude on the part of borrowers. For the fall of prices has been disastrous to those who have borrowed, and any one who has postponed new enterprise has gained by his delay. Moreover, the risks that frighten lenders frighten borrowers too. Finally, in the United States, the vast scale on which new capital enterprise has been undertaken in the last five years has somewhat exhausted for the time being—at any rate so long as the atmosphere of business depression continues—the profitable opportunities for yet further enterprise. By the middle of 1929 new capital undertakings were already on an inadequate scale in the world as a whole, outside the United States. The culminating blow has been the collapse of new investment inside the United States, which to-day is probably 20 to 30 per cent less than it was in 1928. Thus in certain countries the opportunity for new profitable investment is more limited than it was; whilst in others it is more risky.

A wide gulf, therefore, is set between the ideas of lenders and the ideas of borrowers for the purpose of genuine new capital investment; with the result that the savings of the lenders are being used up in financing business losses and distress borrowers, instead of financing new capital works.

At this moment the slump is probably a little overdone for psychological reasons. A modest upward reaction, therefore, may be due at any time. But there cannot be a real recovery, in my judgement, until the ideas of lenders and the ideas of productive borrowers are brought together again; partly by lenders becoming ready to lend on easier terms and over a wider geographical field, partly by borrowers recovering their good spirits and so becoming readier to borrow.

Seldom in modern history has the gap between the two been so wide and so difficult to bridge. Unless we bend our wills and our intelligences, energised by a conviction that this diagnosis is right, to find a solution along these lines, then, if the diagnosis *is* right, the slump may pass over into a depression, accompanied by a sagging price level, which might last for years, with untold damage to the material wealth and to the social stability of every country alike. Only if we seriously seek a solution, will the optimism of my opening sentences be confirmed—at least for the nearer future.

It is beyond the scope of this essay to indicate lines of future policy. But no one can take the first step except the central banking authorities of the chief creditor countries; nor can any one Central Bank do enough acting in isolation. Resolute action by the Federal Reserve Banks of the United States, the Bank of France, and the Bank of England might do much more than most people, mistaking symptoms or aggravating circumstances for the disease itself, will, readily believe. In every way the most effective remedy would be that the Central Banks of these three great creditor nations should join together in a bold scheme to restore confidence to the international long-term loan market; which would serve to revive enterprise and activity everywhere, and to restore prices and profits, so that in due course the wheels of the world's commerce would go round again. And even if France, hugging the supposed security of gold, prefers to stand aside from the adventure of creating new wealth, I am convinced that Great Britain and the United States, likeminded and acting together, could start the machine again within a reasonable time; if that is to say, they were energised by a confident conviction as to what was wrong. For it is chiefly the lack of this conviction which to-day is paralysing the hands of authority on both sides of the Channel and of the Atlantic.

Alvin H. Hansen
(1887-1975)

Alvin Hansen was one of the chief promulgators of Keynesian ideas in the United States. His Harvard seminar developed a whole group of Keynesians who spread Keynesian economics not only throughout the academic community but also throughout the policy community in Washington. Hansen was more than an advocate simply for macroeconomic stabilization policy; he was also an advocate of large government and of increases in government spending for stabilizing the economy, believing these were necessary if the economy was, indeed, to be stabilized.

In this selection you can see those visions. Hansen, writing in 1957, argues that the post-World War II prosperity is attributable to Keynes' theory and to the government guarantee of sufficient aggregate demand.

Alvin H. Hansen. 1957. *The American Economy*. New York: McGraw-Hill Book Company, Inc., pp. 24, 37-41.

The American Economy On The March

The American Economy has undergone a considerable remodeling during the last quarter-century. I begin with what I regard as by far the most important single factor. It is a new factor, never before experienced in American history. And it is this. We have not had a major depression since 1938. Nearly two decades without a serious downturn. We had, indeed, a minor dip in 1949 and again in 1954—light jolts but no serious depression. And we have had virtually continuous full employment since 1941, a period of fifteen years. Now this is something distinctly new, and we would do well to take a good look at this strange and quite novel experience.

I repeat, we have had virtually full employment and booming prosperity for sixteen years. Past experience has been quite different. Throughout our history every eight or nine years we have experienced serious depression and widespread unemployment. Indeed our economy was for a hundred years the most violently fluctuating economy in the world. And in the 1930s we had prolonged depression and seemingly endless stagnation.

The Missing Link: Adequate Aggregate Demand

What, then, is the essence of the American economic revolution of the last fifteen years? The miracle of production? The economy already had *that potential* back in the thirties, though the steam was unfortunately lacking. Now, however, we have seen what the economy can do under the pressure of *adequate aggregate demand*. We now have acquired at least some confidence in the government's responsibility for the maintenance of prosperity and full employment. When the British Conservative Government, under Churchill, announced its assumption of continuing responsibility for high employment in 1944, that Act was regarded as a new venture of government, and so indeed it was. The Employment Act of 1946 set much the same goal for the United States. But it was not until President Eisenhower's statement with respect to the firm determination of his Administration to use the full powers of the government to prevent depression that general bipartisan acceptance of this program was achieved. It is indeed a revolution in men's thinking. And this revolution is in no small part the result of the vigorous economic controversies which have filled the pages of economic journals, and from there spilled out into the public forums, during the last two decades.

The American economic revolution involves not only a high-employment policy but also the introduction of the "welfare state." Indeed the welfare state constitutes a solid foundation upon which to build a full-employment program. It is the welfare state which has furnished us with most of the so-called "built-in stabilizers"—the progressive income tax, social-security payments, farm-support programs, etc. It is the welfare state which provides the continuing support of governmentally sponsored housing programs, rural electrification, and lending and guaranteeing operations. The welfare state is not socialism. Socialism is government ownership and operation of productive enterprise. . . . The welfare state does, however, involve government outlays large enough to permit fiscal policy to play a controlling role in the adjustment of aggregate demand to the productive potential of which the private-enterprise economy is capable. (This is the highly important consideration which is overlooked by those who say that all that is needed is to cut government expenditures together with a *corresponding* cut in taxes.) The government makes large expenditures, but private enterprise does the job. It is this that distinguishes the welfare state from socialism.

Now someone will say that the miracle of production which we have witnessed during the upsurge of the last fifteen years could never have occurred without the resourcefulness of private enterprise, the technical know-how, the technological innovations, and the capital formation necessary to implement the new technique. This is indeed unquestionably true, and it is a fact that should be stressed again and again. Yet even with respect to these factors it is important to note that the cause-and-effect relations are closely intertwined. The government has made a major contribution to ensure adequate aggregate demand. The upsurge related thereto has stimulated population growth, which in turn has contributed to the upsurge. The war and the postwar upsurge have served to stimulate new techniques, and these in turn reinforce the upsurge. And finally, investment in new capital (together with corporate and individual savings to finance it) is a consequence, no less than a cause, of a high and growing national income.

Thus the American economic revolution of the last quarter-century constitutes a laboratory experiment in which the flow of events has tested on a broad front the Keynesian diagnosis and the Keynesian policies.

The problems of a highly developed economy are different, as we have seen, from those of an economy in the earlier stages of industrial development. The advanced industrial society, having attained a high level of technology together with entrepreneurial know-how and worker skills, has equipped itself with a vast accumulation of fixed capital. The underdeveloped economy is capital-poor; the advanced country is capital-rich.

No one will deny that the developed economies of Western Europe and North America have reached, after 150 years of technological progress and capital accumulation, a high level of productive capacity. These countries have, moreover, within them the seeds of continued growth. Yet the output of the United Kingdom fell far below her potential throughout the two inter-war decades, and in the United States the economy performed disastrously below her capacity for more than a decade before Pearl Harbor. How long must an economy fail notoriously to perform before it is generally admitted that something is seriously lacking?

Now it was Keynes' central thesis that the element that was woefully lacking was *adequate aggregate demand.* The classicals had argued that all that was needed was technology and capital, that the economy itself would automatically generate adequate demand. The inter-war experience in the United Kingdom and the deep depression in the United States demonstrated, as conclusively as facts can, that the classical thesis, whatever may have been true of the early days of capitalism, was no longer valid.

But facts convinced no one. Facts alone can never destroy a theory. As President Conant [of Harvard University] has aptly put it, men strive desperately "to modify an old idea to make it accord with new experiments." An outworn theory will not be abandoned until it has been superseded by a better one. "It takes," says Conant, "a new conceptual scheme to cause the abandonment of an old one."

In his *General Theory of Employment, Money and Interest,* Keynes challenged the view that the modern economic system can be *depended* upon to make automatically the adjustments needed to ensure full use of productive resources. The thing that private enterprise can certainly do efficiently and well is to *produce*. The thing that it cannot be *depended* upon to do well is to ensure adequate aggregate demand.

Just as the decade before the Second World War deepened the conviction that the classicals were wrong, so the last fifteen years have strengthened the conviction that Keynes was right with respect to his positive program. Governments throughout Western Europe, and in the United States, have on an unprecedented scale augmented aggregate demand beyond that generated by private enterprise. And all over the free world, but especially in the United States, we have witnessed what the economy can do when it is put under pressure. Government expenditures, government borrowing, government guarantees and lending operations, government policies in the area of social security, agriculture, public power, rural electrification, securities regulation, deposit insurance, and monetary, banking, and fiscal policies have provided much of the *fuel* needed for the full use of the productive capacity created by technology and capital accumulation.

Henry Hazlitt
(1894-1993)

Keynes' ideas provoked serious criticism from business, academia, government, and the press. Some of the most biting criticism came from Henry Hazlitt, whose criticism of the full employment concept you saw previously. In this selection, Hazlitt attacks the concept of the multiplier as a logical construct. He asks if a reduction in savings can lead to an increase in growth. As you read it, it is a useful exercise to think back to Chapter 10 and 11 of your text, and to the modern interpretations of Keynes, and explain how the contradictory roles of saving and spending in the income-generating process are reconciled.

Henry Hazlitt. 1959. *The Failure of the "New Economics."* Princeton, N.J.: Van Nostrand, Chapter XI, pp. 135-52.

The Multiplier

We now come to the strange concept of "the multiplier," about which some Keynesians make more fuss than about anything else in the Keynesian system. Indeed, a whole literature has developed around this concept alone.

Let us try to see what Keynes means by the term.

In given circumstances a definite ratio, to be called the *Multiplier,* can be established between income and investment and, subject to certain simplifications, between the total employment and the employment directly employed on investment.... This further step is an integral part of our theory of employment, since it establishes a precise relationship, given the propensity to consume, between aggregate employment and income and the rate of investment (p. 113). . . .

Now the average propensity to consume, the reader will recall, is "the functional relationship . . . between . . . a given level of income in terms of wage-units, and . . . the expenditure on consumption out of that level of income" (p. 90). So, "if C_w is the amount of consumption and Y_w is income (both measured in wage-units) DC_{10} has the same sign as DY_w but is smaller in amount, [that is], dC_{10} [divided by] dY_{10} is positive and less than unity" (p. 96).

What this means, in simple and numerical terms, is that if out of three units of income, two are spent on consumption the "propensity to consume" will be 2/3.

Now in Chapter 10, and on page 115, Keynes advances to the concept of "the *marginal* propensity to consume." He defines this, however, by precisely the same mathematical expression and notation as he has previously used to express what he now calls "the *average* propensity to consume," [that is] dC_w [divided by] dY_w (p 115). The *marginal* propensity to consume is the relation of the *increase* in consumption to the *increase* in "real income" when the income of the community increases.

The reader might not be inclined to imagine, at first glance, that either the average propensity to consume or the marginal propensity to consume was a matter of much importance so far as the *business cycle* or the *extent of employment* was concerned. Keynes simply tells us that out of a given amount of income, or of increase of income, some, but not all of it, will be spent on consumption, and some, but not all of it, will be saved.

Now economists have long pointed out that the greater the percentage of the national income that is saved and invested, the more rapid, other things being equal, will be the growth in production and the more rapidly, therefore, will the real level of income in the community rise. But just how any significant discovery concerning fluctuations in business and employment could follow from the truism that people will spend something and save something out of their incomes it is difficult to see.

Yet Keynes does think he gets a magical result from this truism. The marginal propensity to consume "is of considerable importance, because it tells us how the next increment of output will *have to be* [. . . my italics] divided between consumption and investment" (p. 115). And from this Keynes derives the magic "investment Multiplier," k. "It tells us that, when there is an increment of aggregate investment, income will increase by an amount which is k times the increment of investment" (p. 115) .

Let us try to find in plainer language what it is that Keynes is saying here. He explains on the next page: "It follows, therefore, that, if the consumption psychology of the community is such that they will choose to consume, [for example], nine-tenths of an increment of income, then the multiplier k is 10; and the total employment caused by [for example] increased public works will be ten times the primary employment provided by the public works themselves" (pp. 116-17).

What Keynes is saying, among other things, is that the more a community *spends* of its income, and the *less* it saves, the faster will its real income grow! Nor do the implications of its own logic frighten him. If a community spends none of its additional income (from, say, the increased public works), but saves all of it, then the public works will give only the additional employment that they themselves provide, and that will be the end of it. But if a community spends *all* of the additional income provided by the public works, then the multiplier is *infinity*. This would mean that a small expenditure on public works would increase income without limit, provided only that the community was not poisoned by the presence of savers.

Keynes does not hesitate to accept this deduction, but he accepts it in a peculiar form. "If, on the other hand, they [the community] seek to consume the whole of any increment of income, there will be no point of stability and *prices will rise without limit*" (italics added, p. 117). But just how did prices get into it? The "propensity to consume," and "the multiplier," we have been assured up to this point, are expressed in terms of "wage-units," which, Keynes assures us, means "real" terms and not money terms. Why didn't we hear anything about the effect on prices until we got to an infinite multiplier? This leads us to still another peculiarity of Keynesian economics (which we shall examine at a later point), which is the assumption that increased activity and employment have no significant effect on prices and wages until "full employment" is reached—and then everything happens at once. Only then does "true inflation" set in.

It is true, however, that the implications of their logic do frighten Keynes and the Keynesians just a little bit. Their multiplier is too good to be true. Moreover, when their schemes are tried, and their multiplier does not miraculously do its multiplying, they badly need an alibi. This is supplied by the doctrine of "leakages."

Among the most important of these leakages are the following: (1) a part of the increment of income is used to pay off debts; (2) a part is saved in the form of idle bank deposits; (3) a part is invested in securities purchased from others, who in turn fail to spend the proceeds; (4) a part is spent on imports, which does not help home employment; (5) a part of the purchases is supplied from excess stocks of consumers' goods, which may not be replaced. By reason of leakages of this sort, the employment process peters out after awhile.

* * * *

But two criticisms of the "multiplier" remain to be made, and both are basic. In the first place, even granting all of Keynes's other peculiar assumptions, it is difficult to understand just why the multiplier (except by sheer assertion) should necessarily be the reciprocal of the marginal propensity to save. If the marginal propensity to consume is 9/10, we are told, the multiplier is 10. Why? How?

We have already tried to guess (p. 139) how Keynes might have arrived at this astonishing notion. But let us take an imaginary illustration. Ruritania is a Keynesian country that has a national income of $10 billion and consumes only $9 billion. Therefore it has a propensity to consume of 9/10. But as in some way it manages to "save" 10 per cent of its income without "investing" the 10 per cent in anything at all, it has unemployment of 10 per cent. Then the

Keynesian government comes to the rescue by spending, not $1 billion, but only $100 million on "investment." For as the "multiplier" is 10 (because Keynes has written out a mathematical formula which *makes* it 10 when the marginal propensity to consume is 9/10), this $100 million dollars worth of direct new employment somehow multiplies itself to $1 billion of total new employment to "fill the gap," and lo! "full employment" is achieved.

(Expressing this in terms of employment, we might say: When the propensity to consume of Ruritania is 9/10 then, unless something is done about it, only 9 million of Ruritania's working force of 10 million are employed. It is then simply necessary to spend enough to employ *directly* 100,000 more persons, and *their* spending, in turn, will ensure a total additional employment of 1 million.)

The question I am raising here is simply *why* such a relationship between the marginal propensity to consume and the multiplier is supposed to hold. Is it some inevitable mathematical deduction? If so, its causal inevitability somehow escapes me. Is it an empirical generalization from actual experience? Then why doesn't Keynes condescend to offer even the slightest statistical verification?

We have already seen that *investment,* strictly speaking, is irrelevant to the "multiplier"— that any extra spending on anything will do. . . . But a still further *reductio ad absurdum* is possible [that is, a pursuit of a logical argument until it becomes ridiculous]. Here is a . . . potent multiplier, and on Keynesian grounds there can be no objection to it. Let Y equal the income of the whole community. Let R equal your (the reader's) income. Let V equal the income of everybody else. Then we find that V is a completely stable function of Y; whereas your income is the active, volatile, uncertain element in the social income. Let us say the equation arrived at is:

$$V = .99999 \, Y$$

Then,
$$Y = .99999 \, Y + R$$
$$.00001 \, Y = R$$
$$Y = 100{,}000 \, R$$

Thus we see that your own personal multiplier is far more powerful than the investment multiplier. To increase social income and thereby cure depression and unemployment, it is only necessary for the government to print a certain number of dollars and give them to you. Your spending will prime the pump for an increase in the national income 100,000 times as great as the amount of your spending itself.

The final criticism of the multiplier that must be made is so basic that it almost makes all the others unnecessary. This is that the multiplier, and the whole unemployment that it is supposed to cure, is based on the tacit assumption of inflexible prices and inflexible wages. Once we assume flexibility in prices and wages, and full responsiveness to the forces of the market, the whole Keynesian system dissolves into thin air. For even if we make the other thoroughly unrealistic assumptions that Keynes makes (even if we assume, for example, that people "save" a third of their incomes by simply sticking the money under the mattress, and not investing it in anything) completely responsive wages and prices would simply mean that wages and prices would fall enough for the former volume of sales to be made at lower prices and for "full employment" to continue at lower wage-rates. When the money was taken out from under the mattress again, it would simply be equivalent to an added money supply and would raise prices and wages again.

I am not arguing here that prices and wages are *in fact* perfectly fluid. But neither, as Keynes assumes, are wage-rates completely rigid under conditions of less than full employment. And to the extent that they *are* rigid, they are so either through the anti-social policy of those who insist on employment only at above-equilibrium wage-rates, or through the very economic ignorance and confusion in business and political circles to which Keynes's theories themselves make so great a contribution. . . .

Abba Lerner
(1903-1982)

The following two selections are a pair, showing the Keynesian/classical debate at its finest, with Abba Lerner, the author of this selection, advocating the Keynesian view and Milton Fried-man, the author of the immediately following selection, advocating the classical view. We see this same pair going at it in the set of micro readings.

Lerner was a strange bird as far as economists go. He went into economics to try to better understand socialist ideas that he championed as a youth. He was trained by Lionel Robbins, one of the strongest proponents of classical economics, and he came to be a firm believer in the market. Then he was converted to Keynesian economics and went about espousing and develop-ing Keynesian ideas with the passion only converts have. His wit, his logic, and his delightfully playful writing style made him one of the key expositors of Keynesian ideas in the United States.

This selection may seem familiar to you; a portion of it is in one of the boxes in the textbook. In the selection, you see the continuation of the story. It explains the policy of functional fi-nance—increasing government spending when output was too low, and decreasing government spending when output was too high.

Abba Lerner. 1951. "The Economic Steering Wheel: The Story of the People's New Clothes," in *Economics of Employment*. New York: McGraw-Hill Book Company, pp. 271-72.

The Economic Steering Wheel:
The Story of the People's New Clothes

Our economic system is frequently put to shame in being displayed before an imaginary visitor from a strange planet. It is time to reverse the procedure. Imagine yourself instead in a Buck Rogers interplanetary adventure, looking at a highway in a City of Tomorrow. The highway is wide and straight, and its edges are turned up so that it is almost impossible for a car to run off the road. What appears to be a runaway car is speeding along the road and veering off to one side. As it approaches the rising edge of the highway, its front wheels are turned so that it gets back onto the road and goes off at an angle, making for the other side, where the wheels are turned again. This happens many times, the car zigzagging but keeping on the highway until it is out of sight. You are wondering how long it will take for it to crash, when another car appears which behaves in the same fashion. When it comes near you it stops with a jerk. A door is opened, and an occupant asks whether you would like a lift. You look into the car and before you can control yourself you cry out, "Why! There's no steering wheel!"

"Of course we have no steering wheel!" says one of the occupants rather crossly. "Just think how it would cramp the front seat. It is worse than an old-fashioned gear-shift lever and it is dangerous. Suppose we had a steering wheel and somebody held on to it when we reached a curb! He would prevent the automatic turning of the wheel, and the car would surely be overturned! And besides, we believe in democracy and cannot give anyone the extreme authority of life and death over all the occupants of the car. That would be dictatorship."

"Down with dictatorship!" chorus the other occupants of the car.

"If you are worried about the way the car goes from side to side," continues the first speaker, "forget it! We have wonderful brakes so that collisions are prevented nine times out of ten. On our better roads the curb is so effective that one can travel hundreds of miles without going off the road once. We have a very efficient system of carrying survivors of wrecks to nearby hospitals and for rapidly sweeping the remnants from the road to deposit them on nearby fields as a reminder to man of the inevitability of death."

You look around to see the piles of wrecks and burned-out automobiles as the man in the car continues. "Impressive, isn't it? But things are going to improve. See those men marking and photographing the tracks of the car that preceded us? They are going to take those pictures into their laboratories and pictures of our tracks, too, to analyze the cyclical characteristics of the curves, their degree of regularity, the average distance from turn to turn, the amplitude of the swings, and so on. When they have come to an agreement on their true nature we may know whether something can be done about it. At present they are disputing whether this cyclical movement is due to the type of road surface or to its shape or whether it is due to the length of the car or the kind of rubber in the tires or to the weather. Some of them think that it will be impossible to avoid having cycles unless we go back to the horse and buggy, but we can't do that because we believe in Progress. Well, want a ride?"

The dilemma between saving your skin and humoring the lunatics is resolved by your awakening from the nightmare, and you feel glad that the inhabitants of your own planet are a little more reasonable. But are they as reasonable about other things as they are about the desirability of steering their automobiles? Do they not behave exactly like the men in the nightmare when it comes to operating their economic system? Do they not allow their *economic* automobile to bounce from depression to inflation in wide and uncontrolled arcs? Through their failure to steer away from unemployment and idle factories are they not just as guilty of public injury and insecurity as the mad motorists of Mars?

Depression and Inflation Can Be Prevented By Regulating the Rate of Spending

The outstanding problem of modern society is just this. All the other really important problems, such as wars and fascism, are either caused or aggravated by the failure to solve this one. What is needed more than anything else is a mechanism which will enable us to regulate our economy so as to maintain a reasonable degree of economic activity: on the one hand to prevent any considerable unemployment of resources and on the other hand to prevent the stresses of the overemployment of resources and the disorganization that we know as inflation. We need a regulator of employment—a mechanism for the maintenance of prosperity.

The instrument that can do this is as readily available as the steering wheel for automobiles, yet it has not been installed and put into operation. Instead, all our universities are engaged in studying and adding to the enormous literature about the path traveled by the economy when no steering wheel is used—the study of the business cycle.

In our present moderately competitive economy based on moderately free enterprise the level of economic activity is determined by how much money is being spent on the goods and services that can be produced. The immediate effect of a decrease in spending is that the goods accumulate on the shopkeeper's shelves. The shopkeeper may reduce the price in an attempt to move the goods, but this is not necessarily the case. He may prefer to let his stocks increase, especially if he believes that he will be able to sell them soon at the normal price. But whether he lowers the price or not, he will reduce his orders to the wholesalers and the manufacturers and there will result a reduction in output (and in the number of workers employed in making the goods). A reduction in the rate of spending is thus followed, after this adjustment, by a smaller supply of goods to be purchased, and if the price was lowered in the first place it will rise again to the normal level when the supply has been reduced in response to the reduction in demand.

The same thing happens in reverse when there is an increase in demand. The shopkeeper's stocks are reduced below normal and he may take advantage of the increase in demand to raise the price. But whether he raises the price or not he will increase his orders to the wholesalers and the manufacturers. There will then be an increase in the amount of goods produced (and in the number of people employed in making them). After this adjustment there will be a greater supply of goods corresponding to the greater demand for them, and if the price was raised when the demand first increased, it will fall again to the normal level when the supply has caught up with the demand. The important effect of an increase or of a decrease in spending is essentially, therefore, to increase or decrease the supply. The effect on prices is only temporary.

But if there are no unemployed resources available when spending increases, it is impossible for employment or output to increase. Prices then must be raised and they do not fall back again to normal. They stay higher. The increased spending cannot be absorbed by an increase in the supply of goods. It then shows itself in higher prices for the same supply of goods.

Nor is this the end of the story. Although the manufacturer cannot increase output where there are no unemployed resources available, the increased orders at higher prices induce manufacturers to *try* to increase their output to take advantage of the unusually high profits. In so doing they try to get men and materials away from each other by offering higher wages and prices (or merely agreeing to demands for higher wages and prices). This raises the money incomes of labor and of the owners of materials and results in a further increase in spending. Increased spending increases incomes, and increased incomes increase spending, and so the process becomes cumulative, with prices rising (and the value of money falling) faster and faster. If this process is permitted to continue by a monetary authority which provides the increasing amount of money that is needed as prices rise, we have an inflation. Inflation disorganizes the economy, works great hardship on persons whose money incomes are fixed or only slowly adjustable, and ruins persons whose savings are cautiously tied to the depreciating money.

The aim of any reasonable regulation of the level of economic activity (which we may call "employment" for short) must be to arrange for the rate of spending to be neither too small (which would cause unemployment) nor too great (which would cause inflation). A satisfactory level (or range) of employment must be chosen, and the total rate of spending must be raised when employment is too low and curtailed when employment rises too high.

Milton Friedman

(1912-)

Milton Friedman, perhaps more than any other economist in this century, kept classical ideas in front of the public. He graduated from Columbia University and went on to teach at the University of Chicago, where he played a big role in establishing Chicago's reputation as a center of classical economic thought. He made major contributions in both micro and macro economics. He was introduced to you earlier in this book.

The selection comes from one of his best known books, Capitalism and Freedom *(1962), which is a set of essays on a variety of economics topics. In this selection he directly responds to Abba Lerner's challenge, which you read in the previous selection. Friedman argues that politics does not let government play the necessary skilled driver for the economic steering wheel, and that we need "some means of keeping the monetary passenger who is in the back seat as ballast from occasionally leaning over and giving the steering wheel a jerk that threatens to send the car off the road."*

Milton Friedman. 1962. *Capitalism and Freedom.* Chicago: University of Chicago Press, pp. 75-79.

Fiscal Policy

Ever since the New Deal, a primary excuse for the expansion of governmental activity at the federal level has been the supposed necessity for government spending to eliminate unemployment. The excuse has gone through several stages. At first, government spending was needed to "prime the pump." Temporary expenditures would set the economy going and the government could then step out of the picture.

When the initial expenditures failed to eliminate unemployment and were followed by a sharp economic contraction in 1937-38, the theory of "secular stagnation" developed to justify a permanently high level of government spending. The economy had become mature, it was argued. Opportunities for investment had been largely exploited and no substantial new opportunities were likely to arise. Yet individuals would still want to save. Hence, it was essential for government to spend and run a perpetual deficit. The securities issued to finance the deficit would provide individuals with a way to accumulate savings while the government expenditures provided employment. This view has been thoroughly discredited by theoretical analysis and even more by actual experience, including the emergence of wholly new lines for private investment not dreamed of by the secular stagnationists. Yet it has left its heritage. The idea may be accepted by none, but the government programs undertaken in its name, like some of those intended to prime the pump, are still with us and indeed account for ever-growing government expenditures.

More recently, the emphasis has been on government expenditures neither to prime the pump nor to hold in check the specter of secular stagnation but as a balance wheel. When private expenditures decline for any reason, it is said, governmental expenditures should rise to keep total expenditures stable; conversely, when private expenditures rise, governmental expenditures should decline. Unfortunately, the balance wheel is unbalanced. Each recession, however minor, sends a shudder through politically sensitive legislators and administrators with their ever present fear that perhaps it is the harbinger of another 1929-33 [one of the worst parts of the Great Depression]. They hasten to enact federal spending programs of one kind of another. Many of the programs do not in fact come into effect until after the recession has passed. Hence, insofar as they do affect total expenditures, on which I shall have more to say later, they tend to exacerbate the succeeding expansion rather than to mitigate the recession. The haste with which spending programs are approved is not matched by an equal haste to repeal them or to eliminate others when the recession is passed and expansion is under way. On the contrary, it is then argued that a "healthy" expansion must not be "jeopardized" by cuts in governmental expenditures. The chief harm done by the balance-wheel theory is therefore not that it has failed to offset recessions, which it has, and not that it has introduced an inflationary bias into governmental policy, which it has done too, but that it has continuously fostered an expansion in the range of governmental activities at the federal level and prevented a reduction in the burden of federal taxes.

In view of the emphasis on using the federal budget as a balance wheel, it is ironic that the most unstable component of national income in the postwar period is federal expenditure, and the instability has not at all been in a direction to offset movements of other expenditure components. Far from being a balance wheel offsetting other forces making for fluctuations, the federal budget has if anything been itself a major source of disturbance and instability.

Because its expenditures are now so large a part of the total for the economy as a whole, the federal government cannot avoid having significant effects on the economy. The first requisite is therefore that the government mend its own fences, that it adopt procedures that will lead to reasonable stability in its own flow of expenditures. If it would do that, it would make a clear contribution to reducing the adjustments required in the rest of the economy. Until it does that, it is farcical for government officials to adopt the self-righteous tones of the schoolmaster keeping unruly pupils in line. Of course, their doing so is not surprising. Passing the buck and blaming others for one's own deficiencies are not vices of which governmental officials have a monopoly.

Even if one were to accept the view that the federal budget should be and can be used as a balance wheel—a view I shall consider in more detail below—there is no necessity to use the expenditure side of the budget for this purpose. The tax side is equally available. A decline in national income automatically reduces the tax revenue of the federal government in greater proportion and thus shifts the budget in the direction of a deficit, and conversely during a boom. If it is desired to do more, taxes can be lowered during recessions and raised during expansions. Of course, politics might well enforce an asymmetry here too, making the declines politically more palatable than the rises.

If the balance-wheel theory has in practice been applied on the expenditure side, it has been because of the existence of other forces making for increased governmental expenditures; in particular, the widespread acceptance by intellectuals of the belief that government should play a larger role in economic and private affairs; the triumph, that is, of the philosophy of the welfare state. This philosophy has found a useful ally in the balance-wheel theory; it has enabled governmental intervention to proceed at a faster pace than would otherwise have been possible.

How different matters might now be if the balance-wheel theory had been applied on the tax side instead of the expenditure side. Suppose each recession had seen a cut in taxes and suppose the political unpopularity of raising taxes in the succeeding expansion had led to resistance to newly proposed governmental expenditure programs and to curtailment of existing ones. We might now be in a position where federal expenditures would be absorbing a good deal less of a national income that would be larger because of the reduction in the depressing and inhibiting effects of taxes.

I hasten to add that this dream is not intended to indicate support for the balance-wheel theory. In practice, even if the effects would be in the direction expected under the balance-wheel theory, they would be delayed in time and spread. To make them an effective offset to other forces making for fluctuations, we would have to be able to forecast those fluctuations a long time in advance. In fiscal policy as in monetary policy, all political considerations aside, we simply do not know enough to be able to use deliberate changes in taxation or expenditures as a sensitive stabilizing mechanism. In the process of trying to do so, we almost surely make matters worse. We make matters worse not by being consistently perverse—that would be easily cured by simply doing the opposite of what seemed at first the thing to do. We make matters worse by introducing a largely random disturbance that is simply added to other disturbances. That is what we seem in fact to have done in the past—in addition, of course to the major mistakes that have been seriously perverse. What I have written elsewhere in respect of monetary policy is equally applicable to fiscal policy: "What we need is not a skillful monetary driver of the economic vehicle continuously turning the steering wheel to adjust to the unexpected irregularities of the route, but some means of keeping the monetary passenger who is in the back seat as ballast from occasionally leaning over and giving the steering wheel a jerk that threatens to send the car off the road."

John Law
(1671-1729)

Perhaps no event in economics so cemented the quantity theory of money into economic think-ing as did the "John Law Escapade." Law was a Scotsman who argued that as long as money was backed up by something real, there could not be "too much money." The French government hired him as an adviser and started issuing assignats—*money backed up by government-owned land in France and abroad. Initially, the result was an economic boom, and Law was labeled a hero. Then, when real production didn't keep up with the increases in money, runaway inflation began. John Law was declared an outlaw and was lucky to escape France alive.*

This short selection is from his book, Money and Trade Considered, *and to some extent we have modernized its style from the 18th century English in which the book was published in 1705. But we have preserved the capitalization of words and some of the now-quaint spelling and punctuation to give the selection the flavor of its initial composition. As you read the selec-tion, you might ask yourself what part of the argument seems correct and what part does not— and why.*

Note that "shillings" and "pounds" were the units of English currency in which Law pro-posed his examples. Also note that Law refers to "a Stone of Wool." A "stone" was at that time, and still is to this day, a British expression for "14 pounds in weight." This definition should not be confused with the fact that English money is also expressed in "pounds."

John Law. 1705. *Money and Trade Considered.* Printed by the heirs and successors of Andrew Anderson, printer to the Queen's Most Excellent Majesty.

The Importance of Money

Domestic and Foreign Trade may be carried on by Barter; But not for so great a value as by Money, nor with so much convenience.

Domestic Trade depends on the Money. A greater Quantity employs more People than a lesser Quantity. A limited Sum can only set a number of People to Work proportional to it, and 'tis with little success Laws are made, for Employing the Poor or Idle in Countries where Money is scarce; Good Laws may bring the Money to full Circulation 'tis capable of, and force it to those Employments that are most profitable to the Country: But no Laws can make it go further, nor can more People be set to Work, without more Money to circulate so as to pay the Wages of a greater number. They may be brought to Work on Credit, and that is not practicable, unless the Credit have a Circulation, so as to supply the Workman with necessaries; If that's supposed, then that Credit is Money, and will have the same effects [as credit] on Home and Foreign Trade.

An Addition to the Money adds to the Value of the Country. So long as Money gives Interest, it is employed; And Money employed brings Profit, though the Employer loses. (*Ex.*) [for example:] If 50 Men are set to Work, to whom 25 *Shillings* is paid *per* day, and the Improvement made by their Labour be only equal to, or worth 15 *Sh[illings]*, yet by so much [that is, 15 shillings] the Value of the Country is increased. But as it is reasonable to suppose their Labour equal to 40 *Sh[illings]*. So much [that is, 40 shillings] is added to the value of the Country, of which the Employer gains 15 *Sh[illings]*. 15 [shillings] may be supposed to equal the Consumption of the Labourers, who before lived on Charity, and 10 *Sh[illings]* remains to them over their Consumption.

If a Stone [English unit of weight] of Wool is worth 10 *Sh[illings]* and made into Cloth worth 2 Pound, the Product is improved to four times the Value it had in Wool [at 10 shillings to the pound, 2 pounds in money equalled 40 shillings]. The Workmen may be supposed to consume more than when they were not employed: Allow one 4th, the Nation is Gainer double the value of the Product. So an Addition to the Money, whether the Employer gains or not, adds to the National Wealth, eases the Country of a number of Poor or idle, proportioned to the Money added, enables them to live better, and to bear a share in the Public with the other People.

The first Branch of Foreign Trade, which is the Export and Import of Goods, depends on the Money. If one half of the People are employed, and the whole Product and Manufacture [is] consumed, More Money, by employing more People, will make an Overplus to Export. If then the Goods imported balance the Goods exported, a great Addition to the Money will employ yet more People, or the same People before employed [will be employed] to more Advantage; which by making a greater, or more valuable, Export, will make a Balance due. So if the Money lessens, a part of the People then employed are set idle, or employed to less advantage, the Product and Manufacture is less, or less valuable; the Export of Consequence less; and a Balance [is] due to Foreigners. . . .

Walter Bagehot
(1826-1877)

Walter Bagehot was a long-time editor of The Economist, *an important popular economic magazine. He was a broad-based economist who saw the boundaries of economics as fluid. He saw little use for pure theory and argued that good economics took account of real-world institutions.*

His most famous work, Lombard Street, *from which this selection is taken, focused on the role of confidence as a necessary foundation of a banking system. This confidence is a psychological phenomenon which makes the conduct of monetary policy an art rather than a science.*

In this article note that Lombard Street is the British equivalent to Wall Street.

Walter Bagehot. "Why Lombard Street is Often Very Dull, and Sometimes Extremely Excited," in *Lombard Street.* London: Kegon Paul and Co., April 1873, pp. 118-123, 150-52.

Why Lombard Street is Often Very Dull, and Sometimes Extremely Excited

Any sudden event which creates a great demand for actual cash may cause, and will tend to cause, a panic in a country where cash is much economised, and where debts payable on demand are large. In such a country an immense credit rests on a small cash reserve, and an unexpected and large diminution of that reserve may easily break up and shatter very much, if not the whole, of that credit. Such accidental events are of the most various nature: a bad harvest, an apprehension of foreign invasion, the sudden failure of a great firm which everybody trusted, and many other similar events, have all caused a sudden demand for cash. And some writers have endeavoured to classify panics according to the nature of the particular accidents producing them. But little, however, is, I believe, to be gained by such classifications. There is little difference in the effect of one accident and another upon our credit system. We must be prepared for all of them, and we must prepare for all of them in the same way—by keeping a large cash reserve.

But it is of great importance to point out that our industrial organisation is liable not only to irregular external accidents, but likewise to regular internal changes; that these changes make our credit system much more delicate at some times than at others; and that it is the recurrence of these periodical seasons of delicacy which has given rise to the notion that panics come according to a fixed rule,—that every ten years or so we must have one of them.

Most persons who begin to think of the subject are puzzled on the threshold. They hear much of "good times" and "bad times," meaning by "good" times in which nearly every one is very well off, and by "bad" times in which nearly every one is comparatively ill off. And at first it is natural to ask why should everybody, or almost everybody, be well off together? Why should there be any great tides of industry, with large diffused profit by way of flow, and large diffused want of profit, or loss, by way of ebb? The main answer is hardly given distinctly in our common books of political economy. These books do not tell you what is the fund out of which large general profits are paid in good times, nor do they explain why that fund is not available for the same purpose in bad times.

Our current political economy does not sufficiently take account of *time* as an element in trade operations; but as soon as the division of labour has once established itself in a community, two principles at once begin to be important, of which time is the very essence. These are—

First. That as goods are produced to be exchanged, it is good that they should be exchanged as quickly as possible.

Secondly. That as every producer is mainly occupied in producing what others want, and not what he wants himself, it is desirable that he should always be able to find, without effort, without delay, and without uncertainty, others who want what he can produce.

In themselves these principles are self-evident. Every one will admit it to be expedient that all goods wanting to be sold should be sold as soon as they are ready; that every man who wants to work should find employment as soon as he is ready for it. Obviously also, as soon as the "division of labour " is really established, there is a difficulty about both of these principles. A produces what he thinks B wants, but it may be a mistake, and B may not want it. A may be able and willing to produce what B wants, but he may not be able to find B—he may not know of his existence.

The general truth of these principles is obvious, but what is not obvious is the extreme greatness of their effects. Taken together, they make the whole difference between times of brisk trade and great prosperity, and times of stagnant trade and great adversity, so far as that prosperity and that adversity are real and not illusory. If they are satisfied, every one knows whom to work for, and what to make, and he can get immediately in exchange what he wants himself. There is no idle labour and no sluggish capital in the whole community, and, in consequence, all which can be produced is produced, the effectiveness of human industry is augmented, and both kinds of producers—both capitalists and labourers—are much richer than usual, because the amount to be divided between them is also much greater than usual.

And there is a partnership in industries. No single large industry can be depressed without injury to other industries; still less can any great group of industries. Each industry when prosperous buys and consumes the produce probably of most (certainly of very many) other industries, and if industry A fails and is in difficulty, industries B, and C, and D, which used to sell to it, will not be able to sell that which they had produced in reliance on A's demand, and in future they will stand idle till industry A recovers, because in default of A there will be no one to buy the commodities which they create. Then as industry buys of C, D, etc., the adversity of B tells on C, D, etc., and as these buy of E, F, etc., the effect is propagated through the whole alphabet. And in a certain sense it rebounds. Z feels the want caused by the diminished custom of A, B, and C, and so it does not earn so much; in consequence, it cannot lay out as much on the produce of A, B, and C, and so these do not earn as much either. In all this money is but an instrument. The same thing would happen equally well in a trade of barter, if a state of barter on a very large scale were not practically impossible, on account of the time and trouble which it would necessarily require. As has been explained, the fundamental cause is that under a system in which every one is dependent on the labour of every one else, the loss of one spreads and multiplies through all, and spreads and multiplies the faster the higher the previous perfection of the system of divided labour, and the more nice and effectual the mode of interchange. And the entire effect of a depression in any single large trade requires a considerable time before it can be produced. It has to be propagated, and to be returned through a variety of industries, before it is complete. Short depressions, in consequence, have scarcely any discernible consequences; they are over before we think of their effects. It is only in the case of continuous and considerable depressions that the cause is in action long enough to produce discernible effects. ......

... The case is worse, because at most periods of great commercial excitement there is some mixture of the older and simpler kind of investing mania. Though the money of saving persons is in the hands of banks, and though, by offering interest, banks retain the command of much of it, yet they do not retain the command of the whole, or anything near the whole; all of it can be used, and much of it is used, by its owners. They speculate with it in bubble companies and in worthless shares, just as they did in the time of the South Sea mania, when there were no banks, and as they would again in England supposing that banks ceased to exist. The mania of 1825 and the mania of 1866 were striking examples of this; in their case to a great extent, as in most similar modern periods to a less extent, the delirium of ancient gambling co-operated with the milder madness of modern overtrading. At the very beginning of adversity, the counters in the gambling mania, the shares in the companies created to feed the mania, are discovered to be worthless; down they all go, and with them much of credit.

The good times too of high prices almost always engender much fraud. All people are most credulous when they are most happy; and when much money has just been made, when some people are really making it, when most people think they are making it, there is a happy opportunity for ingenious mendacity. Almost everything will be believed for a little while, and long before discovery the worst and most adroit deceivers are geographically or legally beyond the reach of punishment. But the harm they have done diffuses harm, for it weakens credit still further.

When we understand that Lombard Street is subject to severe alternations of opposite causes, we should cease to be surprised at its seeming cycles. We should cease too to be surprised at the sudden panics. During the period of reaction and adversity, just even at the last instant of prosperity, the whole structure is delicate. The peculiar essence of our banking system is an unprecedented trust between man and man; and when that trust is much weakened by hidden causes, a small accident may greatly hurt it, and a great accident for a moment may almost destroy it.

Now too that we comprehend the inevitable vicissitudes of Lombard Street, we can also thoroughly comprehend the cardinal importance of always retaining a great banking reserve. Whether the times of adversity are well met or ill met depends far more on this than on any other single circumstance. If the reserve be large, its magnitude sustains credit; and if it be small, its diminution stimulates the gravest apprehensions. And the better we comprehend the importance of the banking reserve, the higher we shall estimate the responsibility of those who keep it.

Irving Fisher
(1867-1947)

Irving Fisher was a professor of economics at Yale University and one of the top economists of the early 1900s. He was considered one of the greatest, if not the greatest, and most colorful of the early American economists. He wrote on a wide variety of topics and held strong views on a number of positions, including the one presented here for a 100 percent deposit reserve money.

This selection shows the opposite side of the reasoning presented by John Law (above). It argues that banks should only be allowed to issue checks if they back them 100 percent with U.S. currency or gold. This proposal would give the government direct control of the money supply. As you read this selection and the selection from John Law, ask yourself where the current U.S. banking system falls in relation to this proposal and whether it would make sense to institute this proposal today.

Wildcat bank notes referred to by Fisher are currency issued by banks located away from cities in the mountains where wildcats live.

Irving Fisher. 1935. *100% Money*. New Haven: The City Printing Company, pp. 3-20.

100 Per Cent Reserves

Introduction

In the United States, as in a few other countries, most of our bills are paid by check—not by money passing from hand to hand.

When a person draws a check, he draws it against what he calls "the money I have in the bank" as shown by his deposit balance on the stub of his check book. The sum of all such balances, on all such stubs in the whole country, i.e., all checking deposits, or what we ordinarily think of as the "money" lying on deposit in banks and *subject to check*, constitutes the chief circulating medium of the United States. This I propose to call "check-book money" as distinct from actual cash or "pocket-book money." Pocket-book money is the more basic of the two. It is visible and tangible; check-book money is not. Its claim to be money and to pass as if it were real money is derived from the belief that it "represents" real money and can be converted into real money on demand by "cashing" a check.

But the chief practical difference between check-book money and pocket-book money is that the latter is bearer money, good in anybody's hands, whereas check-book money requires the special permission of the payee in order to pass.

In 1926, a representative year before the great depression, the total check-book money of the people of the United States, according to one estimate, was 22 billion dollars, whereas, outside of the banks and the United States Treasury, the pocket-book money—that is, the actual physical bearer money in the people's pockets and in the tills of merchants— amounted, all told, to less than 4 billion dollars. Both together made the total circulating medium of the country, in the hands of the public, 26 billion dollars, 4 billions circulating by hand and 22 by check.

Many people imagine that check-book money is really money and really in the bank. Of course, this is far from true.

What, then, is this mysterious check-book money which we mistakenly call our "money in the bank"? It is simply the bank's *promise to furnish* money to its depositors when asked. Behind the 22 billions of checking deposits in 1926, the banks held only some 3 billions in actual money. The remaining 19 billions were assets other than money—assets such as the promissory notes of borrowers and assets such as government bonds and corporation bonds.

In ordinary times, as for instance in 1926, the 3 billions of money were enough to enable the banks to furnish any depositor all the money or "cash" he asked for. But if *all* the depositors had demanded cash at one and the same time, the banks, though they could have gotten together a certain amount of cash by selling their other assets, could not have gotten enough; for there was not enough cash in the entire country to make up the 22 billions. And if all the depositors had demanded *gold* at the same time, there would not have been enough gold in the whole world.

* * * *

. . . [O]ur national circulating medium is now at the mercy of loan transactions of banks; and our thousands of checking banks are, in effect, so many irresponsible private mints.

What makes the trouble is the fact that the bank lends not money but merely a promise to furnish money on demand—money it does not possess. The banks can build upon their meager cash reserves an inverted pyramid of such "credits," that is, check-book money, the volume of which can be inflated and deflated.

It is obvious that such a top-heavy system is dangerous—dangerous to depositors, dangerous to the banks, and above all dangerous to the millions of "innocent bystanders," the general public. In particular, when deflation results, the public is deprived of part of its essential circulating medium through which goods change hands.

There is little practical difference between permitting banks to issue these book credits which perform monetary services, and permitting them to issue paper currency as they did during the "wildcat bank note" period [in the early 19th century]. It is essentially the same unsound practice.

Deposits are the modern equivalent of bank notes. But deposits may be created and destroyed invisibly, whereas bank notes have to be printed and cremated. [Between 1929 and 1933, Fisher wrote, $8 billion in "checkbook money" that was not backed by real assets, was wiped out of the banking system without the general public realizing that "an essential part of the Depression" was this loss from the nation's circulating currency of $8 billion.] If eight billion bank notes had been cremated between 1929 and 1933, the fact could scarcely have been overlooked.

As the system of checking accounts, or checkbook money, based chiefly on loans, spreads from the few countries now using it to the whole world, all its dangers will grow greater. As a consequence, future booms and depressions threaten to be worse than those of the past, unless the system is changed.

The Proposal

Let the government, through an especially created "Currency Commission," turn into cash enough of the assets of every commercial bank to increase the cash reserve of each bank up to 100% of its checking deposits. In other words, let the government, through the Currency Commission, issue this money, and, with it, buy some of the bonds, notes, or other assets of the bank or lend it to the banks on those assets as security. Then all check-book money would have actual money—pocket-book money—behind it.

This new money (Commission currency, or United States notes), would merely give an all-cash backing for the checking deposits and would, of itself, neither increase nor decrease the total circulating medium of the country. A bank which previously had $100,000,000 of deposits subject to check with only $10,000,000 of cash behind them (along with $90,000,000 in securities) would send these $90,000,000 of securities to the Currency Commission in return for $90,000,000 more cash, thus bringing its total cash reserve up to $100,000,000 or 100% of the deposits.

After this substitution of actual money for securities had been completed, the bank would be required to maintain *permanently* a cash reserve of 100% against its demand deposits. In other words, the demand deposits would literally be deposits, consisting of cash held in trust for the depositor.

Thus, the new money would, in effect, be *tied up* by the 100% reserve requirement.

The checking deposit department of the bank would become a mere storage warehouse for bearer money belonging to its depositors and would be given a separate corporate existence as a Check Bank. There would then be no practical distinction between the checking deposits and the reserve. The "money I have in the bank," as recorded on the stub of my check book, would literally be money and literally be in the bank (or near at hand). The bank's deposits could rise to $125,000,000 only if its cash also rose to $125,000,000, i.e., by depositors depositing $25,000,000 more cash, that is, taking that much out of their pockets or tills and putting it into the bank. And if deposits shrank it would mean that depositors withdrew some of their stored-up money, that is, taking it out of the bank and putting it into their pockets or tills. In neither case would there be any change in the total.

So far as this change to the 100% system would deprive the bank of earning assets and require it to substitute an increased amount of non-earning cash, the bank would be reimbursed through a service charge made to its depositors.

Advantages

The resulting advantages to the public would include the following:

1. *There would be practically no more runs on commercial banks;* because 100% of the depositors' money would always be in the bank (or available) awaiting their orders. In practice, less money would be withdrawn than now; we all know of the frightened depositor who shouted to the bank teller, "If you haven't got my money, I want it; if you have, I don't."

2. *There would be far fewer bank failures;* because the important creditors of a commercial bank who would be most likely to make it fail are its depositors and these depositors would be 100% provided for.

3. *The interest-bearing government debt would be substantially reduced;* because a great part of the outstanding bonds of the government would be taken over from the banks by the Currency Commission (representing the government).

4. *Our monetary system would be simplified;* because there would be no longer any essential difference between pocket-book money and check-book money. All of our circulating medium, one hundred per cent of it, would be actual money.

5. *Banking would be simplified;* at present, there is a confusion of ownership. When money is deposited in a checking account, the depositor still thinks of that money as his, though legally it is the bank's. The depositor owns no money in the bank; he is merely a creditor of the bank as a private corporation. Most of the "mystery" of banking would disappear as soon as a bank was no longer allowed to lend out money deposited by its customers, while, at the same time, these depositors were using that money as their money by drawing checks against it. "Mr. Dooley," the Will Rogers of his day, brought out the absurdity of this double use of money on demand deposit when he called a banker "a man who takes care of your money by lending it out to his friends."

6. *Great inflations and deflations would be eliminated;* because banks would be deprived of their present power virtually to mint check-book money and to destroy it; that is, making loans would not inflate our circulating medium and calling loans would not deflate it. The volume of the checking deposits would not be affected any more than when any other sort of loans increased or decreased. These deposits would be part of the total actual money of the nation, and this total could not be affected by being lent from one person to another.

* * *

7. *Booms and depressions would be greatly mitigated;* because these are largely due to inflation and deflation.
8. *Banker-management of industry would almost cease;* because only in depressions can industries in general fall into the hands of bankers.

Of these eight advantages, the first two would apply chiefly to America, the land of bank runs and bank failures. The other six would apply to all countries having check-deposit banking. Advantages "6" and "7" are by far the most important, i.e., the cessation of inflation and deflation of our circulating medium and so the mitigation of booms and depressions in general and the elimination of great booms and depressions in particular.

Objections

Naturally, a new idea, or one which seems new, like this of a 100% system of money and banking, must and should run the gauntlet of criticism .

The questions which seem most likely to be asked by those who will have doubts about the 100% system are:

1. *Would not the transition to the 100% system—the buying up of the assets with new money— immediately increase the circulating medium of the country and increase it greatly?*

Not by a single dollar. It would merely make money completely interconvertible; change existing circulating deposits of imaginary money into circulating deposits of real money.

After the transition (and after the prescribed degree of reflation had been reached), the Currency Commission could increase the quantity of money by buying bonds, and could decrease it by selling, being restricted in each case by the obligation to maintain the prescribed price level or value of the dollar with reasonable accuracy.

But it is worth noting that the maintenance of 100% reserve and the maintenance of a stable price level are distinct; either could, conceivably, exist without the other.

2. *Would there be any valuable assets "behind" the new money?*

The day after the adoption of the 100% system there would be behind the new money transferable by check the very same assets— mostly government bonds—which had been behind the check-book money the day before, although these bonds would now be in the possession of the Currency Commission.

The idea is traditional that all money and deposits must have a "backing" in securities to serve as a safeguard against reckless inflation. Under the present system (which, for contrast, we are to call the "10% system"), whenever the depositor fears that his deposit cannot be paid in actual pocket-book money, the bank can (theoretically) sell the securities for money and use the money to pay the panicky depositor. Very well; under the 100% system there would be precisely the same backing in securities and the same possibility of selling the securities; but in addition there would be the credit of the United States Government. Finally, there would be no panicky depositor, fearful lest he could not convert his deposits into cash.

3. Would not the gold standard be lost?

No more than it is lost already! And no less. The position of gold could be exactly what it is now, its price to be fixed by the government and its use to be confined chiefly to settling international balances.

Furthermore, a return to the kind of gold standard we had prior to 1933 could, if desired, be just as easily accomplished under the 100% system as now; in fact, under the 100% system, there would be a much better chance that the old-style gold standard, if restored, would operate as it was intended.

4. How would the banks get any money to lend?

Just as they usually do now, namely: (1) from their own money (their capital); (2) from the money received from customers and put into savings accounts (not subject to check); and (3) from the money repaid on maturing loans.

In the long run, there would probably be much more money lent; for there would be more savings created and so available for lending. But such an expansion of loans—a normal expansion generated by savings—would not necessarily involve any increase of money in circulation.

The only new limitation on bank loans would be a wholesome one; namely, that no money could be lent unless there was money to lend; that is, the banks could no longer over-lend by manufacturing money out of thin air so as to cause inflation and a boom. Besides the above three sources of loan funds (bank capital, savings, and repayments), it would be possible for the Currency Commission to create new money and pass it on to the banks by buying more bonds. But this additional money would be limited by the fundamental requirement of preventing a rise of prices above the prescribed level, as measured by a suitable index number.

5. Would not the bankers be injured?

On the contrary.

(a) They would share in the general benefits to the country resulting from a sounder monetary system and a returned prosperity; in particular they would receive larger savings deposits;
(b) They would be reimbursed (by service charges or otherwise) for any loss of profits through tying up large reserves;
(c) They would be almost entirely freed from risk of future bank runs and failures.

The bankers will not soon forget what they suffered from their mob race for liquidity in 1931-33—each for himself and the devil take the hindmost. Such a mob movement would be impossible under the 100% system; for a 100% liquidity would be assured at all times and for each bank separately and independently of other banks.

6. Would the plan be a nationalization of money and banking?

Of money, yes; of banking, no.

In Conclusion

The 100% proposal is the opposite of radical. What it asks, in principle, is a return from the present extraordinary and ruinous system of lending the same money 8 or 10 times over, to the conservative safety-deposit system of the old goldsmiths, before they began lending out improperly what was entrusted to them for safekeeping. It was this abuse of trust which, after being accepted as standard practice, evolved into modern deposit banking. From the standpoint of public policy it is still an abuse, no longer an abuse of trust but an abuse of the loan and deposit functions. . . .

Henry C. Simons

(1899-1946)

Henry Simons, together with Frank Knight (to whom you will be introduced in the micro section), was one of the founders of the modern Chicago school of economics. In his work he carefully explored the relationship between government and a laissez-faire economy. He argued strongly that the government should provide the appropriate framework within which competitive forces would be allowed to play but that the government should not enter into the economy after that framework was established.

In this selection we see a recurring theme in classical economics, in Simons' work and in general: the need to establish a framework within which the market economy can function effectively. Here we see the search for such a rule in the 1930s. As you read it, think about monetary policy today—how much it seems guided by rules and how much by discretion.

Henry Simons. 1936. "Rules versus Authorities in Monetary Policy." Abridged from *The Journal of Political Economy*, Vol. 44, No. 1 (February), pp. 1-30.

Rules versus Authorities in Monetary Policy

The monetary problem stands out today as the great intellectual challenge to the liberal faith. For generations we have been developing financial practices, financial institutions, and financial structures which are incompatible with the orderly functioning of a system based on economic freedom and political liberty. Even more disturbing, perhaps, than the institutional trend is the trend of thinking and discussion among special students of money—the fact that economists have become accustomed to deal with monetary problems in a manner which impliedly belies their professed liberalism.

The liberal creed demands the organization of our economic life largely through individual participation in a game *with definite rules*. It calls upon the state to provide a stable framework of rules within which enterprise and competition may effectively control and direct the production and distribution of goods. The essential conception is that of a genuine division of labor between competitive markets and political controls—a division of labor within which competition has a major, or at least proximately primary, place.

A liberal system adapted to modern conditions would be, of course, exceedingly complex by comparison with an authoritarian collectivism. It would involve a large measure of political control: outright collectivism in some areas; deliberate enforcement of competition in others; prevention of extreme inequality, largely via taxation, in the distribution of property, income, and power. Moreover, such a system is attainable, through economic reconstruction, only by years of careful planning and wise legislation; and once realized, however perfectly, it would require continuous modification, with at least minor changes in the rules, to meet new developments and new conditions.

There is thus little point in contrasting a liberal system and a planned economy—except for the coincidence that the latter phrase has been appropriated by reformers who have little sympathy with, and less understanding of, the liberal position.

There is imminent danger, however, that actual governmental policies will undermine irreparably the kind of economic and political life which most of us prefer to the possible alternatives. This danger manifests itself mainly in three ways: (1) in the displacement of price competition by political (governmental or monopoly) control in many areas where such competition, if established, preserved, and properly canalized, is peculiarly competent for promoting the general welfare; (2) in the neglect of the unquestioned positive responsibilities of governments under the free-enterprise system; and (3) in measures and policies which involve delegation of legislative powers and the setting-up of *authorities instead of rules*.

95

It is this danger of substituting authorities for rules which especially deserves attention among students of money. There are, of course, many special responsibilities which may wisely be delegated to administrative authorities with substantial discretionary power; health authorities, for example, cannot well be limited narrowly in their activities by legislative prescriptions. The expedient must be invoked sparingly, however, if democratic institutions are to be preserved; and it is utterly inappropriate in the money field. An enterprise system cannot function effectively in the face of extreme uncertainty as to the action of monetary authorities or, for that matter, as to monetary legislation. We must avoid a situation where every business venture becomes largely a speculation on the future of monetary policy. In the past, governments have grossly neglected their positive responsibility of controlling the currency; private initiative has been allowed too much freedom in determining the character of our financial structure and in directing changes in the quantity of money and money substitutes. On this point there is now little disagreement. In our search for solutions of this problem, however, we seem largely to have lost sight of the essential point, namely, that definite, stable, legislative rules of the game as to money are of paramount importance to the survival of a system based on freedom of enterprise.

Indeed, it may be said that economists, as students of money and banking, have accepted and propagated the first serious heresy among liberals. Managed currency (along with protectionism) is the prototype of all current "planning" schemes—in the sense of all the illiberal connotations of planning. To be sure many economists still protest vigorously against proposals for currency management; but they and their teachers before them joined zealously in the movement for central banking—and it is precisely here that the heresy is clearly manifested.

This unwitting defection among custodians of the liberal faith is explicable, and may be apologized for, in terms of an unfortunate habit of distinguishing too sharply between currency and banking problems, and in terms of a disposition to look upon banking arrangements as merely a detail or subsidiary system within the supposedly automatic mechanism of the gold standard. Only of late is it clearly realized that the money problem has been swallowed up in the credit problem or that gold has long been reduced largely to the status of a decorative symbol within a welter of national policies as to central banking, government finance, and foreign trade.

Liberal economists are now on the defensive. On most fronts, however, their position is, or can be made, very strong intellectually. Conspicuous weakness is to be found only with respect to the problems of money and banking. There is little agreement, and not much relevant discussion, as to how the monetary rules of the game might effectively be altered to prevent or greatly to mitigate the affliction of extreme industrial fluctuations. We cannot effectively answer radical critics of the present system, or expose the stupid schemes of plausible reformers, by saying that the problems which they find in other areas are really just problems of money (although this observation is usually correct and pointed), when we have no good solutions to propose, with some unanimity, in the money field.

Our problem is that of defining an adequate monetary system based on simple rules and of finding the way toward such a system. We cannot seek merely to return to some arrangement of the past. The monetary problem never was solved in the past. There is no adequate system of rules to be found in earlier arrangements—except in the sense that the specific form of the rules was formerly, in a more flexible economy, a matter of less importance. Moreover, we have become so habituated to the fact and to the idea of "management," especially with respect to banking, that we shall find it hard either to reject the palliatives which management offers or even to face squarely our intellectual task.

In a free-enterprise system we obviously need highly definite and stable rules of the game, especially as to money. The monetary rules must be compatible with the reasonably smooth working of the system. Once established, however, they should work mechanically, with the chips falling where they may. To put our present problem as a paradox—we need to design and establish with the greatest intelligence a monetary system good enough so that, hereafter, we may hold to it unrationally—on faith—as a religion, if you please. The utter inadequacy of the old gold standard, either as a definite system of rules or as the basis of a monetary religion, seems beyond intelligent dispute. But if that system lacks peculiarly the virtues which now seem important, they are also patently lacking in most of the systems proposed as substitutes.

The possibilities of genuine economic reconstruction, and the requirements of sound liberal strategy, may be defined in terms of three objectives: (1) restoration of a maximum of competitiveness in industry (including the labor markets); (2) transition to a less preposterous structure of private money contracts; and (3) ultimate establishment of a simple, mechanical rule of monetary policy. As regards this third objective, the writer feels that his earlier persuasion as to the merits of the rule of a fixed quantity of money was fundamentally correct, although the scheme is obviously too simple as a prescription under anything like present conditions. Its limitations, however, have to do mainly with the unfortunate character of our financial structure—with the abundance of what we may call "near-moneys"—with the difficulty of defining money in such manner as to give practical significance to the conception of quantity.

The shortcomings of price-index stabilization, as the fundamental basis of a monetary system, are numerous and serious from either an analytical or an empirical viewpoint. It is easy to maintain that such a rule falls far short of the ideal in monetary arrangements—far too easy, indeed, when those who criticize are not obliged or inclined to define the better rules by comparison with which the one in question is so defective. The advocates of a stable price level (with all the irritating excesses of their advocacy) are proposing a solution which is genuinely consistent with traditional liberal principles—and, precisely on that account, are faring rather badly in the debate which the proposal has provoked among professional economists and journalists. The most vigorous and pungent criticism comes from specialists who themselves have no intelligible solutions to offer and who generally have been spared the suspicion that a solution in terms of definite rules is of any importance.

If price-level stabilization is a poor system, it is, still from a liberal viewpoint, infinitely better than no system at all. And it seems now highly questionable whether any better system is feasible or possible at all within the significant future. Given the present financial structure, and given the present multitude of uncoordinated monetary measures and monetary authorities, is there any other rule of policy around which some order and system might be achieved? How else may the present chaos of private financial practices, central-bank action, fiscal measures, and tariff changes be pulled together into something which resembles a monetary system? How else can we possibly escape from a situation where monetary policy is merely the composite of the uncertain daily actions of an indefinite number of agencies, governmental and private? Some ordering of this chaos is imperative. It may be achieved either by setting up a superior, independent authority or by bringing the totality of monetary measures under the discipline of some rule; and only the advocates of price-index stabilization have offered a feasible way out along the latter lines.

This solution, if unsatisfying, is likewise not simple administratively. Question is often raised as to whether stabilization of a price level is possible. The problem is better formulated, however, when we ask by what agency it might best be undertaken and what methods would be appropriate in its execution.

The task is certainly not one to be intrusted to banking authorities, with their limited powers and restricted techniques, as should be abundantly evident from recent experience. Ultimate control over the value of money lies in fiscal practices—in the spending, taxing, and borrowing operations of the central government. Thus, in an adequate scheme for price level stabilization, the Treasury would be the primary administrative agency; and all the fiscal powers of Congress would be placed behind (and their exercise religiously limited by) the monetary rule. The powers of the government to inject purchasing power through expenditure and to withdraw it through taxation—the powers of expanding and contracting issues of actual currency and other obligations more or less serviceable as money—are surely adequate to price-level control. At present, monetary powers are dispersed indefinitely, among governmental agencies and private institutions, not to mention Congress itself. Since the powers of the legislature are ultimate and decisive, a program looking toward coordination and concentration of responsibility must focus on fiscal policy as its mode of implementation.

The scheme clearly requires the delegation of large administrative powers. The Treasury might be given freedom within wide limits to alter the form of the public debt—to shift from long-term to short-term borrowing or vice versa, to issue and retire demand obligations in a legal-tender form. It might be granted some control over the timing of expenditures. It might be given limited power to alter tax rates by decree and to make refunds of taxes previously collected. How wide and numerous these powers should be, need not concern us here. Any legislation granting such authority, however, must also impose the duty and responsibility of exercising that authority in accordance with a sharply defined policy.

Given the suitable mandate, the grant of administrative powers should err, if at all, on the side of generosity. The more adequately implemented the rule of monetary policy, the easier will be its actual execution. The greater the powers available for its execution, the smaller will be the probable demands for their exercise. If it is clear that the administrative authority is adequately equipped to make the rule effective, then the rule will be, to some extent, self-enforcing, in so far as the actions of enterprisers and speculators come to be predicated upon its enforcement.

Not only must the price-level rule be implemented through fiscal measures; it must also serve as a control upon all governmental measures which have significant monetary effects. In other words, it must be accepted by the community, and obeyed by legislatures as the guiding principle of government finance—as the basic criterion of sound fiscal policy. While the rule cannot wisely be written into our fundamental law, it must provide the same sort of limitation and mandate as would a constitutional provision. As things stand now, there is almost nothing which a dominant party may not do or leave undone financially, without rebuke. (There is still some moral pressure, to be sure, against the outright issuance of paper money; but this only invites evasion through the use of short maturities and through resort to the inelegant expedient of paying the banks to create money for the Treasury.) A federal administration can now spend far beyond its revenues and grossly debase the currency without even placing itself on the defensive before public opinion. On the other hand, the "principles" to which reactionaries would have us return are perhaps worse than none at all. That the old moral prohibitions have lost their force is here not altogether an occasion for regret. But we can not get along without some such rules—without some moral sanctions and mandates which politicians must obey in matters of finance. And there is probably nothing more promising than the idea of a stable price level as a symbol articulating deep-rooted sentiments and as a source of discipline in fiscal practice.

The following observations may now be submitted, to define the author's general position, and to guard against misinterpretation:

1. A democratic, free-enterprise system implies, and requires for its effective functioning and survival, a stable framework of definite rules, laid down in legislation and subject to change only gradually and with careful regard for the vested interests of participants in the economic game. It is peculiarly essential economically that there should be a minimum of uncertainty for enterprisers and investors as to monetary conditions in the future—and, politically, that the plausible expedient of setting up "authorities" instead of rules, with respect to matters of such fundamental importance, be avoided, or accepted only as a very temporary arrangement. The most important objective of a sound liberal policy, apart from the establishment of highly competitive conditions in industry and the narrow limitation of political control over relative prices, should be that of securing a monetary system governed by definite rule.

2. To assure adequate moral pressure of public opinion against legislative (and administrative) tinkering, the monetary rules must be definite, simple (at least in principle), and expressive of strong, abiding, pervasive, and reasonable popular sentiments. They should be designed to permit the fullest and most stable employment, to facilitate adjustment to such basic changes (especially in technology) as are likely to

occur, and, secondarily, to minimize inequities as between debtors and creditors; but the problems here, while of first importance, should be conceived and dealt with mainly as problems of a transition period. Once well established and generally accepted as the basis of anticipations, any one of many different rules (or sets of rules) would probably serve about as well as another.

3. The responsibility for carrying out the monetary rules should be lodged in a federal authority, endowed with large administrative powers but closely controlled in their exercise by a sharply defined policy. The powers of the monetary authority should have to do primarily exclusively with fiscal arrangements—with the issue and retirement of paper money (open market operations in government securities) and perhaps with the relation between government revenues and expenditures; in other words, the monetary rules should be implemented entirely by, and in turn should largely determine, fiscal policy.

4. Political control in this sphere should be confined exclusively to regulation of the quantity of money and near-money, the *direction* of investment (the allocation of investment funds) being left to the control of competition and kept as far as possible outside the influence of political agencies (or central banks).

5. A liberal program of monetary reform should seek to effect an increasingly sharp differentiation between money and private obligations and, especially, to minimize the opportunities for the creation of effective money substitutes (whether for use as circulating media or in hoards) by private corporations. The abolition of private deposit banking is clearly the appropriate first step in this direction and would bring us in sight of the goal; but such a measure, to be really effective, must be accompanied, or followed closely, by drastic limitation on the formal borrowing powers of all private corporations and especially upon borrowing at short term.

6. A monetary rule of maintaining the constancy of some price index, preferably an index of prices of competitively produced commodities, appears to afford the only promising escape from present monetary chaos and uncertainties. A rule calling for outright fixing of the total quantity of money, however, definitely merits consideration as a perhaps preferable solution in the more distant future. At least, it may provide a point of departure for fruitful academic discussion.

John Maynard Keynes
(1883-1946)

Keynes' economics was often criticized for its inflationary aspects. Keynes, however, did not consider himself a pro-inflation economist. In this brief selection we see Keynes making arguments against inflation. First he argues that the Allies (the countries allied with Britain, the United States, and the other nations who fought against Germany and its allies in World War I) caused inflation in Germany after World War I because of their impossible reparations demands (demands that Germany and its allies make monetary and other restitution for the harm resulting from the war). That argument would make any classical economist proud.

John Maynard Keynes. 1932. *Essays in Persuasion*. New York: Harcourt Brace, pp. 77-79.

Inflation and Deflation

1. Inflation (1919)

Lenin is said to have declared that the best way to destroy the Capitalist System was to debauch the currency. By a continuing process of inflation, Governments can confiscate, secretly and unobserved, an important part of the wealth of their citizens. By this method they not only confiscate, but they confiscate *arbitrarily*; and, while the process impoverishes many, it actually enriches some. The sight of this arbitrary rearrangement of riches strikes not only at security, but at confidence in the equity of the existing distribution of wealth. Those to whom the system brings windfalls, beyond their deserts and even beyond their expectations or desires, become "profiteers," who are the object of the hatred of the bourgeoisie, whom the inflationism has impoverished, not less than of the proletariat. As the inflation proceeds and the real value of the currency fluctuates wildly from month to month, all permanent relations between debtors and creditors, which form the ultimate foundation of capitalism, become so utterly disordered as to be almost meaningless; and the process of wealth-getting degenerates into a gamble and a lottery.

Lenin was certainly right. There is no subtler, no surer means of overturning the existing basis of Society than to debauch the currency. The process engages all the hidden forces of economic law on the side of destruction, and does it in a manner which not one man in a million is able to diagnose.

In the latter stages of the war [World War I begin in 1914 and ended in 1918], all the belligerent Governments practised, from necessity or incompetence, what a Bolshevist might have done from design. Even now, when the war is over, most of them continue out of weakness the same malpractices. But further, the Governments of Europe, being many of them at this moment reckless in their methods as well as weak, seek to direct on to a class known as "profiteers" the popular indignation against the more obvious consequences of their vicious methods. These "profiteers" are, broadly speaking, the entrepreneur class of capitalists, that is to say, the active and constructive element in the whole capitalist society, who in a period of rapidly rising prices cannot but get rich quick whether they wish it or desire it or not. If prices are continually rising, every trader who has purchased for stock or owns property and plant inevitably makes profits. By directing hatred against this class, therefore, the European Governments are carrying a step further the fatal process which the subtle mind of Lenin had consciously conceived. The profiteers are a consequence and not a cause of rising prices. By combining a popular hatred of the class of entrepreneurs with the blow already given to social security by the violent and arbitrary disturbance of contract and of the established equilibrium of wealth which is the inevitable result of inflation, these Governments are fast rendering impossible a continuance of the social and economic order of the nineteenth century. But they have no plan for replacing it.

Paul Samuelson and Robert Solow

(Paul Samuelson: 1915-)
(Robert Solow: 1924-)

Paul Samuelson is the first American economist to win a Nobel prize (1970). His Foundations of Economic Analysis *(1947) is a classic and his principles of economics text,* Economics: An Introductory Analysis *(1948 and many subsequent editions), set the stage, as of the 1950s, for how principles of economics would be taught in the United States. He has written on a wide variety of topics and is still regarded as one of the preeminent economists of our time.*

Robert Solow, together with Paul Samuelson, made MIT (the Massachusetts Institute of Technology) into what was considered the top economics program during their stay there. Solow wrote on a variety of theories, including capital theory and growth, and his writing is the epitome of clarity and wit. More recently he has focused on the social limitations that cultural aspects place on labor markets, and has been a key expositor of Keynesian economics. Solow is also a Nobel prize winner (1987).

The piece by Samuelson and Solow is a famous article in economics because it introduced the Phillips curve into U.S. economic thinking. As you read it, notice the limitations that the authors suggest about the use of the Phillips curve for policy.

Note that they talk about the "NRA." That was the National Recovery Administration, a government agency early in the presidency of Franklin D. Roosevelt, designed to regulate industry for economic reform and recovery from the Great Depression. In 1935 the Supreme Court declared it unconstitutional.

Paul Samuelson and Robert Solow. 1959. "Problems of Achieving and Maintaining a Stable Price Level." *American Economic Review,* (December), pp. 136, 189, 191-94.

Policy Implications of the Phillips Curve

Consider . . . the question of the relation between money wage changes and the degree of unemployment. We have A. W. Phillips' interesting paper on the U. K. history since the Civil War (our Civil War, that is!). His findings are remarkable, even if one disagrees with his interpretations.

In the first place, the period 1861-1913, during which the trade-union movement was rather weak, shows a fairly close relationship between the per cent change in wage rates and the fraction of the labor force unemployed. Due allowance must be made for sharp import-price-induced changes in the cost of living, and for the normal expectation that wages will be rising faster when an unemployment rate of 5 per cent is reached on the upswing than when it is reached on the downswing. In the second place, with minor exceptions, the same relationship that fits for 1861-1913 also seems to fit about as well for 1913-48 and 1948-57. And finally Phillips concludes that the money wage level would stabilize with 5 per cent unemployment; and the rate of increase of money wages would be held down to the 2-3 per cent rate of productivity increase with about 2 per cent of the labor force unemployed.

In spite of all its deficiencies, we think the accompanying scatter diagram in Figure 1 [shown below] is useful. Where it does not provide answers, it at least asks interesting questions. We have plotted the yearly percentage changes of average hourly earnings in manufacturing, including supplements (Rees's data) against the annual average percentage of the labor force unemployed.

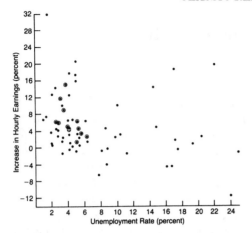

FIGURE 1
Phillips Scatter Diagram for the U.S.

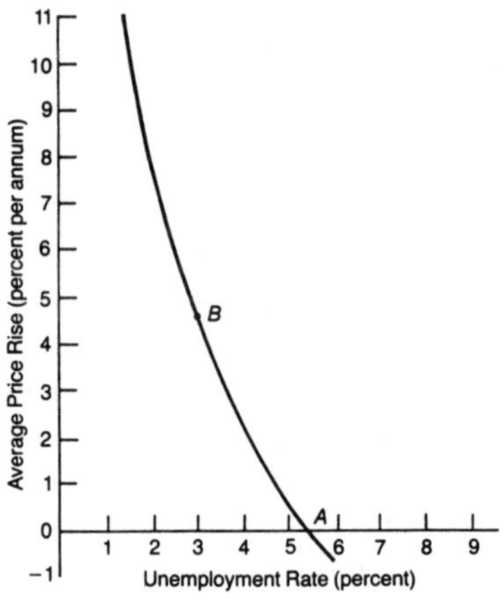

FIGURE 2
Modified Phillips Curve for U.S. (This shows the menu of choice between difference degrees of unemployment and a price stability, as roughly estimated from last twenty-five years of American data.)

The first defect to note is the different coverages represented in the two axes. Duesenberry has argued that postwar wage increases in manufacturing on the one hand and in trade, services, etc., on the other, may have quite different explanations: union power in manufacturing and simple excess demand in the other sectors. It is probably true that if we had an unemployment rate for manufacturing alone, it would be somewhat higher during the postwar years than the aggregate figure shown. Even if a qualitative statement like this held true over the whole period, the increasing weight of services in the total might still create a bias. Another defect is our use of annual increments and averages, when a full-scale study would have to look carefully into the nuances of timing.

A first look at the scatter is discouraging; there are points all over the place. But perhaps one can notice some systematic effects. In the first place, the years from 1933 to 1941 appear to be *sui generis* [unique]: money wages rose or failed to fall in the face of massive unemployment. One may attribute this to the workings of the New Deal (the 20 per cent wage increase of 1934 must represent the NRA codes); or alternatively one could argue that by 1933 much of the unemployment had become structural, insulated from the functioning labor market, so that in effect the vertical axis ought to be moved over to the right. This would leave something more like the normal pattern.

The early years of the first World War also behave atypically although not so much so as 1933-39. This may reflect cost-of-living increases, the rapidity of the increase in demand, a special tightness in manufacturing, or all three.

But the bulk of the observations—the period between the turn of the century and the first war, the decade between the end of that war [1918] and the Great Depression, and the most recent ten or twelve years—all show a rather consistent pattern. Wage rates do tend to rise when the labor market is tight, and the tighter the faster. What is most interesting is the strong suggestion that the relation, such as it is, has shifted upward slightly but noticeably in the forties and fifties. On the one hand, the first decade of the century and the twenties seem to fit the same pattern. Manufacturing wages seem to stabilize absolutely when 4 or 5 per cent of the labor force is unemployed; and wage increases equal to the productivity increase of 2 to 3 per cent per year is the normal pattern at about 3 per cent unemployment. This is not so terribly different from Phillips' results for the U. K., although the relation holds there with a greater consistency. When we translate the Phillips' diagram showing the American pattern of wage increase against degree of unemployment into a related diagram showing the different levels of unemployment

102

that would be "needed" for each degree of price level change, we come out with guesses like the following:

1. In order to have wages increase at no more than the 2-1/2 per cent per annum characteristic of our productivity growth, the American economy would seem on the basis of twentieth-century and postwar experience to have to undergo something like 5 to 6 per cent of the civilian labor force's being unemployed. That much unemployment would appear to be the cost of price stability in the years immediately ahead.

2. In order to achieve the nonperfectionist's goal of high enough output to give us no more than 3 per cent unemployment, the price index might have to rise by as much as 4 to 5 per cent per year. That much price rise would seem to be the necessary cost of high employment and production in the years immediately ahead.

All this is shown in our price-level modification of the Phillips curve, Figure 2 [shown above]. The point A, corresponding to price stability, is seen to involve about 5-1/2 per cent unemployment; whereas the point B, corresponding to 3 per cent unemployment, is seen to involve a price rise of about 4 1/2 per cent per annum. We rather expect that the tug of war of politics will end us up in the next few years somewhere in between these selected points. We shall probably have some price rise and some excess unemployment.

Aside from the usual warning that these are simply our best guesses we must give another caution. All of our discussion has been phrased in short-run terms, dealing with what might happen in the next few years. It would be wrong, though, to think that our Figure 2 menu that relates obtainable price and unemployment behavior will maintain its same shape in the longer run. What we do in a policy way during the next few years might cause it to shift in a definite way.

Thus, it is conceivable that after they had produced a low-pressure economy, the believers in demand-pull might be disappointed in the short run; i.e., prices might continue to rise even though unemployment was considerable. Nevertheless, it might be that the low-pressure demand would so act upon wage and other expectations as to shift the curve downward in the longer run—so that over a decade, the economy might enjoy higher employment with price stability than our present-day estimate would indicate.

But also the opposite is conceivable. A low-pressure economy might build up within itself over the years larger and larger amounts of structural unemployment (the reverse of what happened from 1941 to 1953 as a result of strong war and postwar demands). The result would be an upward shift of our menu of choice, with more and more unemployment being needed just to keep prices stable.

Since we have no conclusive or suggestive evidence on these conflicting issues, we shall not attempt to give judgment on them. Instead we venture the reminder that, in the years just ahead, the level of attained growth will be highly correlated with the degree of full employment and high-capacity output.

But what about the longer run? If the per annum rate of technical progress were about the same in a low- and high-pressure economy, then the initial loss in output in going to the low-pressure state would never be made up; however, in relative terms, the initial gap would not grow but would remain constant as time goes by. If a low-pressure economy could succeed in improving the efficiency of our productive factors, some of the loss of growth might be gradually made up and could in long enough time even be more than wiped out. On the other hand, if such an economy produced class warfare and social conflict and depressed the level of research and technical progress, the loss in growth would be compounded in the long run.

A final disclaimer is in order. We have not here entered upon the important question of what feasible institutional reforms might be introduced to lessen the degree of disharmony between full employment and price stability. These could of course involve such wide-ranging issues as direct price and wage controls, antiunion and antitrust legislation, and a host of other measures hopefully designed to move the American Phillips' curves downward and to the left.

Milton Friedman

(1912-)

Milton Friedman, to whom you were introduced earlier, has played a continuing role in economic debates over the past 50 years. In the late 1960s he predicted the Phillips curve tradeoff would be illusory, and helped introduce the natural rate long-run Phillips curve into economists' thinking.

In this selection, which is taken from his Nobel prize speech (1976), he goes beyond that. He argues that there is a third stage, in which the interdependence between politics and economics will mean that the Phillips curve will become positively, not negatively, sloped.

Milton Friedman. 1977. "Inflation and Unemployment." *Journal of Political Economy*, No. 3, pp. 454-60, 464-71.

The Stages of the Phillips Curve

Stage 1: Negatively Sloping Phillips Curve

Professional analysis of the relation between inflation and unemployment has gone through two stages since the end of World War II and is now entering a third. The first stage was the acceptance of a hypothesis associated with the name of A. W. Phillips that there is a stable negative relation between the level of unemployment and the rate of change of wages—high levels of unemployment being accompanied by falling wages, low levels of unemployment by rising wages. The wage change in turn was linked to price change by allowing for the secular increase in productivity and treating the excess of price over wage cost as given by a roughly constant markup factor.

Figure 1 illustrates this hypothesis, where I have followed the standard practice of relating unemployment directly to price change, short-circuiting the intermediate step through wages.

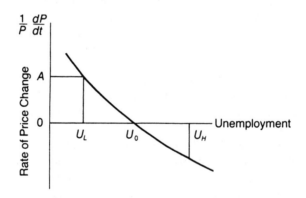

FIGURE 1
Simple Phillips Curve

Extracted from "Inflation and Unemployment," *Journal of Political Economy*, 85, No. 3 (1977), 454–60, 464–71. ©The Nobel Foundation.

Unfortunately for this hypothesis, additional evidence failed to conform with it. Empirical estimates of the Phillips curve relation were unsatisfactory. More important, the inflation rate that appeared to be consistent with a specified level of unemployment did not remain fixed: in the circumstances of the post-World War II period, when governments everywhere were seeking to promote "full employment," it tended in any one country to rise over time and to vary sharply among countries. Looked at the other way, rates of inflation that had earlier been associated with low levels of unemployment were experienced along with high levels of unemployment. The phenomenon of simultaneous high inflation and high unemployment increasingly forced itself on public and professional notice, receiving the unlovely label of "stagflation."

Some of us were skeptical from the outset about the validity of a stable Phillips curve, primarily on theoretical rather than empirical grounds. What mattered for employment, we argued, was not wages in dollars or pounds or kronor but real wages—what the wages would buy in goods and services. Low unemployment would, indeed, mean pressure for a higher real wage—but real wages could be higher even if nominal wages were lower, provided that prices were still lower. Similarly, high unemployment would, indeed, mean pressure for a lower real wage—but real wages could be lower, even if nominal wages were higher, provided prices were still higher.

There is no need to assume a stable Phillips curve in order to explain the apparent tendency for an acceleration of inflation to reduce unemployment. That can be explained by the impact of *unanticipated* changes in nominal demand on markets characterized by (implicit or explicit) long-term commitments with respect to both capital and labor. Long-term labor commitments can be explained by the cost of acquiring information by employers about employees and by employees about alternative employment opportunities plus the specific human capital that makes an employee's value to a particular employer grow over time and exceed his value to other potential employers.

Only surprises matter. If everyone anticipated that prices would rise at, say, 20 percent a year, then this anticipation would be embodied in future wage (and other) contrasts, real wages would then behave precisely as they would if everyone anticipated no price rise, and there would be no reason for the 20 percent rate of inflation to be associated with a different level of unemployment than a zero rate. An unanticipated change is very different, especially in the presence of long-term commitments—themselves partly a result of the imperfect knowledge whose effect they enhance and spread over time. Long-term commitments mean, first, that there is not instantaneous market clearing (as in markets for perishable foods) but only a lagged adjustment of both prices and quantity to changes in demand or supply (as in the house-rental market); second, that commitments entered into depend not only on current observable prices but also on the prices expected to prevail throughout the term of the commitment.

Stage 2: Natural Rate Hypothesis

Proceeding along these lines, we (in particular, E. S. Phelps and myself) developed an alternative hypothesis that distinguished between the short-run and long-run effects of unanticipated changes in aggregate nominal demand. Start from some initial stable position and let there be, for example, an unanticipated acceleration of aggregate nominal demand. This will come to each producer as an unexpectedly favorable demand for his product. In an environment in which changes are always occurring in the relative demand for different goods, he will not know whether this change is special to him or pervasive. It will be rational for him to interpret it as at least partly special and to react to it by seeking to produce more to sell at what he now perceives to be a higher than expected market price for future output. He will be willing to pay higher nominal wages than he had been willing to pay before in order to attract additional workers. The real wage that matters to him is the wage in terms of the price of his product, and he perceives that price as higher than before. A higher nominal wage can therefore mean a lower *real* wage as perceived by him.

To workers, the situation is different: what matters to them is the purchasing power of wages not over the particular good they produce but over all goods in general. Both they and their employers are likely to adjust more slowly their perception of prices in general—because it is more costly to acquire information about that—than their perception of the price of the particular good they produce. As a result, a rise in nominal wages may be perceived by workers as a rise in real wages and hence call forth an increased supply at the same time that it is perceived by employers as a fall in real wages and hence calls forth an increased offer of jobs. Expressed in terms of the average of perceived future prices, real wages are lower; in terms of the perceived future average price, real wages are higher.

But this situation is temporary: let the higher rate of growth of aggregate nominal demand and of prices continue, and perceptions will adjust to reality. When they do, the initial effect will disappear and then even be reversed for a time as workers and employers find themselves locked into inappropriate contracts. Ultimately, employment will be back at the level that prevailed before the assumed unanticipated acceleration in aggregate nominal demand. . . . .

This analysis is, of course, oversimplified. It supposes a single unanticipated change whereas, of course, there is a continuing stream of unanticipated changes; it does not deal explicitly with lags, or with overshooting, or with the process of formation of anticipations. But it does highlight the key points: what matters is not inflation per se but unanticipated inflation; there is no stable trade-off between inflation and unemployment; there is a "natural rate of unemployment" which is consistent with the real forces and with accurate perceptions; unemployment can be kept below that level only by an accelerating inflation; or above it only by accelerating deflation.

The "natural rate of unemployment," a term I introduced to parallel Knut Wicksell's "natural rate of interest," is not a numerical constant but depends on "real" as opposed to monetary factors—the effectiveness of the labor market, the extent of competition or monopoly, the barriers or encouragements to working in various occupations, and so on.

For example, the natural rate has clearly been rising in the United States for two major reasons. First, women, teenagers, and part-time workers have been constituting a growing fraction of the labor force. These groups are more mobile in employment than other workers, entering and leaving the labor market, shifting more frequently between jobs. As a result, they tend to experience higher average rates of unemployment. Second, unemployment insurance and other forms of assistance to unemployed persons have been made available to more categories of workers and have become more generous in duration and amount. Workers who lose their jobs are under less pressure to look for other work, will tend to wait longer in the hope, generally fulfilled, of being recalled to their former employment, and can be more selective in the alternatives they consider. Further, the availability of unemployment insurance makes it more attractive to enter the labor force in the first place, and so may itself have stimulated both the growth that has occurred in the labor force as a percentage of the population and its changing composition.

The determinants of the natural rate of unemployment deserve much fuller analysis for both the United States and other countries. So also do the meaning of the recorded unemployment figures and the relation between the recorded figures and the natural rate. These issues are all of the utmost importance for public policy. However, they are side issues for my present limited purpose. . . .

Stage 3: A Positively Sloped Phillips Curve?

Although the second stage is far from having been fully explored, let alone fully absorbed into the economic literature, the course of events is already producing a move to a third stage. In recent years higher inflation has often been accompanied by higher, not lower, unemployment, especially for periods of several years in length. A simple statistical Phillips curve for such periods seems to be positively sloped, not vertical. The third stage is directed at accommodating this apparent empirical phenomenon. To do so, I suspect that it will have to include in the analysis the interdependence of economic experience and political developments. It will have to treat at least some political phenomena not as independent variables—as exogenous variables in econometric jargon—but as themselves determined by economic events—as endogenous variables. The second stage was greatly influenced by two major developments in economic theory of the past few decades—one, the analysis of imperfect information and of the cost of acquiring information, pioneered by George Stigler; the other, the role of human capital in determining the form of labor contracts, pioneered by Gary Becker. The third stage will, I believe, be greatly influenced by a third major development—the application of economic analysis to political behavior, a field in which pioneering work has also been done by Stigler and Becker as well as by Kenneth Arrow, Duncan Black, Anthony Downs, James Buchanan, Gordon Tullock, and others.

* * * *

Conclusion

One consequence of the Keynesian revolution of the 1930s was the acceptance of a rigid absolute wage level, and a nearly rigid absolute price level, as a starting point for analyzing short-term economic change. It came to be taken for granted that these were essentially institutional data and were so regarded by economic agents, so that changes in aggregate nominal demand would be reflected almost entirely in output and hardly at all in prices. The age-old confusion between absolute prices and relative prices gained a new lease on life.

In this intellectual atmosphere it was understandable that economists would analyze the relation between unemployment and *nominal* rather than *real* wages and would implicitly regard changes in anticipated *nominal* wages as equal to changes in anticipated *real* wages. Moreover, the empirical evidence that initially suggested a stable relation between the level of unemployment and the rate of change of nominal wages was drawn from a period when, despite sharp short-period fluctuations in prices, there was a relatively stable long-run price level and when the expectation of continued stability was widely shared. Hence these data flashed no warning signals about the special character of the assumptions.

The hypothesis that there is a stable relation between the level of unemployment and the rate of inflation was adopted by the economics profession with alacrity. It filled a gap in Keynes's theoretical structure. It seemed to be the "one equation" that Keynes himself had said "we are . . . short." In addition, it seemed to provide a reliable tool for economic policy, enabling the economist to inform the policymaker about the alternatives available to him.

As in any science, so long as experience seemed to be consistent with the reigning hypothesis it continued to be accepted, although, as always, a few dissenters questioned its validity.

But as the '50s turned into the '60s, and the '60s into the '70s, it became increasingly difficult to accept the hypothesis in its simple form. It seemed to take larger and larger doses of inflation to keep down the level of unemployment. Stagflation reared its ugly head.

Many attempts were made to patch up the hypothesis by allowing for special factors such as the strength of trade unions. But experience stubbornly refused to conform to the patched-up versions.

A more radical revision was required. It took the form of stressing the importance of surprises—of differences between actual and anticipated magnitudes. It restored the primacy of the distinction between real and nominal magnitudes. There is a natural rate of unemployment at any time determined by real factors. This natural rate will tend to be attained when expectations are on the average realized. The same real situation is consistent with any absolute level of prices or of price change, provided allowance is made for the effect of price change on the real cost of holding money balances. In this respect, money is neutral. On the other hand, unanticipated changes in aggregate nominal demand and in inflation will cause systematic errors of perception on the part of employers and employees alike that will initially lead unemployment to deviate in the opposite direction from its natural rate. In this respect, money is not neutral. However, such deviations are transitory, though it may take a long chronological time before they are reversed and finally eliminated as anticipations adjust.

The natural-rate hypothesis contains the original Phillips curve hypothesis as a special case and rationalizes a far broader range of experience, in particular the phenomenon of stagflation. It has by now been widely though not universally accepted.

However, the natural-rate hypothesis in its present form has not proved rich enough to explain a more recent development—a move from stagflation to slumpflation. In recent years, higher inflation has often been accompanied by higher unemployment—not lower unemployment, as the simple Phillips curve would suggest, nor the same unemployment, as the natural-rate hypothesis would suggest.

This recent association of higher inflation with higher unemployment may reflect the common impact of such events as the oil crisis, or independent forces that have imparted a common upward trend to inflation and unemployment.

However, a major factor in some countries and a contributing factor in others may be that they are in a transitional period—this time to be measured by quinquennia [5-year periods] or decades, not [single] years. The public has not adapted its attitudes or its institutions to a new monetary environment. Inflation tends not only to be higher but also increasingly volatile and to be accompanied by widening government intervention into the setting of prices. The growing volatility of inflation and the growing departure of relative prices from the values that market forces alone would set combine to render the economic system less efficient, to introduce frictions in all markets, and, very likely, to raise the recorded rate of unemployment.

On this analysis, the present situation cannot last. It will either degenerate into hyperinflation and radical change, or institutions will adjust to a situation of chronic inflation, or governments will adopt policies that will produce a low rate of inflation and less government intervention into the fixing of prices.

I have told a perfectly standard story of how scientific theories are revised. Yet it is a story that has far-reaching importance.

Government policy about inflation and unemployment has been at the center of political controversy. Ideological war has raged over these matters. Yet the drastic change that has occurred in economic theory has not been a result of ideological warfare. It has not resulted from divergent political beliefs or aims. It has responded almost entirely to the force of events: brute experience proved far more potent than the strongest of political or ideological preferences.

The importance for humanity of a correct understanding of positive economic science is vividly brought out by a statement made nearly two hundred years ago by Pierre S. du Pont, a deputy from Nemours to the French National Assembly, speaking, appropriately enough, on a proposal to issue additional assignats—the fiat money of the French Revolution: "Gentlemen, it is a disagreeable custom to which one is too easily led by the harshness of the discussions, to assume evil intentions. It is necessary to be gracious as to intentions; one should believe them good, and apparently they are; but we do not have to be gracious at all to inconsistent logic or to absurd reasoning. Bad logicians have committed more involuntary crimes than bad men have done intentionally ."

James M. Buchanan and Richard E. Wagner
(James M. Buchanan: 1919-)
(Richard E. Wagner: 1941-)

James Buchanan has played an important role in extending the boundaries of economics to include politics. His work spawned a school—the public choice school of economics—which emphasizes that government decisions are reflections of politics, not the good of society and that government failures are as likely as market failures. His most famous work is the Calculus of Consent, *written jointly with Gordon Tullock. In 1986, he won a Nobel Prize for his contribution.*

Richard Wagner is an important member of that public choice school and he has done significant work on the implications of public choice ideas for macroeconomics.

In this selection they consider those implications and argue that "Keynesianism" represents a substantial disease that over the long run can prove fatal for the survival of democracy.

James M. Buchanan and Richard E. Wagner. 1978. *The Consequences of Mr. Keynes.* London: Institute of Economic Affairs, pp. 13-17, 18, 23, 27.

The Consequences of Mr. Keynes

Visions of the Economic Order: Classical and Keynesian

The Classical or pre-Keynesian notions of prudent fiscal conduct were reasonably summarized by drawing an analogy between the state and the family. It was another British intellectual 'export,' Adam Smith, who noted that 'What is prudence in the conduct of every private family, can scarce be folly in that of a great kingdom.' Prudent financial conduct by the state was conceived in basically the same image as that for the family. Frugality, not profligacy, was the cardinal virtue, and this norm assumed practical shape in the widely shared principle that public budgets should be in balance, if not in surplus, and that deficits were to be tolerated only in extraordinary circumstances. Substantial and continuing deficits were interpreted as the mark of fiscal folly. Principles of sound family and business practice were deemed equally relevant to the fiscal affairs of the state.

During this period, a free-enterprise economy was generally held as being characterized by 'Say's Equality.' While fluctuations in economic activity would occur in such an economy, they would set in motion self-correcting forces that would operate to restore prosperity. Within this economic framework, the best action for government was simply to avoid injecting additional sources of instability into the economy. The profligacy of government was one latent source of disturbance, and it was considered important that this governmental proclivity should be restrained. Avoiding such sources of instability, along with keeping debt and taxes low so as to promote thrift and saving, was the way to achieve prosperity. A balanced or surplus budget was one of the practical rules that reflected such constraints and beliefs. Such siren songs as the 'paradox of thrift' were yet to come.

From Classical Stability to Keynesian Instability

The idea that the spontaneous co-ordination of economic activities within a system or markets would generally produce economic stability was replaced in the Keynesian vision by the idea of an inherently unstable economy. Say's Equality was deemed inapplicable. The Keynesian paradigm was one of an economy ultimately haunted by gluts and secular stagnation. The prosperous co-ordination of economic activities was a razor's edge. The economic order is as likely to be saddled with substantial unemployment as it is to provide full employment. An important element in the Keynesian paradigm was the absence of an equilibrating process by which inconsistencies among the plans of the participants in the economic process became self-correcting. Prosperity, accordingly, could be assured only through deliberate efforts of government to help the economy avoid the buffeting forces of inflation and recession. 'Fine tuning' became the ideal of Keynesian economic policy.

The Keynesian message, in other words, contained two central features. One was the image of an inherently unstable economy, ungoverned by some 'natural law' of a generally smooth co-ordination of economic activities. The other was of government as having both the obligation and the ability to offset this instability so as to bring about a more smoothly functioning economic order. The notion of an unstable economy whose performance could be improved through the manipulation of public budgets produced a general principle that budgets *need not* be in balance: indeed, they *should not* be in balance, since that would mean government was failing in its duty. Some years of deficit and others of surplus were both necessary to, and evidence of, corrective macro-economic management. A stable relation between revenues and expenditures, say a relatively constant rate of surplus, would indicate a failure of government to carry out its managerial duties.

The Idealised Environment For Keynesian Economic Policy

While Lord Keynes published his *General Theory* in 1936, his presuppositions did not infuse themselves into generally held understandings or beliefs for about a generation in America, though sooner in Britain, much as he anticipated in a famous passage on the time-lag between the articulation of an idea and its influence on policy. While the Keynesian vision of the nature of our economic order and the proper pattern of budgetary policy gained dominance in academia in the 1940s and 1950s, it did not filter into the general climate of American opinion until the 1960s. With this conversion or shift in generally-held perspectives or beliefs, macroeconomic engineering became the province of government.

As developed by the economists who advocated macro-economic engineering, fiscal policy would be devoted to smoothing out cycles in private economic activity. Fiscal policy would be guided by the same principle during both recession and inflation. Deficits would be created during recession and surpluses during inflation, with the object of smoothing out peaks and troughs. The policy precepts of Keynesian economics were alleged to be wholly symmetrical. In depressed economic conditions, budget deficits would be required to restore full employment and prosperity. When inflation threatened, budget surpluses would be appropriate. The time-honoured norm of budget balance was thus jettisoned, but, in the pure logic Keynesian policy, there was no one-way departure. It might even be said that Keynesian economics did not destroy the principle of a balanced budget, but only lengthened the time-period over which it applied, from a calendar year to the period of a business cycle. In this way, rational public policy would operate to promote a more prosperous and stable economy during both recession and inflation.

While the idealised setting for the symmetrical application of Keynesian economic policy is familiar, the political setting within which the policy is to be formulated and implemented is much less familiar. We have now learned that mere exhortations to politicians to promote prosperity do not guarantee they will do so: they may lack the knowledge required to promote such an outcome, or the incentive to act in the required manner, or both. In other words, the actions of politicians on budgetary policy as well as on other types of policy depend upon both the knowledge politicians have and the incentives they confront.

Keynes's Defective Assumptions

Keynes largely begged questions pertaining to knowledge. Central to his approach was the presumption that economists could possess knowledge sufficient to enable them to give advice which, if acted upon, would facilitate the coordination of human activities within the economic order. This extremely questionable assumption about knowledge melded nicely with his normative assumptions about political conduct. Keynes was an elitist, and he operated under what his biographer called the 'presuppositions of Harvey Road'—that governmental policy, and economic policy in particular, would be made by a relatively small group of wise and enlightened people. Keynes did not consider the application of his policy prescriptions in a contemporary democratic setting—in which government is tempted to yield to group pressures to retain or return to power. Rather, the small group of enlightened men who made economic policy would, he assumed, subconsciously—even if in defiance of historical experience—always tend to act in accordance with the 'public interest', even when this might run foul of constituency, sectional or other organised pressures.

In the unreal economic and political environment envisaged by Keynes, there could be little or no question raised about the application of the Keynesian policy instruments. To secure a stable, prosperous economy, expenditures would be expanded and contracted symmetrically. Budget deficits would be created during periods of sluggish economic activity, and surpluses as the pace of economic activity became too quick. There would be no political pressures, he implicitly supposed, operating to render the surpluses fictional and the deficits disproportionately large or ill-timed. The ruling elite would be guided by the presuppositions of Harvey Road; they would not act as competitors for electoral favour in a democratic political environment.

There was little awareness that the dictates of political survival might run contrary to the requirements of macro-economic engineering (assuming for now that the economic order is aptly described by the Keynesian paradigm). It was tacitly assumed either that the political survival of politicians was automatically strengthened as they came to follow more fully the appropriate fiscal policies, or that the ruling elite would act without regard to their political fortunes. But what happens when we make non-Keynesian assumptions about politics? What if we commence from the assumption that elected politicians respond to pressures emanating from constituents and the state bureaucracy? When this shift of perspective is made in the political setting for analysis, the possibilities that policy precepts may unleash political biases cannot be ignored.

Keynesian Presuppositions, Democratic Politics, and Economic Policy

Anyone, citizens no less than politicians, would typically like to live beyond his means. Individual citizens generally face a personal or household budget constraint which prevents them from acting on this desire, although some counterfeit and others go bankrupt. In the century before the shift in belief wrought by the Keynesian revolution, politicians acted as if they sensed a similar constraint when making the nation's budgetary choices.

Contemporary political institutions, however, are constrained differently because of the general belief in the Keynesian vision. This shift in constraints due to the shift in general beliefs alters the character of governmental budgetary policy. While there is little political resistance to budget deficits, there is substantial resistance to budget surpluses. Hence, fiscal policy will tend to be applied asymmetrically: deficits will be created frequently, but surpluses will materialise only rarely. This bias results from the shift in the general, public impression or understanding of the Western economic order, and of the related rules of thumb held generally by the citizenry as to what constitutes prudent, reasonable, or efficacious conduct by government in running its budget. Old-fashioned beliefs about the virtue of the balanced-budget rule and of redeeming public debt during periods of prosperity became undermined by Keynesian ideas, and lost their hold upon the public. In consequence, debt reduction lost its claim as a guiding rule. Budget surpluses lost their *raison d' etre* [reason for being]. Deficits allow politicians to increase spending without having directly and openly to raise taxes. There is little obstacle to such a policy. Surpluses, on the other hand, require government to raise taxes without increasing spending—a programme far more capable of stimulating political opposition than budget deficits, especially once the constraining norm of debt retirement had receded from public consciousness.

Keynesian Economics in Political Democracy

The grafting of Keynesian economics onto the fabric of a political democracy has wrought a significant revision in the underlying fiscal constitution. The result has been a tendency toward budget deficits and, consequently, once the workings of democratic political institutions are taken into account, inflation. Democratic governments will generally respond more vigorously in correcting for unemployment than in correcting for inflation. Budgetary adjustments aimed at the prevention or control of inflation will rarely be observed as the result of deliberate policy. Budget deficits will come to be the general rule, even when inflation is severe. In slack years, when deficits might seem warranted by strict application of the Keynesian precepts, the size of these deficits will become disproportionately large. Moreover, the perceived cost of government will generally be lower than the real cost because of the deficit financing. As a consequence, there will also be a relative increase in the size of the government sector in the economy. Budget deficits, inflation, and the growth of government—all are intensified by the Keynesian destruction of former constitutional principles of sound finance.

Conclusion

Why does Camelot lie in ruins? Intellectual error of monumental proportion has been made, and not exclusively by the politicians. Error also lies squarely with the economists. The 'academic scribbler' who must bear substantial responsibility is Lord Keynes, whose thinking was uncritically accepted by establishment economists in both America and Britain. The mounting historical evidence of the ill-effects of Keynes's ideas cannot continue to be ignored. Keynesian economics has turned the politicians loose; it has destroyed the effective constraint on politicians' ordinary appetites to spend and spend without the apparent necessity to tax.

A sober assessment suggests that, politically, Keynesianism represents a substantial disease that over the long run can prove fatal for the survival of democracy.

William H. Hutt
(1899-1988)

During the Keynesian period in the 1950s and 1960s, very few economists found it possible to maintain the classical views. One of those who did maintain consistency throughout his entire career was William Hutt, who wrote a variety of insightful criticisms of Keynesian economics. Hutt's arguments are grounded in classical economics with deep roots in laissez-faire and natural rights, and in Hayekian Austrian economics. The Austrian interpretation of the classical economic policy position is a much broader-based presentation of the classical position presented in the text. Born and educated in London, he spent much of his life as an academic in South Africa and his The Crises of the Color Bar *(1964) is an interesting examination of economics and race relations.*

He devoted his life, however, to attacking Keynesian economic ideas and his important books include Theory of Idle Resource, A Rehabilitation of Say's Law, *and* The Keynesian Episode *(1963), from which this selection is drawn.*

William Harold Hutt. 1963. *Keynesianism—Retrospect and Prospect.* Chicago: Henry Regnery, pp. 39-43.

The Keynesian Episode

Generalizing boldly, it can be said that there have been two kinds of diagnosis: the orthodox and the Keynesian. The orthodox diagnosis places the blame on a disco-ordination expressed through prices being fixed at levels which are inconsistent with full employment under uninflated money income; and it prescribes the adjustment of prices in order to achieve full employment and stability. The Keynesian diagnosis blames lack of purchasing power or lack of "effective demand" and it prescribes (in formulae which often obscure the true nature of the prescription) the creation of additional purchasing power which will raise final prices and thereby reduce real costs. I shall argue that this second diagnosis diverts attention from the crucial issues and that the remedy associated with it is harmful.

To me, the course of the great depression of the thirties had provided an empirical demonstration of the soundness of the classical analysis and synthesis (not of its all-sufficiency or infallibility) At the same time *it had demonstrated equally clearly how unacceptable, for a variety of socio-psychological reasons, disinterested teachings had become.* I was prompted by these circumstances to write my *Economists and the Public.* In that book, I dealt with the problem of authority in economic science, and the reasons for the current unacceptability of teaching in the classical tradition. It seems to me that, at the same time, others were unconsciously groping for some *more acceptable* substitute for the old economic teachings. Naturally, the Keynesians will not be easy to convince that the mere palatability of their theories had any influence upon them. They interpreted the great depression in the opposite way. To them it was the great practical refutation of the classical system of thought or fundamental parts of it. I make this point simply to show how diametrically my own reactions to the economic experience of the inter-war period have differed.

To consider the *consequences* of Keynesian policies, one can hardly avoid discussing the phenomenon of creeping inflation. But as I have already conceded, not all Keynesians will agree that the tacit approval of inflation is implied by their teachings. I must therefore ask those readers who may feel that I am here misrepresenting Keynesian thought to withhold their judgment at this stage. They will readily admit that, wherever Keynesian ideas have been influential in policy, inflation has in fact been experienced; and in this chapter I am concerned with the apparent results of that policy. They may well object that Keynesian maxims must not be held to be responsible for the inflationary experiences to which I shall be referring. But I shall try to convince them that, if they take that line, they are assuming that imposed restrictions or controls can effectively repress forces which would otherwise be expressed in open inflation, whilst I hope to make it clear in due course that the repression of inflation merely destroys its crude co-ordinative power. Hence the reasonableness of *my assumption* in this chapter that the full employment which the world has witnessed since the thirties is attributable to inflation and not to other virtues of Keynesian policy must be judged from arguments which will be developed in later chapters.

The issue can be summarized as follows: The Keynesians have centered attention upon the possibility that, in the equation PT--MV, an increase in MV (i.e., in M or in V) may cause an increase, not in P but in T (output) owing to the release of withheld capacity. Economists have always known that an increase in MV *could* result not only in an increase in P but subsequently in an increase in T; and this has been explicitly recognized at least since the days of Hume. But since Hume and before Keynes, it was almost always tacitly accepted that was a very bad way of increasing T (as compared with co-ordination through price adjustment).

In Keynes' earlier writings, the possibility of a rise in prices was ignored and stability of the scale of prices was accepted as the ideal. Subsequently, however, the argument *seems* to have developed that, whilst prices will rise as increased expenditure stimulates output, the inflation is nevertheless defensible. It is assumed that, up to the point of full employment, output will increase in sufficient measure to make inflation a lesser evil than withheld capacity. Had the assumption been unambiguously enunciated in these terms, subsequent controversies would have been more fruitful. The main issue would have boiled down to the effectiveness and justice of inflation as a means of releasing capacity, in comparison with other means available.

The Keynesians seem often to be claiming that their remedy in some way creates stability. Yet if a tolerable scale of prices (or any form of convertibility) is to be maintained, the "maintenance of effective demand" seems inevitably to lead to a boom; and hence either to the necessity for a period of drastic general price adjustments or to a period of depression. For just as cost rigidity downwards is the main cause of the persistence of depression (in the absence of inflation), so is the very much less marked cost rigidity upwards, which is experienced during an inflation, the main cause which prolongs a boom. The lag of cost-increases below revenue-increases explains why inflation succeeds in stimulating outputs—the *real boom;* and the fact that the flow of residual incomes (generally speaking, entrepreneurial incomes) increases relatively to the flow of wage and other contractual incomes and contains an illusory element (due to capital gains—caused by interest below the natural—tending to be treated as income), explains in part why inflation can so easily induce a *speculative boom* (through causing exaggerated predictions of yields).

Obviously, then, we are unable to draw a common (and politically very popular) Keynesian conclusion, namely, that if wage receipts rise as rapidly as residual receipts, the boom can be prolonged. What *is* true, and this is the truth which is often missed, is that if ,wage-rates and other costs were perfectly flexible upwards, it would not pay to indulge in inflation. Inflation would then be purposeless, ceasing to have any co-ordinative tendency (although it might certainly continue through mere habit, like continuance with a drug which has been known to give relief in the past). For as I shall be reiterating in this work, the public's expectations tend to force the scale of prices towards the level to which it is believed that policy is aiming (drift being regarded as one policy). Anticipated inflation becomes pointless; and the use of the monetary system as an instrument of "national policy" is practicable only as long as the public do not understand or can be deceived about objectives.

Indeed, the degree of inflation needed (in any given situation with unemployment) to bring relative prices into co-ordination, increases in proportion to the extent to which the inflation can be forecast. In the absence of *"controls"* which, if politically tolerable, would make the inflationary remedy redundant, the so-called "maintenance of effective demand" can succeed only when the majority of people can be misled into thinking that the expansion of credit is about to cease or that it will be much more moderate than it is destined to be. Unless this deception is possible, those who are in a position to raise prices and wage-rates will do so in advance of the declining value of the money unit so that the original degree of withheld capacity will tend to be perpetuated.

Inflation once commenced appears, indeed, to be self-perpetuating and, in the Keynesian atmosphere, inevitable. Theoretically there is no limit to the extent to which V can rise for this reason. But if M does not increase, and the monetary authority does not in fact intend to increase it, it seems likely that wrong expectations will soon be corrected; for as prices rise (through the *increasing* V) more money units will be required for the same real volume of transactions and more demanded therefore. In the present age, however, monetary authorities nearly always remove this deflationary barrier to the private reinforcement of their policy. For by this time they have all forgotten the simple lessons which economists learned in the days of the pre-1844 currency controversies, and it appears to be their unmistakable duty to respond to the *"obviously legitimate"* demand for money so expressed. Moreover, it has been noticed that, in so far as any inflation is initiated or enforced *via* budget deficits, each deficit tends to generate an inflation of government expenditure in anticipation of revenue, and hence to cause a succession of further deficits.

In practice, it is seldom possible to resort to inflation merely as a transition from an era of dislocating rigidity to an era of price flexibility. Raising the general scale of prices can hardly serve as a stepping stone to a regime in which it will be possible to establish a defined measuring rod of value as well as maintain full employment. *For the institutional setup which permits the rigidities evaded by the inflation will remain un-reformed.* Withheld capacity will return and further inflation will be demanded on the same old grounds.

It is, I think, for this reason that, even during the practice of inflation itself, some concrete recognition of the true remedy seems often to be discernible; for whilst the depreciation of the money unit is in progress, it is almost universally accompanied by measures to prevent, or at least to discourage direct disco-ordination of the price system. It is recognized that antisocial sectionalist action to force up wage-rates and prices, unless checked, would cause *runaway* inflations. But the required checks are usually imposed, not in the form of strict antimonopoly control or action to prevent trade-unions from reducing aggregate uninflated wages, but by the crude expedients of price control, moral exhortations to industry, commerce and organized labor, and very occasionally wage-ceilings.

Perhaps the strongest objection to the attempt to maintain coordination by "maintaining effective demand" is, then, that it removes (a) pressures to co-ordinating adjustments within the existing framework of institutions and (b) the incentive to fundamental reform of the framework. The politicians may feel that far-reaching reforms are needed. But cheap money eases things for the time being and enables them to procrastinate. For this reason it permits the survival of distortions in the price structure or concomitant distortions in the form taken by production functions. This is partly because it *obscures* the inherent contradictions and inconsistencies in the functioning of economic institutions due to sectionalist pricing, but partly because it *destroys the collective incentive* to refashion institutions. Perpetual recourse to the line of least resistance results in unplanned institutional modifications which stand as powerful, semipermanent obstacles to a more efficient, just and stable social order.

I have already referred to the easy solution which inflation offers to the problems created by disco-ordination. It is because the method is so easy that the great nations have been able superficially to eradicate virtually all signs of the "trade cycle"—beyond minor recessions and up-swings-since the 1930's, without any attempts at major institutional reform. What "sound finance" *did* do in the pre-Keynesian era was to create every incentive to reprice services and products the sale of which was being held up, as well as to create a strong social motive to eradicate practices which reduced the flow of uninflated income. In the private sphere, the pressures were fairly successful, and had it not been for contrary action by the State, they could, I believe, have rescued the economy— without inflation— from the great depression. But the reaction of governments was, typically enough, to impose further disco-ordination. For instance, the multitude of relatively small-scale withholdings of capacity throughout the world which had developed during the 1920's had caused so serious a contraction in uninflated demand that large-scale State-imposed output and trade restrictions were resorted to (at that time mainly valorization schemes and tariffs). The repercussions of the situation caused by these measures aggravated the decline in uninflated world demand. There was then an enhanced incentive for cheap money. But the degree of inflation which was possible before the general abandonment of convertibility in the 'thirties could not, as B. H. Beckhart has pointed out, "bring about that readjustment of retail and wholesale prices and costs, on the basis of which any substantial improvement in business must be rounded." It is precisely because there could have been no other way out if there had been perseverance with "sound finance," that the demand for direct co-ordination and institutional reform may well have become irresistible (especially if the bulk of the economists had recognized the necessity and pressed for the reforms required).

The actual working of the mechanism of value determination certainly needed re-designing. Difficult institutional changes were called for —not simple monetary panaceas, but carefully planned structural adjustments based on patient, painstaking studies of the psychological, sociological and political resistances likely to be encountered. No attempts whatsoever have been made at such replanning.

It is possible to achieve a money unit of stable value without the general problem of economic co-ordination having been successfully solved. But if so, it must be at the expense of *more conspicuous forms of* waste, including unemployment. Only if the problems of inflation and disco-ordination are tackled simultaneously is it possible for "sound money" to accompany "full employment." *Hence, seriously to advocate the cessation of inflation is to recommend far-reaching but perfectly obvious reforms of a nonmonetary kind.* Wise monetary policy *demands* non-monetary co-ordination; and that means in practice reforms to achieve such flexibility of values and prices as permits the free allocation of means to ends (whether those ends are expressed individually or collectively).

Franco Modigliani

(1918-)

Franco Modigliani is a professor of economics at the Massachusetts Institute of Technology and is one of the foremost macroeconomists of our day. He and his many former students are an influential force in both modern macroeconomic theory and macroeconomic modeling. He won a Nobel prize in 1985.

He was elected president of the American Economic Association in 1977 and the following is excerpted from his presidential address. In this selection he discusses the debate between Keynesian and classical thinking (He calls classicals "monetarists," which is what they were called in the 1970s.) He argues that the classicals' objections to Keynesian theory, while justified, do not overturn that theory.

Franco Modigliani. 1977. "The Monetarist Controversy, or Should We Forsake Stabilization Policies?" *American Economic Review*, Volume 67 (March), pp. 1-8, 12, 14, 15, 17, 18.

The Monetarist Controversy, or Should We Forsake Stabilization Policies?

In recent years and especially since the onset of the current depression, the economics profession and the lay public have heard a great deal about the sharp conflict between "monetarists and Keynesians" or between "monetarists and fiscalists." The difference between the two "schools" is generally held to center on whether the money supply or fiscal variables are the major determinants of aggregate economic activity, and hence the most appropriate tool of stabilization policies.

My central theme is that this view is quite far from the truth, and that the issues involved are of far greater practical import. There are in reality no serious analytical disagreements between leading monetarists and leading nonmonetarists. Milton Friedman was once quoted as saying, "We are all Keynesians, now," and I am quite prepared to reciprocate that "we are all monetarists"—if by monetarism is meant assigning to the stock of money a major role in determining output and prices. Indeed, the list of those who have long been monetarists in this sense is quite extensive, including among others John Maynard Keynes as well as myself, as is attested by my 1944 and 1963 articles.

In reality the distinguishing feature of the monetarist school and the real issues of disagreement with nonmonetarists is not monetarism, but rather the role that should probably be assigned to stabilization policies. Nonmonetarists accept what I regard to be the fundamental practical message of *The General Theory:* that a private enterprise economy using an intangible money *needs* to be stabilized, *can* be stabilized, and therefore *should* be stabilized by appropriate monetary and fiscal policies. Monetarists by contrast take the view that there is no serious need to stabilize the economy, that even if there were a need, it could not be done, for stabilization policies would be more likely to increase than to decrease instability; and, at least some monetarists would, I believe, go so far as to hold that, even in the unlikely event that stabilization policies could on balance prove beneficial, the government should not be trusted with the necessary power.

I propose first to review the main arguments bearing on the *need* for stabilization policies, that is, on the likely extent of instability in the absence of such policies, and then to examine the issue of the supposed destabilizing effect of pursuing stabilization policies.

* * * *

The Early Keynesians

The early disciples of the new Keynesian gospel, still haunted by memories of the Great Depression, frequently tended to outdo Keynes' pessimism about potential instability. Concern with liquidity traps fostered the view that the demand for money was highly interest elastic; failure to distinguish between the short- and long-run marginal propensity to save led to overestimating the long-run saving rate, thereby fostering concern with stagnation, and to underestimating the short-run propensity, thereby exaggerating the short-run multiplier. Interest rates were supposed to affect, at best, the demand for long-lived fixed investments, and the interest elasticity was deemed to be low. Thus, shocks were believed to produce a large response. Finally, investment demand was seen as capriciously controlled by "animal spirits," thus providing an important source of shocks. All this justified calling for very active stabilization policies. Furthermore, since the very circumstances which produce a large response to demand shocks also produce a large response to *fiscal* and a small response to *monetary* actions, there was a tendency to focus on fiscal policy as the main tool to keep the economy at near full employment.

The Phillips Curve

In the two decades following *The General Theory,* there were a number of developments of the Keynesian system including dynamization of the model, the stress on taxes versus expenditures and the balanced budget multiplier, and the first attempts at estimating the critical parameters through econometric techniques and models. But for present purposes, the most important one was the uncovering of a "stable" statistical relation between the rate of change of wages and the rate of unemployment, which has since come to be known as the Phillips curve. This relation, and its generalization by Richard Lipsey to allow for the effect of recent inflation, won wide acceptance even before an analytical underpinning could be provided for it, in part because it could account for the "puzzling" experience of 1954 and 1958, when wages kept rising despite the substantial rise in unemployment. It also served to dispose of the rather sterile "cost push"—"demand pull" controversy.

In the following years, a good deal of attention went into developing theoretical foundations for the Phillips curve, in particular along the lines of search models (for example, Edmund Phelps et al.). This approach served to shed a new light on the nature of unemployment by tracing it in the first place to labor turnover and search time rather than to lack of jobs as such: in a sense unemployment is all frictional—at least in developed countries. At the same time it clarified how the availability of more jobs tends to reduce unemployment by increasing vacancies and thus reducing search time.

Acceptance of the Phillips curve relation implied some significant changes in the Keynesian framework which partly escaped notice until the subsequent monetarists' attacks. Since the rate of change of wages decreased smoothly with the rate of unemployment, there was no longer a unique Full Employment but rather a whole family of possible equilibrium rates, each associated with a different rate of inflation (and requiring, presumably, a different long-run growth of money). It also impaired the notion of a stable underemployment equilibrium. A fall in demand could still cause an initial rise in unemployment but this rise, by reducing the growth of wages, would eventually raise the real money supply, tending to return unemployment to the equilibrium rate consistent with the given long-run growth of money.

But at the practical level it did not lessen the case for counteracting lasting demand disturbances through stabilization policies rather than by relying on the slow process of wage adjustment to do the job, at the cost of protracted unemployment and instability of prices. Indeed, the realm of stabilization policies appeared to expand in the sense that the stabilization authority had the power of choosing the unemployment rate around which employment was to be stabilized, though it then had to accept the associated inflation. Finally, the dependence of

118

wage changes also on past inflation forced recognition of a distinction between the short- and the long-run Phillips curve, the latter exhibiting the long-run equilibrium rate of inflation implied by a *maintained* unemployment rate. The fact that the long-run tradeoff between unemployment and inflation was necessarily less favorable than the short-run one, opened up new vistas of "enjoy-it-now, pay-later" policies, and even resulted in an entertaining literature on the political business cycle and how to stay in the saddle by riding the Phillips curve (see for example, Ray Fair, William Nordhaus).

The Monitarists' Attack

The Stabilizing Power of the Hicksian Mechanism

The monetarists' attack on Keynesianism was directed from the very beginning not at the Keynesian framework as such, but at whether it really implied a need for stabilization. It rested on a radically different empirical assessment of the value of the parameters controlling the stabilizing power of the Hicksian mechanism and of the magnitude and duration of response to shocks, given a stable money supply. And this different assessment in turn was felt to justify a radical downgrading of the *practical relevance* of the Keynesian framework as distinguished from its *analytical validity*.

* * * *

The Demise of Wage Rigidity and the Vertical Phillips Curve

. . . The most serious challenge came in Friedman's 1968 [A.E.A.] Presidential Address, building on ideas independently put forth also by Phelps (1968). Its basic message was that, despite appearances, wages were in reality perfectly flexible and there was accordingly *no* involuntary unemployment. The evidence to the contrary, including the Phillips curve, was but a statistical illusion resulting from failure to differentiate between price changes and *unexpected* price changes.

Friedman starts out by reviving the Keynesian notion that, at any point of time, there exists a unique full-employment rate which he labels the "natural rate." An unanticipated fall in demand in Friedman's competitive world leads firms to reduce prices and also output and employment along the short-run marginal cost curve—unless the nominal wage declines together with prices. But workers, failing to judge correctly the current and prospective fall in prices, misinterpret the reduction of nominal wages as a cut in *real* wages. Hence, assuming a positively sloped supply function, they reduce the supply of labor. As a result, the effective real wage rises to the point where the resulting decline in the demand for labor matches the reduced supply. Thus, output falls not because of the decline in demand, but because of the entirely voluntary reduction in the supply of labor, in response to erroneous perceptions. Furthermore, the fall in employment can only be temporary, as expectations must soon catch up with the facts, at least in the absence of new shocks. The very same mechanism works in the case of an increase in demand, so that the responsiveness of wages and prices is the same on either side of the natural rate.

The upshot is that Friedman's model also implies a Phillips-type relation between inflation, employment or unemployment, and past inflation—provided the latter variable is interpreted as a reasonable proxy for expected inflation. But it turns the standard explanation on its head: instead of (excess) employment causing inflation, it is (the unexpected component of) the rate of inflation that causes excess employment.

One very basic implication of Friedman's model is that the coefficient of price expectations should be precisely unity. This specification implies that whatever the shape of the short-run Phillips curve—a shape determined by the relation between expected and actual price changes, and by the elasticity of labor supply with respect to the perceived real wage—the long-run curve *must be vertical.*

Friedman's novel twist provided a fresh prop for the claim that stabilization policies are not really needed, for, with wages flexible, except possibly for transient distortions, the Hicksian mechanism receives powerful reinforcement from changes in the real money supply. Similarly, the fact that full employment was a razor edge provided new support for the claim that stabilization policies were bound to prove destabilizing.

The Macro Rational Expectations Revolution

But the death blow to the already badly battered Keynesian position was to come only shortly thereafter by incorporating into Friedman's model the so-called rational expectation hypothesis, or *REH*. Put very roughly, this hypothesis, originally due to John Muth, states that rational economic agents will endeavor to form expectations of relevant future variables by making the most efficient use of all information provided by past history. It is a fundamental and fruitful contribution that has already found many important applications, for example, in connection with speculative markets, and as a basis for some thoughtful criticism by Robert Lucas (1976) of certain features of econometric models. What I am concerned with here is only its application to macro-economics, or *MREH* [macroeconomic rational expectation hypothesis] associated with such authors as Lucas (1972), Thomas Sargent (1976), and Sargent and Neil Wallace (1976).

The basic ingredient of *MREH is* the postulate that the workers of Friedman's model hold rational expectations, which turns out to have a number of remarkable implications: (i) errors of price expectations, which are the only source of departure from the natural state, cannot be avoided but they can only be short-lived and random. In particular, there cannot be persistent unemployment above the natural rate for this would imply high serial correlation between the successive errors of expectation, which is inconsistent with rational expectations; (ii) any attempts to stabilize the economy by means of stated monetary or fiscal rules are bound to be totally ineffective because their effect will be fully discounted in rational expectations; (iii) nor can the government successfully pursue *ad hoc* measures to offset shocks. The private sector is already taking care of any anticipated shock; therefore government policy could conceivably help only if the government information was better than that of the public, which is impossible, by the very definition of rational expectations. Under these conditions, *ad hoc* stabilization policies are most likely to produce instead further destabilizing shocks.

These are clearly remarkable conclusions, and a major rediscovery—for it had all been said 40 years ago by Keynes in a well-known passage of *The General Theory:*

> If, indeed, labour were always in a position to take action (and were to do so), whenever there was less than full employment, to reduce its money demands by concerted action to whatever point was required to make money so abundant relatively to the wage-unit that the rate of interest would fall to a level compatible with full employment, we should, in effect, have monetary management by the Trade Unions, aimed at full employment, instead of by the banking systems. [P. 267]

The only novelty is that *MREH* replaces Keynes' opening "if" with a "since."

If one accepts this little amendment, the case against stabilization policies is complete. The economy is inherently pretty stable—except possibly for the effect of government messing around. And to the extent that there is a small residual instability, it is beyond the power of human beings, let alone the government, to alleviate it.

* * * *

The Overall Effectiveness of Postwar Stabilization Policies

Even granted that a smooth money supply will not produce a very stable world and that there is therefore room for stabilization policies, monetarists will still argue that we should nonetheless eschew such policies. They claim, first, that allowing for unpredictably variable lags and unforseeable future shocks, we do not know enough to successfully design stabilization policies, and second, that the government would surely be incapable of choosing the appropriate policies or be politically willing to provide timely enforcement. Thus, in practice, stabilization polices will result in destabilizing the economy much of the time.

This view is supported by two arguments, one logical and one empirical. The logical argument is the one developed in Friedman's [A.E.A.] Presidential Address (1968). An attempt at stabilizing the economy at full employment is bound to be destabilizing because the full employment or natural rate is not known with certainty and is subject to shifts in time; and if we aim for the incorrect rate, the result must perforce be explosive inflation or deflation. By contrast, with a constant money supply policy, the economy will automatically hunt for, and eventually discover, that shifty natural rate, wherever it may be hiding.

This argument, I submit, is nothing but a debating ploy. It rests on the preposterous assumption that the only alternative to a constant money growth is the pursuit of a very precise unemployment target which will be adhered to indefinitely no matter what, and that if the target is off in the second decimal place, galloping inflation is around the corner. In reality, all that is necessary to pursue stabilization policies is a rough target range that includes the warranted rate, itself a range and not a razor edge; and, of course, responsible supporters of stabilization policies have long been aware of the fact that the target range needs to be adjusted in time on the basis of foreseeable shift in the warranted range, as well as in the light of emerging evidence that the current target is not consistent with price stability. It is precisely for this reason that I, as well as many other nonmonetarists, would side with monetarists in strenuous opposition to recent proposals for a target unemployment rate rigidly fixed by statute (although there is nothing wrong with Congress committing itself and the country to work toward the eventual achievement of some target unemployment rate through *structural* changes rather than aggregate demand policies).

Clearly, even the continuous updating of targets cannot guarantee that errors can be avoided altogether or even that they will be promptly recognized; and while errors persist, they will result in some inflationary (or deflationary) pressures. But the growing inflation to which Friedman refers is, to repeat, a crawl not a gallop. One may usefully recall in this connection the experience of 1965-70 referred to earlier, with the further remark that the existence of excess employment was quite generally recognized at the time, and failure to eliminate it resulted overwhelmingly from political considerations and not from a wrong diagnosis.

There remains then only the empirical issue: have stabilization policies worked in the past and will they work in the future? Monetarists think the answer is negative and suggest, as we have seen, the misguided attempts at stabilization, especially through monetary policies, are responsible for much of the observed instability. The main piece of evidence in support of this contention is the Great Depression, an episode well documented through the painstaking work of Friedman and Anna Schwartz, although still the object of dispute (see, for example, Peter Temin). But in any event, that episode while it may attest to the power of money, is irrelevant for present purposes since the contraction of the money supply was certainly not part of a comprehensive stabilization program in the post-Keynesian sense.

* * *

What Macro Stabilization Policies can Accomplish, and How

[Arguing] that the adherence to a stable money growth path through much of 1974 bears a major responsibility for the sharp contraction does not per se establish that the policy was mistaken. The reason is that the shock that hit the system in 1973-74 was not the usual type of demand shock which we gradually learned to cope with, more or less adequately. It was, instead, a supply or price shock, coming from a cumulation of causes, largely external. This poses an altogether different stabilization problem. In particular, in the case of demand shocks, there exists in principle an ideal policy which avoids all social costs, namely to offset completely the shock thus, at the same time, stabilizing employment and the price level. There may be disagreement as to whether this target can be achieved and how, but not about the target itself.

But in the case of supply shocks, there is no miracle cure—there is no macro policy which can both maintain a stable price level and keep employment at its natural rate. To maintain stable prices in the face of the exogenous price shock, say a rise in import prices, would require a fall in all domestic output prices; but we know of no macro policy by which domestic prices can be made to fall except by creating enough slack, thus putting downward pressure on wages. And the amount of slack would have to be substantial in view of the sluggishness of wages in the face of unemployment. If we do not offset the exogenous shock completely, then the initial burst, even if activated by an entirely transient rise in some prices, such as a once and for all deterioration in the terms of trade, will give rise to further increases, as nominal wages rise in a vain attempt at preserving real wages; this secondary reaction too can only be cut short by creating slack. In short, once a price shock hits, there is no way of returning to the initial equilibrium except after a painful period of both above equilibrium unemployment and inflation.

There are, of course, in principle, policies other than aggregate demand management to which we might turn, and which are enticing in view of the unpleasant alternatives offered by demand management. But so far such policies, at least those of the wage-price control variety, have proved disappointing. The design of better alternatives is probably the greatest challenge presently confronting those interested in stabilization. However, these policies fall outside my present concern. Within the realm of aggregate demand management, the only choice open to society is the cruel one between alternative feasible paths of inflation and associated paths of unemployment, and the best the macroeconomist can offer is policies designed to approximate the chosen path.

Conclusion

To summarize, the monetarists have made a valid and most valuable contribution in establishing that our economy is far less unstable than the early Keynesians pictured it and in rehabilitating the role of money as a determinant of aggregate demand. They are wrong, however, in going as far as asserting that the economy is sufficiently shockproof that stabilization policies are not needed. They have also made an important contribution in pointing out that such policies might in fact prove destabilizing. This criticism has had a salutary effect on reassessing what stabilization policies can and should do, and on trimming down fine-tuning ambitions. But their contention that postwar fluctuations resulted from an unstable money growth or that stabilization policies decreased rather than increased stability just does not stand up to an impartial examination of the postwar record of the United States and other industrialized countries. Up to 1974, these policies have helped to keep the economy reasonably stable by historical standards, even though one can certainly point to some occasional failures.

The serious deterioration in economic stability since 1973 must be attributed in the first place to the novel nature of the shocks that hit us, namely, supply shocks. Even the best possible aggregate demand management cannot offset such shocks without a lot of unemployment together with a lot of inflation. But, in addition, demand management was far from the best. This failure must be attributed in good measure to the fact that we had little experience or even an adequate conceptual framework to deal with such shocks; but at least from my reading of the record, it was also the result of failure to use stabilization policies, including too slavish adherence to the monetarists' constant money growth prescription.

We must therefore, categorically reject the monetarist appeal to turn back the clock forty years by discarding the basic message of *The General Theory*. We should instead concentrate our efforts in an endeavor to make stabilization policies even more effective in the future than they have been in the past.

John Maynard Keynes
(1883-1946)

It is only fitting that we give the last word in this macroeconomic section to Keynes. (From descriptions of him, it is likely that, if he were alive, he would have had it.) In this selection he reflects on the implications of his General Theory *and finds it "moderately conservative in its implications." He argues that what it calls for is a "somewhat comprehensive socialization of investment" as the only means of securing an approximation to full employment. That policy was far too radical for most politicians and they went with the less intrusive monetary and fiscal policy. Thus, monetary and fiscal policies became known as Keynesian policies even though he did not specifically advocate them in the* General Theory.

The selection ends with "the madmen in authority" quotation, one of the most famous in all economics.

John Maynard Keynes. 1936. *The General Theory of Employment Interest and Money.* London: Macmillan, pp. 377-84.

Concluding Notes on the Social Philosophy Towards Which the General Theory Might Lead

The General Theory of Employment

In some respects the foregoing theory is moderately conservative in its implications. For whilst it indicates the vital importance of establishing certain central controls in matters which are now left in the main to individual initiative, there are wide fields of activity which are unaffected. The State will have to exercise a guiding influence on the propensity to consume partly through its scheme of taxation, partly by fixing the rate of interest, and partly, perhaps, in other ways. Furthermore, it seems unlikely that the influence of banking policy on the rate of interest will be sufficient by itself to determine an optimum rate of investment. I conceive, therefore, that a somewhat comprehensive socialisation of investment will prove the only means of securing an approximation to full employment; though this need not exclude all manner of compromises and of devices by which public authority will co-operate with private initiative. But beyond this no obvious case is made out for a system of State Socialism which would embrace most of the economic life of the community. It is not the ownership of the instruments of production which it is important for the State to assume. If the State is able to determine the aggregate amount of resources devoted to augmenting the instruments and the basic rate of reward to those who own them, it will have accomplished all that is necessary. Moreover, the necessary measures of socialisation can be introduced gradually and without a break in the general traditions of society.

Our criticism of the accepted classical theory of economics has consisted not so much in finding logical flaws in its analysis as in pointing out that its tacit assumptions are seldom or never satisfied, with the result that it cannot solve the economic problems of the actual world. But if our central controls succeed in establishing an aggregate volume of output corresponding to full employment as nearly as is practicable, the classical theory comes into its own again from this point onwards. If we suppose the volume of output to be given, *i.e.* to be determined by forces outside the classical scheme of thought, then there is no objection to be raised against the classical analysis of the manner in which private self-interest will determine what in particular is produced, in what proportions the factors of production will be combined to produce it, and how the value of the final product will be distributed between them. Again, if we have dealt otherwise with the problem of thrift, there is no objection to be raised against the modern classical theory as to the degree of consilience [concurrence] between private and public advantage in conditions of perfect and imperfect competition respectively. Thus, apart from the necessity of central controls to bring about an adjustment between the propensity to consume and the inducement to invest, there is no more reason to socialise economic life than there was before.

To put the point concretely, I see no reason to suppose that the existing system seriously misemploys the factors of production which are in use. There are, of course, errors of foresight; but these would not be avoided by centralising decisions. When 9,000,000 men are employed out of 10,000,000 willing and able to work, there is evidence that the labour of these 9,000,000 men is misdirected. The complaint against the present system is not that these 9,000,000 men ought to be employed on different tasks, but that tasks should be available for the remaining 1,000,000 men. It is in determining the volume, not the direction, of actual employment that the existing system has broken down.

Thus I agree with Gesell that the result of filling in the gaps in the classical theory is not to dispose of the "Manchester System," but to indicate the nature of the environment which the free play of economic forces requires if it is to realise the full potentialities of production. The central controls necessary to ensure full employment will, of course, involve a large extension of the traditional functions of government. Furthermore, the modern classical theory has itself called attention to various conditions in which the free play of economic forces may need to be curbed or guided. But there will still remain a wide field for the exercise of private initiative and responsibility. Within this field the traditional advantages of individualism will still hold good.

Let us stop for a moment to remind ourselves what these advantages are. They are partly advantages of efficiency—the advantages of decentralisation and of the play of self-interest. The advantage to efficiency of the decentralisation of decisions and of individual responsibility is even greater, perhaps, than the nineteenth century supposed; and the reaction against the appeal to self-interest may have gone too far. But, above all, individualism, if it can be purged of its defects and its abuses, is the best safeguard of personal liberty in the sense that, compared with any other system, it greatly widens the field for the exercise of personal choice. It is also the best safeguard of the variety of life, which emerges precisely from this extended field of personal choice, and the loss of which is the greatest of all the losses of the homogeneous or totalitarian state. For this variety preserves the traditions which embody the most secure and successful choices of former generations; it colours the present with the diversification of its fancy; and, being the handmaid of experiment as well as of tradition and of fancy, it is the most powerful instrument to better the future.

Whilst, therefore, the enlargement of the functions of government, involved in the task of adjusting to one another the propensity to consume and the inducement to invest, would seem to a nineteenth-century publicist or to a contemporary American financier to be a terrific encroachment on individualism, I defend it, on the contrary, both as the only practicable means of avoiding the destruction of existing economic forms in their entirety and as the condition of the successful functioning of individual initiative.

For if effective demand is deficient, not only is the public scandal of wasted resources intolerable, but the individual enterpriser who seeks to bring these resources into action is operating with the odds loaded against him. The game of hazard which he plays is furnished with many zeros, so that the players *as a whole* will lose if they have the energy and hope to deal all the cards. Hitherto the increment of the world's wealth has fallen short of the aggregate of positive individual savings; and the difference has been made up by the losses of those whose courage and initiative have not been supplemented by exceptional skill or unusual good fortune. But if effective demand is adequate, average skill and average good fortune will be enough.

The authoritarian state systems of to-day seem to solve the problem of unemployment at the expense of efficiency and of freedom. It is certain that the world will not much longer tolerate the unemployment which, apart from brief intervals of excitement, is associated—and, in my opinion, inevitably associated—with present-day capitalistic individualism. But it may be possible by a right analysis of the problem to cure the disease whilst preserving efficiency and freedom.

Is the fulfillment of these ideas a visionary hope? Have they insufficient roots in the motives which govern the evolution of political society? Are the interests which they will thwart stronger and more obvious than those which they will serve?

I do not attempt an answer in this place. It would need a volume of a different character from this one to indicate even in outline the practical measures in which they might be gradually clothed. But if the ideas are correct—an hypothesis on which the author himself must necessarily base what he writes— it would be a mistake, I predict, to dispute their potency over a period of time. At the present moment people are unusually expectant of a more fundamental diagnosis; more particularly ready to receive it; eager to try it out, if it should be even plausible. But apart from this contemporary mood, the ideas of economists and political philosophers, both when they are right and when they are wrong, are more powerful than is commonly understood. Indeed the world is ruled by little else. Practical men, who believe themselves to be quite exempt from any intellectual influences, are usually the slaves of some defunct economist. Madmen in authority, who hear voices in the air, are distilling their frenzy from some academic scribbler of a few years back. I am sure that the power of vested interests is vastly exaggerated compared with the gradual encroachment of ideas. Not, indeed, immediately, but after a certain interval; for in the field of economic and political philosophy there are not many who are influenced by new theories after they are twenty-five or thirty years of age, so that the ideas which civil servants and politicians and even agitators apply to current events are not likely to be the newest. But, soon or late, it is ideas, not vested interests, which are dangerous for good or evil.

ICROECONOMICS

Issues in Supply and Demand
Nassau Senior: Value and the Forces of Demand and Supply 128
Thorstein Veblen: The Theory of the Leisure Class 131
John Kenneth Galbraith: The Dependence Effect 134
Joan Robinson: Increasing and Diminishing Returns 137
F. A. Hayek: Economics and Knowledge 142

Competition, Market Structure, and the Firm
Alfred Marshall: Competition 145
John Stuart Mill: Competition and Custom 148
Frank H. Knight: The Price System and the Economic Process 150
John Kenneth Galbraith: The Development of Monopoly Theory 153
C. Northcote Parkinson: Parkinson's Law or the Rising Pyramid 156
Ronald Coase: The Nature of the Firm 160

Private Property, Factor Markets, and Distribution
Sir John Hicks: Wage Theory: Basic Forces 163
David Ricardo: Rent 167
Frank H. Knight: Profit 170
John Stuart Mill: Private Property Has Not Had A Fair Trial 172
Henry George: Progress and Poverty: Preface 173

Micro Policy Debates
George Stigler: A Sketch of the History of Truth in Teaching 176
John Stuart Mill: The Subjection of Women 180
Jack Hirshleifer: The Sumptuary Manifesto 184
Milton Friedman: The Relation between Economic Freedom and
    Political Freedom 187
Abba Lerner: Review of *Capitalism and Freedom* by Milton Friedman 189
George Stigler: An Academic Episode 191

International and Development
Thomas R. Malthus: The Theory of Population 194
Frédéric Bastiat: Petition of the Candlemakers 196
Adam Smith: Restraints on Trade and the Invisible Hand 199

Nassau Senior

(1790-1864)

Nassau Senior was an important economist in the development of classical economics in Britain during the early 1800s. He was the son of a vicar and was educated at Oxford, where he was later a professor of political economy. He also served as a professor at Kings College, London, but was forced to resign when he advocated confiscating some of the revenues of the Established Church of Ireland which were devoted to the benefit of the Roman Catholics. He is now also known for advocating keeping a strict division between the science of economics and the art of economics, in which policy matters were discussed.

His main work, from which this selection is taken, is An Outline of the Science of Political Economy.

Nassau W. Senior. 1836 (1951). *An Outline of the Science of Political Economy*. New York: Augustus N. Kelly, pp. 13-17.

Value and the Forces of Demand and Supply

Value defined.—Our definition of Wealth, as comprehending all those things, and those things only which have *Value*, requires us to explain at some length the signification which we attribute to the word Value; especially as the meaning of that word has been the subject of long and eager controversy. We have already stated that we use the word VALUE in its popular acceptation, as signifying *that quality in anything which fits it to be given and received in exchange;* or, in other words, to be lent or sold, hired or purchased.

So defined, Value denotes a relation reciprocally existing between two objects, and the precise relation which it denotes is the quantity of the one which can be obtained in exchange for a given quantity of the other. It is impossible, therefore, to predicate value of any object, without referring, expressly or tacitly, to some other objects in which its value is to be estimated; or, in other words, of which a certain quantity can be obtained in exchange for a certain quantity of the object in question.

We have already observed that the substance which at present is most desired, or, in other words, possesses the highest degree of value, is the diamond. By this we meant to express that there is no substance of which a given quantity will exchange for so large a quantity of every other commodity. When we wished to state the value of the king of Persia's bracelet, we stated first the amount of gold, and afterwards of English labour, which it would command in exchange. If we had attempted to give a perfect account of its value, we could have done so only by enumerating separately the quantity of every other article of wealth which could be obtained in exchange for it. Such an enumeration, if it could have been given, would have been a most instructive commercial lesson, for it would have shown not only the value of the diamond in all other commodities, but the reciprocal value of all other commodities in one another. If we had ascertained that a diamond weighing an ounce would exchange for one million five hundred thousand tons of Hepburn coal, or one hundred thousand tons of Essex wheat, or two thousand five hundred tons of English foolscap paper, we might have inferred that the coal, wheat, and paper would mutually exchange in the same proportions in which they were exchangeable for the diamond, and that a given weight of paper would purchase six hundred times as much coal, and forty times as much wheat.

Demand and Supply.—The causes which determine the reciprocal values of commodities, or, in other words, which determine that a given quantity of one shall exchange for a given quantity of another, must be divided into two sets[:] those which occasion the one to be limited in supply and useful, (using that word to express the power of occasioning pleasure and preventing pain), and those which occasion those attributes to belong to the other. In ordinary language, the *force* of the causes which give utility to a commodity is generally indicated by the word *Demand;* and the *weakness* of the obstacles which limit the quantity of a commodity by the word *Supply.*

Thus the common statement that commodities exchange in proportion to the Demand and Supply of each, means that they exchange in proportion to the force of weakness of the causes which give utility to them respectively, and to the weakness or force of the obstacles by which they are respectively limited in supply.

Unfortunately, however, the words Demand and Supply have not been always so used. Demand is sometimes used as synonymous with consumption, as when an increased production is said to generate an increased demand; sometimes it is used to express not only the desire to obtain a commodity, but the power to give the holder of it something which will induce him to part with it. "A Demand," says Mr. Mill, *(Political Economy, p.* 23, 3d edition), "means the will to purchase and the power of purchasing." Mr. Malthus, Definitions in *Political Economy,* p. 244, states that "Demand for commodities has two distinct meanings: one in regard to its extent, or the quantity of commodities purchased; the other in regard to its intensity, or the sacrifice which the demanders are able and willing to make in order to satisfy their wants."

Demand.—Neither of these expressions appears to be consistent with common usage. It must be admitted that the word Demand is used in its ordinary sense when we say that a deficient wheat harvest increases the Demand for oats and barley. But this proposition is not true if we use the word Demand in any other sense than as expressing the increased utility of oats and barley; or, in other words, the increased desire of the community to obtain them. The deficiency of wheat would not give to the consumers of oats and barley any increased power of purchasing them, nor would the quantity purchased or consumed be increased. The mode of consumption would be altered; instead of being applied to the feeding of horses, or to the supply of stimulant liquids, a certain portion of them would be used as human food. And, as the desire to eat is more urgent than the desire to feed horses, or drink beer or spirits, the desire to obtain oats and barley, or, in other words, the pleasure given, or the pain averted, by the possession of a given quantity of them or, in other words, the utility of a given quantity of them, would increase. A fact, which, in ordinary language, would be expressed by saying, that the demand for them was increased.

But though the vagueness with which the word Demand has been used renders it an objectionable term, it is too useful and concise to be given up; but we shall endeavour never to use it in any other signification than as expressing the utility of a commodity; or, what is the same, for we have seen that all utility is relative, the degree in which its possession is desired.

Supply.—We cannot complain of equal vagueness in the use of the word Supply. In ordinary language, as well as in the writings of Political Economists, it is used to signify the quantity of a commodity actually brought to market. The complaint is, not that the word Supply has been used in this sense, but that, when used in this sense, it has been considered as a cause of value, except in a few cases, or for very short periods. We have shown, in the examples of coats and waistcoats, and gold and silver, that the reciprocal value of any two commodities depends, not on the quantity of each brought to market, but on the comparative force of the obstacles which in each case oppose any increase in that quantity. When, therefore, we represent increase or diminution of supply as affecting value, we must be understood to mean not a mere positive increase or diminution, but an increase or diminution occasioned by a diminution or increase of the obstacles by which the supply is limited.

Intrinsic and Extrinsic Causes of the Value of a Commodity.—To revert to our original proposition, the reciprocal Values of any two commodities must be determined by two sets of causes; those which determine the Demand and Supply of the one, and those which determine the Demand and Supply of the other. The causes which give utility to a commodity and limit it in supply may be called the *intrinsic* causes of its value; those which limit the supply and occasion the utility of the commodities for which it is to be exchanged, may be called the *extrinsic* causes of its value. Gold and silver are now exchanged for one another in Europe in the proportion of one ounce of gold for about sixteen ounces of silver. This proportion must arise partly from the causes which give utility to gold and limit its supply, and partly from those which create the utility and limit the supply of silver. When talking of the value of gold we may consider the first set of causes affect gold only so far as it is said to be exchanged for silver, which may be called one of its specific values; the aggregate of its specific values forming its general value. If while the causes which give utility to silver and limit it in supply were unaltered, those which affect gold should vary; if, for instance, fashion should require every well-dressed man to have all his buttons of pure gold, or the disturbances in South America should permanently stop all the gold works of Brazil and Columbia [the author means Colombia], and thus (as would be the case) intercept five-sixths of our supplies of gold, the reciprocal values of gold and silver would in time be materially varied. Though silver would be unaltered both as to its utility and as to its limitation in supply, a given quantity of it would exchange for a less quantity of gold, in the proportion perhaps of twenty to one, instead of sixteen to one. As between one another the rise and fall of gold and silver would precisely correspond, silver would fall and gold would rise one-fourth. But the fall of silver would not be general but specific; though fallen as estimated in gold, it would command precisely the same quantities as before of all other commodities. The rise of gold would be more general; a given quantity of it would command one-fourth more not only of silver, but of all other commodities. The holder of a given quantity of silver would be just as rich as before for all purposes except the purchase of gold; the holder of a given quantity of gold would be richer than before for all purposes.

The circumstances by which each different class of commodities is invested with utility and limited in supply are subject to perpetual variation. Sometimes one of the causes alone varies. Sometimes they both vary in the same direction; sometimes in opposite directions. In the last case the opposite variations, wholly or partially neutralize one another.

The effects of an increased Demand concurrent with increased obstacles to Supply, and of diminished Demand concurrent with increased facility of Supply, are well exemplified by hemp. Its average price before the revolutionary war, exclusive of duty, did not exceed £30 per ton. The increased Demand, occasioned by a maritime war, and the natural obstacles to a proportionate increase of Supply, raised it, in the year 1796, to above £50 a ton; at about which price it continued during the next twelve years. But in 1808, the rupture between England and the Baltic powers, the principal source of our supplies, suddenly raised it to £118 a ton, being nearly four times the average price in peace. At the close of the war, both the extraordinary demand and the extraordinary obstacles to the supply ceased together, and the price fell to about its former average.

Thorstein Veblen

(1857-1929)

One of the most colorful of all American economists was Thorstein Veblen. He was the son of a Wisconsin farmer of Norwegian descent, and he never felt comfortable in academic society. In his writing he looked at the customs of his time with a particularly discerning eye, creating such well known terms as "conspicuous consumption" and "pecuniary emulation." He did not endear himself to presidents of universities by calling them "captains of erudition." His unconventionalism led to his leaving a variety of positions after only a few years in each, and he taught variously at the University of Chicago, Stanford, the University of Missouri, and The New School for Social Research (New York City). His most famous book is The Theory of the Leisure Class *(1899), from which this selection is taken.*

Thorstein Veblen. 1899. *The Theory of the Leisure Class.* New York: The Viking Press, Inc., pp. 36-37, 70, 71, 230-32

The Theory of the Leisure Class

But it is otherwise with the superior pecuniary class, with which we are here immediately concerned. For this class also the incentive to diligence and thrift is not absent; but its action is so greatly qualified by the secondary demands of pecuniary emulation, that any inclination in this direction is practically overborne and any incentive to diligence tends to be of no effect. The most imperative of these secondary demands of emulation, as well as the one of widest scope, is the requirement of abstention from productive work. This is true in an especial degree for the barbarian stage of culture. During the predatory culture labour comes to be associated in men's habits of thought with weakness and subjection to a master. It is therefore a mark of inferiority, and therefore comes to be accounted unworthy of man in his best estate. By virtue of this tradition labour is felt to be debasing, and this tradition has never died out. On the contrary, with the advance of social differentiation it has acquired the axiomatic force due to ancient and unquestioned prescription.

In order to gain and to hold the esteem of men it is not sufficient merely to possess wealth or power. The wealth or power must be put in evidence, for esteem is awarded only on evidence. And not only does the evidence of wealth serve to impress one's importance on others and to keep their sense of his importance alive and alert, but it is of scarcely less use in building up and preserving one's self-complacency. In all but the lowest stages of culture the normally constituted man is comforted and upheld in his self-respect by "decent surroundings" and by exemption from "menial offices." Enforced departure from his habitual standard of decency, either in the paraphernalia of life or in the kind and amount of his everyday activity, is felt to be a slight upon his human dignity, even apart from all conscious consideration of the approval or disapproval of his fellows.

The archaic theoretical distinction between the base and the honorable in the manner of a man's life retains very much of its ancient force even to-day. So much so that there are few of the better class who are not possessed of an instinctive repugnance for the vulgar forms of labour. We have a realizing sense of ceremonial uncleanness attaching in an especial degree to the occupations which are associated in our habits of thought with menial service. It is felt by all persons of refined taste that a spiritual contamination is inseparable from certain offices that are conventionally required of servants. Vulgar surroundings, mean (that is to say, inexpensive) habitations, and vulgarly productive occupations are unhesitatingly condemned and avoided. They are incompatible with life on a satisfactory spiritual plane—with "high thinking." From the days of the Greek philosophers to the present, a degree of leisure and of exemption from contact with such industrial processes as serve the immediate everyday purposes of human life has even been recognized by thoughtful men as a prerequisite to a worthy or beautiful, or even a blameless, human lift. In itself and in its consequences the life of leisure is beautiful and ennobling in all civilized men's eyes.

This direct, subjective value of leisure and of other evidences of wealth is no doubt in great part secondary and derivative. It is in part a reflex of the utility of leisure as a means of gaining the respect of others, and in part it is the result of a mental substitution. The performance of labour has been accepted as a conventional evidence of inferior force; therefore it comes itself, by a mental short-cut, to be regarded as intrinsically base.

* * * *

The ceremonial differentiation of the dietary is best seen in the use of intoxicating beverages and narcotics. If these articles of consumption are costly, they are felt to be noble and honorific. Therefore the base classes, primarily the women, practice an enforced continence with respect to these stimulants, except in countries where they are obtainable at a very low cost. From archaic times down through all the length of the patriarchal regime it has been the office of the women to prepare and administer these luxuries, and it has been the perquisite of the men of gentle birth and breeding to consume them. Drunkenness and the other pathological consequences of the free use of stimulants therefore tend in their turn to become honorific, as being a mark, at the second remove, of the superior status of those who are able to afford the indulgence. Infirmities induced by over-indulgence are among some peoples freely recognized as manly attributes. It has even happened that the name for certain diseased conditions of the body arising from such an origin has passed into everyday speech as a synonym for "noble" or "gentle." It is only at a relatively early stage of culture that the symptoms of expensive vice are conventionally accepted as marks of a superior status, and so tend to become virtues and command the deference of the community; but the reputability that attaches to certain expensive vices long retains so much of its force as to appreciably lessen the disapprobation visited upon the men of the wealthy or noble class for any excessive indulgence. The same invidious distinction adds force to the current disapproval of any indulgence of this kind on the part of women, minors, and inferiors. This invidious traditional distinction has not lost its force even among the more advanced peoples of to-day. Where the example set by the leisure class retains its imperative force in the regulation of the conventionalities, it is observable that the women still in great measure practice the same traditional concern with regard to stimulants.

It has already been noticed that modern economic institutions fall into two roughly distinct categories—the pecuniary and the industrial. The like is true of employments. Under the former head are employments that have to do with ownership or acquisition; under the latter head, those that have to do with workmanship or production. As was found in speaking of the growth of institutions, so with regard to employments. The economic interests of the leisure class lie in the pecuniary employments; those of the working classes lie in both classes of employments, but chiefly in the industrial. Entrance to the leisure class lies through the pecuniary employments.

These two classes of employments differ materially in respect of the aptitudes required for each; and the training which they give similarly follows two divergent lines. The discipline of the pecuniary employments acts to conserve and to cultivate certain of the predatory aptitudes and the predatory animus. It does this both by educating those individuals and classes who are occupied with these employments and by selectively repressing and eliminating those individuals and lines of descent that are unfit in this respect. So far as men's habits of thought are shaped by the competitive process of acquisition and tenure; so far as their economic functions are comprised within the range of ownership of wealth as conceived in terms of exchange value, and its management and financiering through a permutation of values; so far their experience in economic life favours the survival and accentuation of the predatory temperament and habits of thought. Under the modern, peaceable system, it is of course the peaceable range of predatory habits and aptitudes that is chiefly fostered by a life of acquisition. That is to say, the pecuniary employments give proficiency in the general line of practices comprised under fraud, rather than in those that belong under the more archaic method of forcible seizure.

These pecuniary employments, tending to conserve the predatory temperament, are the employments which have to do with ownership—the immediate function of the leisure class proper—and the subsidiary functions concerned with acquisition and accumulation. These cover that class of persons and that range of duties in the economic process which have to do with the ownership of enterprises engaged in competitive industry; especially those fundamental lines of economic management which are classed as financiering operations. To these may be added the greater part of mercantile occupations. In their best and clearest development these duties make up the economic office of the "captain of industry." The captain of industry is an astute man rather than an ingenious one, and his captaincy is a pecuniary rather than an industrial captaincy. Such administration of industry as he exercises is commonly of a permissive kind. The mechanically effective details of production and of industrial organization are delegated to subordinates of a less "practical" turn of mind,—men who are possessed of a gift for workmanship rather than administrative ability. So far as regards their tendency in shaping human nature by education and selection, the common run of non-economic employments are to be classed with the pecuniary employments. Such are politics and ecclesiastical and military employments.

The pecuniary employments have also the sanction of reputability in a much higher degree than the industrial employments. In this way the leisure-class standards of good repute come in to sustain the prestige of those aptitudes that serve the invidious purpose; and the leisure-class scheme of decorous living, therefore, also furthers the survival and culture of the predatory traits. Employments fall into a hierarchical gradation of reputability. Those which have to do immediately with ownership on a large scale are the most reputable of economic employments proper. Next to these in good repute come those employments that are immediately subservient to ownership and financiering,—such as banking and the law. Banking employments also carry a suggestion of large ownership, and this fact is doubtless accountable for a share of the prestige that attaches to the business. The profession of the law does not imply large ownership; but since no taint of usefulness, for other than the competitive purpose, attaches to the lawyer's trade, it grades high in the conventional scheme. The lawyer is exclusively occupied with the details of predatory fraud, either in achieving or in checkmating chicane, and success in the profession is therefore accepted as marking a large endowment of that barbarian astuteness which has always commanded men's respect and fear. Mercantile pursuits are only half-way reputable, unless they involve a large element of ownership and a small element of usefulness. They grade high or low somewhat in proportion as they serve the higher or the lower needs; so that the business of retailing the vulgar necessaries of life descends to the level of the handicrafts and factory labour. Manual labour, or even the work of directing mechanical processes, is of course on a precarious footing as regards respectability.

A qualification is necessary as regards the discipline given by the pecuniary employments. As the scale of industrial enterprise grows larger, pecuniary management comes to bear less of the character of chicane and shrewd competition in detail. That is to say, for an ever-increasing proportion of the persons who come in contact with this phase of economic life, business reduces itself to routine in which there is less immediate suggestion of overreaching or exploiting a competitor. The consequent exemption from predatory habits extends chiefly to subordinates employed in business. The duties ownership and administration are virtually untouched by this qualification. . . .

John Kenneth Galbraith

(1908-)

In the 1960s, two economists with contrasting views were best known to the general public. One was Milton Friedman, known for his conservative or libertarian views; the other was John Kenneth Galbraith, known for his liberal views. Galbraith followed in the steps of earlier liberal economists who favored a larger government role in the economy, but his writing ability quickly led him away from technical economics into writing for the general public. This had two effects: it made him extremely well known, and it meant that his provocative ideas had little influence on the actual movement of the profession. The profession discussed his ideas, but somehow few of them became incorporated into economic thinking. He is a prolific author, and three of his most famous books are American Capitalism, The Affluent Society, *and* The New Industrial State. *This selection, taken from* The Affluent Society, *discusses the "dependence effect," an idea that parallels and further develops Veblen's notion of "conspicuous consumption." Specifically, Galbraith argues that the process of production creates wants and then satisfies them. Thus, it is an open question whether the production has made humankind better off, because if it had not created wants, humankind would not know what it was missing.*

Note that in the selection he mentions "Messrs. Batten, Barton, Durstine & Osborn." "Messrs." is an old-fashioned abbreviation used in front of a series of names to mean more than one Mr.— that is, a number of people all of whom individually could be called "Mr." Galbraith's point in mentioning these people is that Batten, Barton, Durstine & Osborn was, and still is, a prominent New York advertising agency.

John Kenneth Galbraith. 1952. *The Affluent Society*. Boston: Houghton Mifflin, pp. 126-131.

The Dependence Effect

The notion that wants do not become less urgent the more amply the individual is supplied is broadly repugnant to common sense. It is something to be believed only by those who wish to believe. Yet the conventional wisdom must be tackled on its own terrain. Intertemporal comparisons of an individual's state of mind do rest on doubtful grounds. Who can say for sure that the deprivation which afflicts him with hunger is more painful than the deprivation which afflicts him with envy of his neighbor's new car? In the time that has passed since he was poor his soul may have become subject to a new and deeper searing. And where a society is concerned, comparisons between marginal satisfactions when it is poor and those when it is affluent will involve not only the same individual at different times but different individuals at different times. The scholar who wishes to believe that with increasing affluence there is no reduction in the urgency of desires and goods is not without points for debate. However plausible the case against him, it cannot be proven. In the defense of the conventional wisdom this amounts almost to invulnerability.

However, there is a flaw in the case. If the individual's wants are to be urgent they must be original with himself. They cannot be urgent if they must be contrived for him. And above all they must not be contrived by the process of production by which they are satisfied. For this means that the whole case for the urgency of production, based on the urgency of wants, falls to the ground. One cannot defend production as satisfying wants if that production creates the wants.

Were it so that a man on arising each morning was assailed by demons which instilled in him a passion sometimes for silk shirts, sometimes for kitchenware, sometimes for chamber pots, and sometimes for orange squash, there would be every reason to applaud the effort to find the goods, however odd, that quenched this flame. But should it be that his passion was the result of his first having cultivated the demons, and should it also be that his effort to allay it stirred the demons to ever greater and greater effort, there would be question as to how rational was his solution. Unless restrained by conventional attitudes, he might wonder if the solution lay with more goods or fewer demons.

So it is that if production creates the wants it seeks to satisfy, or if the wants emerge *pari passu* [concurrent] with the production, then the urgency of the wants can no longer be used to defend the urgency of the production. Production only fills a void that it has itself created.

II

The point is so central that it must be pressed. Consumer wants can have bizarre, frivolous, or even immoral origins, and an admirable case can still be made for a society that seeks to satisfy them. But the case cannot stand if it is the process of satisfying wants that creates the wants. For then the individual who urges the importance of production to satisfy these wants is precisely in the position of the onlooker who applauds the efforts of the squirrel to keep abreast of the wheel that is propelled by his own efforts.

That wants are, in fact, the fruit of production will now be denied by few serious scholars. And a considerable number of economists, though not always in full knowledge of the implications, have conceded the point. In the observation cited at the end of the preceding chapter Keynes noted that needs of "the second class," i.e., those that are the result of efforts to keep abreast or ahead of one's fellow beings "may indeed be insatiable; for the higher the general level the higher still are they." And emulation has always played a considerable role in the views of other economists of want creation. One man's consumption becomes his neighbor's wish. This already means that the process by which wants are satisfied is also the process by which wants are created. The more wants that are satisfied the more new ones are born.

However, the argument has been carried farther. A leading modern theorist of consumer behavior, Professor Duesenberry, has stated explicitly that "ours is a society in which one of the principal social goals is a higher standard of living.... [This] has great significance for the theory of consumption ... the desire to get superior goods takes on a life of its own. It provides a drive to higher expenditure which may even be stronger than that arising out of the needs which are supposed to be satisfied by that expenditure." The implications of this view are impressive. The notion of independently established need now sinks into the background. Because the society sets great store by ability to produce a high living standard, it evaluates people by the products they possess. The urge to consume is fathered by the value system which emphasizes the ability of the society to produce. The more that is produced the more that must be owned in order to maintain the appropriate prestige. The latter is an important point, for, without going as far as Duesenberry in reducing goods to the role of symbols of prestige in the affluent society, it is plain that his argument fully implies that the production of goods creates the wants that the goods are presumed to satisfy.

III

The even more direct link between production and wants is provided by the institutions of modern advertising and salesmanship. These cannot be reconciled with the notion of independently determined desires, for their central function is to create desires—to bring into being wants that previously did not exist. This is accomplished by the producer of the goods or at his behest. A broad empirical relationship exists between what is spent on production of consumers' goods and what is spent in synthesizing the desires for that production. A new consumer product must be introduced with a suitable advertising campaign to arouse an interest in it. The path for an expansion of output must be paved by a suitable expansion in the advertising budget. Outlays for the manufacturing of a product are not more important in the strategy of modern business enterprise than outlays for the manufacturing of demand for the product. None of this is novel. All would be regarded as elementary by the most retarded student in the nation's most primitive school of business administration. The cost of this want formation is formidable.

In 1956 total advertising expenditure—though, as noted, not all of it may be assigned to the synthesis of wants—amounted to about ten billion dollars. For some years it had been increasing at a rate in excess of a billion dollars a year. Obviously, such outlays must be integrated with the theory of consumer demand. They are too big to be ignored.

But such integration means recognizing that wants are dependent on production. It accords to the producer the function both of making the goods and of making the desires for them. It recognizes that production, not only passively through emulation, but actively through advertising and related activities, creates the wants it seeks to satisfy.

The businessman and the lay reader will be puzzled over the emphasis which I give to a seemingly obvious point. The point is indeed obvious. But it is one which, to a singular degree, economists have resisted. They have sensed, as the layman does not, the damage to established ideas which lurks in these relationships. As a result, incredibly, they have closed their eyes (and ears) to the most obtrusive of all economic phenomena, namely modern want creation.

This is not to say that the evidence affirming the dependence of wants on advertising has been entirely ignored. It is one reason why advertising has so long been regarded with such uneasiness by economists. Here is something which cannot be accommodated easily to existing theory. More previous scholars have speculated on the urgency of desires which are so obviously the fruit of such expensively contrived campaigns for popular attention. Is a new breakfast cereal or detergent so much wanted if so much must be spent to compel in the consumer the sense of want? But there has been little tendency to go on to examine the implications of this for the theory of consumer demand and even less for the importance of production and productive efficiency. These have remained sacrosanct. More often the uneasiness has been manifested in a general disapproval of advertising and advertising men, leading to the occasional suggestion that they shouldn't exist. Such suggestions have usually been ill received.

And so the notion of independently determined wants still survives. In the face of all the forces of modern salesmanship it still rules, almost undefiled, in the textbooks. And it still remains the economist's mission—and on few matters is the pedagogy so firm—to seek unquestioningly the means for filling these wants. This being so, production remains of prime urgency. We have here, perhaps, the ultimate triumph, of the conventional wisdom in its resistance to the evidence of the eyes. To equal it one must imagine a humanitarian who was long ago persuaded of the grievous shortage of hospital facilities in the town. He continues to importune the passers-by for money for more beds and refuses to notice that the town doctor is deftly knocking over pedestrians with his car to keep up the occupancy.

And in unraveling the complex we should always be careful not to overlook the obvious. The fact that wants can be synthesized by advertising, catalyzed by salesmanship, and shaped by the discreet manipulations of the persuaders shows that they are not very urgent. A man who is hungry need never be told of his need for food. If he is inspired by his appetite, he is immune to the influence of Messrs. Batten, Barton, Durstine & Osborn. The latter are effective only with those who are so far removed from physical want that they do not already know what they want. In this state alone men are open to persuasion.

IV

The general conclusion of these pages is of such importance for this essay that it had perhaps best be put with some formality. As a society becomes increasingly affluent, wants are increasingly created by the process by which they are satisfied. This may operate passively. Increases in consumption, the counterpart of increases in production, act by suggestion or emulation to create wants. Or producers may proceed actively to create wants through advertising and salesmanship. Wants thus come to depend on output. In technical terms it can no longer be assumed that welfare is greater at an all-round higher level of production than at a lower one. It may be the same. The higher level of production has, merely, a higher level of want creation necessitating a higher level of want satisfaction. There will be frequent occasion to refer to the way wants depend on the process by which they are satisfied. It will be convenient to call it the Dependence Effect.

Joan Robinson

(1903-1983)

Probably the most famous woman economist of the 20th century, Joan Robinson was involved in most of the important debates in economics that occurred during her lifetime. Her early work on imperfect competition (which she later felt was not important) made it into the textbooks, and remains there today. She was also one of the key players in the Keynesian revolution and it was the force of her arguments that won many converts to Keynesian economics.

Her insightful thinking makes her writing on a variety of topics almost essential reading for economists. Always extremely outspoken, as she became older she became increasingly scornful of what she called "orthodox," or "bastard," economics. In the early 1980s, many economists believed that she should be at the top of the list for Nobel prize winners and, when she did not receive a Nobel, there was much talk about sexism.

It may have been sexism, but probably it was as much her outspoken political and anti-mainstream economics views as it was her gender that kept her from winning the award. Still, it is important to recognize the amount of discrimination against women that existed during most of her life and how forceful a personality a woman had to have to be a success within the male-dominated profession. Thus, Joan Robinson deserves a high place of honor in the profession— Nobel prize or not.

This selection is not easy reading. It challenges a number of concepts which you are probably only now beginning to absorb as you read the textbook. Specifically, the concept of irreversibility challenges the timeless framework of analysis provided in the textbook. We include it in this set of readings to give you a sense of how much more analysis there is out there. Introductory economics is only the introduction to a wide and fascinating field.

Joan Robinson. 1971. *Economic Heresies: Some Old-Fashioned Questions in Economic Theory*. New York: Basic Books, pp. 52-63.

Increasing and Diminishing Returns

The expression "increasing and diminishing returns to scale" implies some kind of symmetry between these phenomena but in origin they have nothing in common. The notion of diminishing returns was developed from Ricardo's theory of rent; increasing returns, from Adam Smith's principle that the division of labor depends upon the extent of the market.

The classical economists were concerned with a process of historical development. A number of confusions and contradictions have arisen from the neoclassical attempt to squeeze their concepts into the mechanical equilibrium of a stationary state.

The concept of constant returns to scale, in the technical sense, means that each physical input required for a given output —man-hours of labor of specific skill and energy, machines of specific types, materials, sites, and so forth—can be regarded as homogeneous within itself, and that a given proportionate increase in each input will bring about an equal proportionate increase in output. Diminishing returns arise from the fact that some inputs, in particular those that are given by nature, cannot be increased at will. To produce a certain proportionate increase in output then requires a more than proportionate increase in *other* factors. There are still conditions of constant returns in a technical sense; *if* all factors were increased, output would increase in the same proportion. On the other hand, the economies of large-scale production which give rise to increasing returns operate by changing the nature of the inputs. Output per man-hour grows as work becomes more specialized; equipment can be designed to produce a larger output at lower cost, larger supplies of materials can be more finely graded, and so forth. It is not a question of the proportions in which given physical inputs are used but rather a question of the specification of the inputs themselves. When some inputs have to be provided on a large minimum scale—say a railway network—strictly constant returns can be realized only for increases in output which

137

are a multiple of the capacity of the indivisible inputs. For ranges of increases in between there are increasing returns due to suboptimal utilization of the input. (To make the Walrasian system work we have to assume divisibility of all factors—otherwise the services of some items would fall to a zero price just after they had been built at great expense.) This concept is logically distinguishable from the economies of specialization but the two are likely to be mixed up together in any actual case.

The main difficulty about these conceptions is connected with time. A change (in output, in prices, or in costs) is an event, taking place at a particular moment, that alters the situation in which the change took place.

Irreversibility

The notion of a functional relationship between output and costs can make sense only in strictly short-period analysis. When the specification of inputs and of methods of work remains unchanged from year to year, output may rise and fall, as more of variable inputs are applied to one that is fixed, up and down a supply curve which remains independent of the direction of change. Such conditions may be approximately fulfilled when the amount of output of a particular crop depends upon the application of man-hours of work, over a yearly cycle, to a particular area of agricultural land. There must have been irreversible investments made in the past in clearing the land, in drainage, irrigation, and so forth; but once the investment has been made, productive capacity is kept intact in the course of operating it, so that henceforth investment is indistinguishable from the "natural resources" in which it is embedded; the short-period situation is quasipermanent. Similarly, in industry with given equipment, output per head may fall or rise as older plant is bought into or put out of use.

But a long-period supply curve is a very treacherous concept. *To increase* productive capacity requires investment. The larger capacity will exist at a later date than the smaller capacity which preceded it. In general it will be different in its technical nature, for three reasons. First, technical change is continually going on in the industrial economies. New plants will embody techniques formerly untried. Second, the mere fact of expanding capacity involves technical adaptations even when they are applications of general principles already known. (The notion of a "book of blueprints" exhibiting "the state of technical knowledge" has played a part in doctrinal controversy, not in realistic analysis. In reality techniques are blueprinted only when they are about to be used.)

Third, large installations often require investments of a quasipermanent type which alter the whole situation forever after.

Marshall was uneasily aware of the problem of irreversibility. He thought of an *increase* in output as taking place through time. A lower point on his falling supply curve is at a later date. When output has once expanded from A to B, a retraction of output back to B would take place at lower costs than obtained when B was the rate of output in the first place. This was a way of smuggling technical progress, learning by doing, and irreversible investment into the static theory.

The most important example of this way of thinking was the "infant industry case" as an exception to the presumption in favor of free trade. It is sufficiently obvious that when one country is trying to catch up upon the advanced technology of another, it must protect its industry from lower-cost competition until it has cut its teeth. In the process of development the scale of industry may grow but the main point is not the scale but the *time* that it takes for workers and managers to learn the business and for accumulation to provide the installations that it requires. Since there was no room for time in the neoclassical model, the argument had to be framed in terms of economies of scale. This, like Marshall's irreversible supply curve, is an example of common sense breaking in and thereby wrecking the logical structure of the equilibrium model.

Economists have not much emphasized the opposite kind of irreversibility—the destruction of resources, the devastation of amenities, and the accumulation of poison in air and water. Pigou

138

made a great point of "external diseconomies" such as the smoke nuisance but, within the confines of his stationary state, he could not emphasize *permanent* losses. It has been left rather to the natural scientists to sound the alarm, while orthodox economists, unperturbed, continue to elaborate the presumption in favor of laissez faire.

"Marginal Products"

A second problem presented by the concepts of diminishing and increasing returns, was concerned with the relation of "marginal products" to factor prices. In the Walrasian stationary state, the haggling of the market and recombination of factors are supposed to settle all marginal productivities and all hire-prices by a simultaneous process. There is, in a certain sense, a rising marginal cost for each commodity; if the output of any one commodity were to be increased, it would have to attract factors of production from other uses so that their price in terms of the commodity in question would have to be raised. But such an increase in output is only notional. When the supplies of all factors of production are given, output of one commodity can increase only if other outputs are reduced. A change in the pattern of demand means that some factors of production are released, where demand has fallen, to be transferred to the production of the commodities for which demand has risen. Before we can say what happens to the price of a commodity of which output rises, we must know what specific factors of production are released by the fall in output of other commodities.

To find the marginal product of a specific factor, say a certain type of machine, we have to consider what output would be lost if a unit of this factor were withdrawn. This loss is the reduction in output of the commodity that this machine was used to make minus the increase in output of other things due to deploying the labor and other factors cooperating with the machine in other uses. The physical marginal product is thus a very complex entity, while the value of the marginal product has no unambiguous meaning, since the pattern of prices, of factors and commodities, is altered by the change in productive capacity. Thus it is hard to understand what is meant by saying that a factor (say a part of machines of a particular type) receives a reward (say, the hire-price per machine year) equal to the value of its marginal product.

Marginal product in Ricardo's scheme has a quite different meaning. In the simplest form of Ricardo's model, the only output is "corn," which stands for all agricultural produce, and it is the only wage good. Capitalist farmers are accumulating corn in order to expand future output. To employ a man from harvest to harvest requires a specific investment of corn—the wage fund— which is equal to the wage bill for a year. Labor and capital are inseparable—the unit of input is a man-year of work together with the investment of corn in advancing a year's wage. Capitalist farmers maximize profits by deploying labor in such a way as to equalize the intensive and extensive margins of cultivation, that is, so that the additional output of corn from adding a man-year of work on the best land is not less than can be obtained by increasing the area of cultivation (neglecting the cost of breaking in new ground). Thus marginal product per man-year falls as employment and output expand over successively less fertile land. (Rent absorbs the difference in the productivity of better and worse land, so that the farmer receives the same average return for each man he employs.) Now, the marginal product of an additional man employed provides the wage per man-year *and* the profit on the capital required to employ him. It is far from being the case that each "factor" separately receives its marginal product. Man-plus-capital earns the marginal product (which is equal to the product of a man-year of work on marginal, no-rent land). The wage-bill for the man-year is deducted from this product and what remains is the profit on the capital required to employ a man. The principle remains the same when capital includes equipment and stocks of materials, though the problem of valuation is then not so simple as when output and capital are made of the same stuff.

In Ricardo's scheme, the corn-wage was fixed by the needs of subsistence, so that as output per man (net of rent) was falling, the rate of profit on capital was being eroded. If we like to postulate a constant rate of profit on capital, then, in such a case, the real wage would be falling with the marginal productivity of a man-plus-capital as total employment increases.

Marshall understood the difference between marginal productivity in Ricardo and in Walras but he made it very difficult for his readers to see the point.

Economies of Scale

The application of the idea of marginal productivity to the case of increasing returns caused even more trouble. Marshall thought of the economies of scale as mainly internal to an individual firm operating a single plant. There were also eastern economies due to the development of an industry as a whole. He did not think of any limit to economies of scale. "As the industry grows, the firm grows." Thus (at constant money-wage rates) cost per unit of output was a decreasing function of output. But he maintained that prices are equal to average cost including an allowance for normal profit. Thus prices must fall with costs. However for each firm, marginal cost is less than average cost; therefore less than price.

This was Marshall's famous dilemma. How can competitive conditions be reconciled with increasing returns?

Pigou tried to rescue Marshall by postulating an optimum size of firm at which long-period costs are at a minimum. Then, to enjoy normal profits, the firm must be working beyond the point of minimum cost to just such an extent that the excess of marginal cost (which is equated to price) over long-period average cost is sufficient to yield the required profit. When price is higher and output is greater than this, supernormal profits are attracting in new competition and forcing the firm back. Contrariwise when output is less. To make room for increasing returns, Pigou then had to rely upon purely external economies, or "economies of large scale to the industry." Each firm was always working under conditions of rising marginal cost, but an increase in the number of firms would lower average cost at the minimum for all of them. (This is a simplified account of an intricate argument which was broken off before it was resolved.) This fanciful construction, although it was demolished by Piero Sraffa more than forty years ago, is still used as the basis of the "theory of the firm" in modern textbooks.

The next problem was to introduce the "laws of returns" into a theory of the relative prices of commodities.

In the Walrasian stationary state all supplies of factors are physically specified and fixed in amount. Each pattern of demand then produces a particular pattern of relative prices. (In the P.O.W. camp, if there were a larger proportion of Sikhs, who do not smoke, the cigarette prices of other items in the parcels would generally be higher.) Pigou did not think of physical factors (except "land") as being specified and fixed; nor did he go to the other extreme (which came into fashion after his time) of thinking of the stock of capital equipment as a large lump of putty. He did think of the total of "resources" as being somehow given.

Formalizing Marshall's vague suggestions, he identified industries with commodities, and he divided the industries into those where diminishing returns predominate, so that the supply price of the commodity is rising with output, and those where economies of scale to the industry predominate, so that supply price is falling.

A change in the pattern of demand would release "resources" from some commodities to be embodied in means of production for other commodities. This put into his head the idea that to reduce the output of commodities "subject to diminishing returns" and transfer resources to commodities "subject to increasing returns," by a system of taxes and subsidies, would bring about an increase in total real output and in welfare. However, he soon recognized that this was based upon a false symmetry between increasing and diminishing returns. A reduction in demand for a commodity produced with the aid of a scarce factor reduces the rent of the factor. This is a transfer of wealth, not a saving of cost to society.

Abstracting from scarce factors, what remained of the argument seems to be as follows. Each commodity is produced by a competitive industry which sells it at a price corresponding to its cost of production including normal profits. Some commodities are more susceptible to increasing returns than others, so that if "resources" were moved between industries to take advantage of the difference, the loss of economies of scale in those where output was reduced would be less than the gain where output was increased. The pattern of demand is strongly affected by relative prices (in general, commodities are substitutes for each other) so that demand would be shifted by taxing some commodities and subsidizing others (the net revenue being zero). Total money income is given (there is full employment of workers at constant wage rates and a fixed total of "waiting" receiving a given rate of interest). The price to the consumer of taxed commodities would be raised by little, if anything, more than the tax (because they have little economies of scale to lose) while the price to the consumer of the subsidized commodities would be reduced by more than the subsidy, because of the gain of economies. Thus the real income of consumers would be increased.

This argument was never treated seriously as a recommendation for policy and nowadays it seems to have dropped out of the canon of orthodox teaching. Pigou put it forward as an example of the theoretical exceptions to the rule that perfect competition, in conditions of laissez faire, produces the optimum distribution of given resources between alternative uses. Here again common sense was breaking in, but he managed to catch it and wrap it up in the assumptions of static equilibrium before it could do much harm.

All these difficulties and confusions connected with the concepts of diminishing and increasing returns arise from the neoclassical attempt to escape from time. When we set the argument in what I have called the Marshallian model—a growing economy with a constant normal rate of profit on capital—they appear much less intractable. Irreversibility is no problem. Time marches in; there is no need to pretend that the past is the same thing as the future. In the Marshallian model, the dilemma between competition and falling costs disappears. If the normal rate of profit is constant, as the economy expands, it follows that as output per head rises, money prices fall relatively to money-wage rates. By assuming a constant rate of profit Marshall has assumed that prices are kept in line with costs; competition may be highly imperfect, in the sense that each firm has considerable freedom in setting prices; the number of independent firms in any one market may be falling; but still the economy is competitive in the broad sense; all he needs is to assume that firms generally prefer to take advantage of falling costs to expand sales rather than to try to hog a monopolistic profit by restricting the growth of output. In this model there is no great importance to be attached to the distinction between economies of scale and technical progress, nor between economies internal to a firm, economies accruing to an industry producing a particular commodity or economies resulting from the general development of industry, transport, distribution, and finance. As time rolls on, output of all kinds is increasing; productivity rises more for some commodities than others and relative prices alter accordingly. So long as the rate of profit on capital is constant through time, long-run normal prices are governed by costs. The forces of demand—the distribution of purchasing power, needs and tastes of the consumers, and persuasive skill of salesmanship—influence the composition of output. The only effects of demand upon prices arise where there are bottlenecks created by specialized factors of production in limited supply which cannot be broken by technical innovations or where economies of scale are concentrated upon a particular commodity. Only thus does the composition of output react upon costs of production and so on relative prices. Supply-price rising and falling with the sale of output of particular commodities then appears as a quite minor complication. (Marshall, it seems, puffed it up all out of proportion in order to bring supply and demand into the forefront of his doctrines).

But once we bring historical time into the argument, it is not so easy to present the free play of the market as an ideal mechanism for maximizing welfare and securing social justice. Marshall himself admitted that accumulation and employment depend upon expectations of an uncertain future. His short-period theory is a theory of instability and in historical terms his theory of distribution based on "rewards" of "factors of production" becomes meaningless. Economic history is notoriously a scene of conflicting interests, which is just what the neoclassical economists did not want to discuss.

F. A. Hayek

(1899-1992)

You have been introduced to F. A. Hayek in an earlier reading. Here, we see a selection from another of Hayek's famous articles—this one concerns economics and knowledge. In it Hayek argues that the concept of equilibrium is tautological, with people having perfect knowledge, and that the interesting aspects of economics concern the acquisition of knowledge and the disequilibrium adjustment. Markets are useful because they process knowledge and push towards equilibrium, not because they achieve *equilibrium.*

F. A. Hayek. 1936. *Economica*, IV (new series, 1937), pp. 33-54.

Economics and Knowledge

The ambiguity of the title of this paper is not accidental. Its main subject is, of course, the role which assumptions and propositions about the knowledge possessed by the different members of society play in economic analysis. But this is by no means unconnected with the other question which might be discussed under the same title—the question to what extent formal economic analysis conveys any knowledge about what happens in the real world. Indeed, my main contention will be that the tautologies, of which formal equilibrium analysis in economics essentially consists, can be turned into propositions which tell us anything about causation in the real world only in so far as we are able to fill those formal propositions with definite statements about how knowledge is acquired and communicated. In short, I shall contend that the empirical element in economic theory—the only part which is concerned not merely with implications but with causes and effects and which leads therefore to conclusions which, at any rate in principle, are capable of verification —consists of propositions about the acquisition of knowledge. . . .

As I have already suggested, the reason for this seems to me to be that we have to deal here only with a special aspect of a much wider question which we ought to have faced at a much earlier stage. Questions essentially similar to those mentioned arise in fact as soon as we try to apply the system of tautologies—those series of propositions which are necessarily true because they are merely transformations of the assumptions from which we start and which constitute the main content of equilibrium analysis—to the situation of a society consisting of several independent persons. I have long felt that the concept of equilibrium itself and the methods which we employ in pure analysis have a clear meaning only when confined to the analysis of the action of a single person and that we are really passing into a different sphere and silently introducing a new element of altogether different character when we apply it to the explanation of the interactions of a number of different individuals.

I am certain that there are many who regard with impatience and distrust the whole tendency, which is inherent in all modern equilibrium analysis, to turn economics into a branch of pure logic, a set of self-evident propositions which, like mathematics or geometry, are subject to no other test but internal consistency. But it seems that, if only this process is carried far enough, it carries its own remedy with it. In distilling from our reasoning about the facts of economic life those parts which are truly a priori [true on its face], we not only isolate one element of our reasoning as a sort of Pure Logic of Choice in all its purity but we also isolate, and emphasize the importance of, another element which has been too much neglected. My criticism of the recent tendencies to make economic theory more and more formal is not that they have gone too far but that they have not yet been carried far enough to complete the isolation of this branch of logic and to restore to its rightful place the investigation of causal processes, using formal economic theory as a tool in the same way as mathematics.

* * * *

In the usual presentations of equilibrium analysis it is generally made to appear as if these questions of how the equilibrium comes about were solved. But, if we look closer, it soon becomes evident that these apparent demonstrations amount to no more than the apparent proof of what is already assumed. The device generally adopted for this purpose is the assumption of a perfect market where every event becomes known instantaneously to every member. It is necessary to remember here that the perfect market which is required to satisfy the assumptions of equilibrium analysis must not be confined to the particular markets of all the individual commodities; the whole economic system must be assumed to be one perfect market in which everybody knows everything. The assumption of a perfect market, then, means nothing less than that all the members of the community, even if they are not supposed to be strictly omniscient, are at least supposed to know automatically all that is relevant for their decisions. It seems that that skeleton in our cupboard, the "economic man," whom we have exorcised with prayer and fasting, has returned through the back door in the form of a quasi omniscient individual.

The statement that, if people know everything, they are in equilibrium is true simply because that is how we define equilibrium. The assumption of a perfect market in this sense is just another way of saying that equilibrium exists but does not get us any nearer an explanation of when and how such a state will come about. It is clear that, if we want to make the assertion that, under certain conditions, people will approach that state, we must explain by what process they will acquire the necessary knowledge. Of course, any assumption about the actual acquisition of knowledge in the course of this process will also be of a hypothetical character. But this does not mean that all such assumptions are equally justified. We have to deal here with assumptions about causation, so that what we assume must not only be regarded as possible (which is certainly not the case if we just regard people as omniscient) but must also be regarded as likely to be true; and it must be possible, at least in principle, to demonstrate that it is true in particular cases.

The significant point here is that it is these apparently subsidiary hypotheses or assumptions that people do learn from experience, and about how they acquire knowledge, which constitute the empirical content of our propositions about what happens in the real world. They usually appear disguised and incomplete as a description of the type of market to which our proposition refers; but this is only one, though perhaps the most important, aspect of the more general problem of how knowledge is acquired and communicated. The important point of which economists frequently do not seem to be aware is that the nature of these hypotheses is in many respects rather different from the more general assumptions from which the Pure Logic of Choice starts. The main differences seem to me to be two:

First, the assumptions from which the Pure Logic of Choice starts are facts which we know to be common to all human thought. They may be regarded as axioms which define or delimit the field within which we are able to understand or mentally to reconstruct the processes of thought of other people. They are therefore universally applicable to the field in which we are interested— although, of course, where *in concreto* [in reality] the limits of this field are is an empirical question. They refer to a type of human action (what we commonly call "rational," or even merely "conscious," as distinguished from "instinctive" action) rather than to the particular conditions under which this action is undertaken. But the assumptions or hypotheses, which we have to introduce when we want to explain the social processes, concern the relation of the thought of an individual to the outside world, the question to what extent and how his knowledge corresponds to the external facts. And the hypotheses must necessarily run in terms of assertions about causal connections, about how experience creates knowledge.

Second, while in the field of the Pure Logic of Choice our analysis can be made exhaustive, that is, while we can here develop a formal apparatus which covers all conceivable situations, the supplementary hypotheses must of necessity be selective, that is, we must select from the infinite variety of possible situations such ideal types as for some reason we regard as specially relevant to conditions in the real world. Of course, we could also develop a separate science, the subject matter of which was *per definitionem* [by definition] confined to a "perfect market" or some similarly defined object, just as the Logic of Choice applies only to persons who have to allot limited means among a variety of ends. For the field so defined our propositions would again become a priori true but for such a procedure we should lack; the justification which consists in the assumption that the situation in the real world is similar to what we assume it to be. . . .

But, to revert to the special problem I have been discussing, the amount of knowledge different individuals must possess in order that equilibrium may prevail (or the "relevant" knowledge they must possess): we shall get nearer to an answer if we remember how it can become apparent either that equilibrium did not exist or that it is being disturbed. We have seen that the equilibrium connections will be severed if any person changes his plans, either because his tastes change (which does not concern us here) or because new facts become known to him. But there are evidently two different ways in which he may learn of new facts that make him change his plans, which for our purposes are of altogether different significance. He may learn of the new facts as it were by accident, that is, in a way which is not a necessary consequence of his attempt to execute his original plan, or it may be inevitable that in the course of his attempt he will find that the facts are different from what he expected. It is obvious that, in order that he may proceed according to plan, his knowledge needs to be correct only on the points on which it will necessarily be confirmed or corrected in the course of the execution of the plan. But he may have no knowledge of things which, if he possessed it, would certainly affect his plan.

The conclusion, then, which we must draw is that the relevant knowledge which he must possess in order that equilibrium may prevail is the knowledge which he is bound to acquire in view of the position in which he originally is, and the plans which he then makes. It is certainly not all the knowledge which, if he acquired it by accident, would be useful to him and lead to a change in his plan. We may therefore very well have a position of equilibrium only because some people have no chance of learning about facts which, if they knew them, would induce them to alter their plans. Or, in other words, it is only relative to the knowledge which a person is bound to acquire in the course of the attempt to carry out his original plan that an equilibrium is likely to be reached.

Alfred Marshall

(1842-1924)

We introduced you to Alfred Marshall at the beginning of this book. In this selection, taken from his Principles of Economics, *you get a somewhat better feel for the "Marshallian approach" than you did in the earlier selection. The Marshallian approach combines common sense, institutional knowledge, and some broad concepts of economic theory. Thus competition for Marshall is not the perfect competition of Chapter 25 in the textbook; rather, it is the real-world competition of Chapter 28 in the textbook.*

The first edition of the Principles *came out in 1890, more than a hundred years ago. When you read this selection, you should remember that an Englishman of that time took certain things for granted that we today see as prejudiced or biased. It is not only that he never mentions "she"; it is also that he assumes certain people are "primitive" and speaks of "backward races" and "backward countries," and you may find other references that seem strange to you. This quality in Marshall does not affect the true substance of his character or the strengths of "the Marshallian approach."*

Alfred Marshall. 1890 (8th edition: 1920). *Principles of Economics*. London: Macmillan & Co., Ltd., pp. 4-8.

Competition

It is often said that the modern forms of industrial life are distinguished from the earlier by being more competitive. But this account is not quite satisfactory. The strict meaning of competition seems to be the racing of one person against another, with special reference to bidding for the sale or purchase of anything. This kind of racing is no doubt both more intense and more widely extended than it used to be: but it is only a secondary, and one might almost say, an accidental consequence from the fundamental characteristics of modern industrial life.

There is no one term that will express these characteristics adequately. They are, as we shall presently see, a certain independence and habit of choosing one's own course for oneself, a self-reliance; a deliberation and yet a promptness of choice and judgment, and a habit of forecasting the future and of shaping one's course with reference to distant aims. They may and often do cause people to compete with one another; but on the other hand they may tend, and just now indeed they are tending, in the direction of cooperation and combination of all kinds [of] good and evil. But these tendencies towards collective ownership and collective action are quite different from those of earlier times, because they are the result not of custom, not of any passive drifting into association with one's neighbours, but of free choice by each individual of that line of conduct which after careful deliberation seems to him the best suited for attaining his ends, whether they are selfish or unselfish.

The term "competition" has gathered about it evil savour, and has come to imply a certain selfishness and indifference to the well-being of others. Now it is true that there is less deliberate selfishness in early than in modern forms of industry; but there is also less deliberate unselfishness. It is deliberateness, and not selfishness, that is the characteristic of the modern age.

For instance, while custom in a primitive society extends the limits of the family, and prescribes certain duties to one's neighbours which fall into disuse in a later civilization, it also prescribes an attitude of hostility to strangers. In a modern society the obligations of family kindness become more intense, though they are concentrated on a narrower area; and neighbours are put more nearly on the same footing with strangers. In ordinary dealings with both of them the standard of fairness and honesty is lower than in some of the dealings of a primitive people with their neighbours: but it is much higher than in their dealings with strangers. Thus it is the ties of neighbourhood alone that have been relaxed: the ties of family are in many ways stronger than before, family affection leads to much more self-sacrifice and devotion than it used to do; and sympathy with those who are strangers to us is a growing source of a kind of deliberate unselfishness, that never existed before the modern age. That country which is the birthplace of modern competition devotes a larger part of its income than any other to charitable uses, and spent twenty millions on purchasing the freedom of the slaves in the West Indies.

In every age poets and social reformers have tried to stimulate the people of their own time to a nobler life by enchanting stories of the virtues of the heroes of old. But neither the records of history nor the contemporary observation of backward races, when carefully studied, give any support to the doctrine that man is on the whole harder and harsher than he was; or that he was ever more willing than he is now to sacrifice his own happiness for the benefit of others in cases where custom and law have left him free to choose his own course. Among races, whose intellectual capacity seems not to have developed in any other direction, and who have none of the originating power of the modern business man, there will be found many who show an evil sagacity in driving a hard bargain in a market even with their neighbours. No traders are more unscrupulous in taking advantage of the necessities of the unfortunate than are the corn-dealers and money-lenders of the East.

Again, the modern era has undoubtedly given new openings for dishonesty in trade. The advance of knowledge has discovered new ways of making things appear other than they are, and has rendered possible many new forms of adulteration. The producer is now far removed from the ultimate consumer; and his wrong-doings are not visited with the prompt and sharp punishment which falls on the head of a person who, being bound to live and die in his native village, plays a dishonest trick on one of his neighbours. The opportunities for knavery are certainly more numerous than they were; but there is no reason for thinking that people avail themselves of a larger proportion of such opportunities than they used to do. On the contrary, modern methods of trade imply habits of trustfulness on the one side and a power of resisting temptation to dishonesty on the other, which do not exist among a backward people. Instances of simple truth and personal fidelity are met with under all social conditions: but those who have tried to establish a business of modern type in a backward country find that they can scarcely ever depend on the native population for filling posts of trust. It is even more difficult to dispense with imported assistance for work, which calls for a strong moral character, than for that which requires great skill and mental ability. Adulteration and fraud in trade were rampant in the middle ages to an extent that is very astonishing, when we consider the difficulties of wrong-doing without detection at that time.

In every stage of civilization, in which the power of money has been prominent, poets in verse and prose have delighted to depict a past truly "Golden Age," before the pressure of mere material gold had been felt. Their idyllic pictures have been beautiful, and have stimulated noble imaginations and resolves; but they have had very little historical truth. Small communities with simple wants for which the bounty of nature has made abundant provisions, have indeed sometimes been nearly free from care about their material needs, and have not been tempted to sordid ambitions. But whenever we can penetrate to the inner life of a crowded population under primitive conditions in our own time, we find more want, more narrowness, and more hardness than was manifest at a distance: and we never find a more widely diffused comfort alloyed by less suffering than exists in the western world to-day. We ought therefore not to brand the forces, which have made modern civilization, by a name which suggests evil.

It is perhaps not reasonable that such a suggestion should attach to the term "competition"; but in fact it does. In fact, when competition is arraigned, its anti-social forms are made prominent; and care is seldom taken to inquire whether there are not other forms of it, which are so essential to the maintenance of energy and spontaneity, that their cessation might probably be injurious on the balance to social well being. The traders or producers, who find that a rival is offering goods at a lower price than will yield them a good profit, are angered at his intrusion, and complain of being wronged; even though it may be true that those who buy the cheaper goods are in greater need than themselves, and that the energy and resourcefulness of their rival is a social gain. In many cases the "regulation of competition" is a misleading term, that veils the formation of a privileged class of producers, who often use their combined force to frustrate the attempts of an able man to rise from a lower class than their own. Under the pretext of repressing anti-social competition, they deprive him of the liberty of carving out for himself a new career, where the services rendered by him to the consumers of the commodity would be greater than the injuries, that he inflicts on the relatively small group which objects to his competition.

If competition is contrasted with energetic co-operation in unselfish work for the public good, then even the best forms of competition are relatively evil; while its harsher and meaner forms are hateful. And in a world in which all men were perfectly virtuous, competition would be out of place; but so also would be private property and every form of private right. Men would think only of their duties; and no one would desire to have a larger share of the comforts and luxuries of life than his neighbours. Strong producers could easily bear a touch of hardship; so they would wish that their weaker neighbours, while producing less should consume more. Happy in this thought, they would work for the general good with all the energy, the inventiveness, and the eager initiative that belonged to them; and mankind would be victorious in contests with nature at every turn. Such is the Golden Age to which poets and dreamers may look forward. But in the responsible conduct of affairs, it is worse than folly to ignore the imperfections which still cling to human nature.

History in general, and especially the history of socialistic ventures, shows that ordinary men are seldom capable of pure ideal altruism for any considerable time together; and that the exceptions are to be found only when the masterful fervour of a small band of religious enthusiasts makes material concerns to count for nothing in comparison with the higher faith.

No doubt men, even now, are capable of much more unselfish service than they generally render: and the supreme aim of the economist is to discover how this latent social asset can be developed most quickly, and turned to account most wisely. But he must not decry competition in general, without analysis: he is bound to retain a neutral attitude towards any particular manifestation of it until he is sure that, human nature being what it is, the restraint of competition would not be more anti-social in its working than the competition itself.

We may conclude then that the term "competition" is not well suited to describe the special characteristics of industrial life in the modern age. We need a term that does not imply any moral qualities, whether good or evil, but which indicates the undisputed fact that modern business and industry are characterized by more self-reliant habits, more forethought, more deliberate and free choice. There is not any one term adequate for this purpose: but *Freedom of Industry and Enterprise,* or more shortly, *Economic Freedom,* points in the right direction; and it may be used in the absence of a better. Of course this deliberate and free choice may lead to a certain departure from individual freedom when co-operation or combination seems to offer the best route to the desired end. The questions how far these deliberate forms of association are likely to destroy the freedom in which they had their origin and how far they are likely to be conducive to the public weal, lie beyond the scope of the present volume.

John Stuart Mill

(1806-1873)

The textbook emphasizes that reality is influenced by three invisible forces—the invisible hand, the invisible foot, and the invisible handshake. Various economists combine these three forces in various ways.

John Stuart Mill was the dominant figure in mid-19th century British political economy. He took the formal classical economics of earlier economists and made it into a broader, more humanistic economics, in which the invisible handshake was given a much greater role to play than it had played earlier. He was a progressive thinker and a person who, while he believed in liberty for the individual, understood that historical circumstances can place individuals in positions where they have no liberty.

In this selection Mill discusses the role of the invisible handshake, giving it significant importance: it limits competition and the competitive process can only be understood given an understanding of a society's culture and customs.

John Stuart Mill. 1849 (1909). Principles of Political Economy. London: Longmans Green, pp. 242-47.

Competition and Custom

It would be a great misconception of the actual course of human affairs, to suppose that competition exercises in fact unlimited sway. I am not speaking of monopolies, either natural or artificial, or of any interferences of authority with the liberty of production or exchange. I speak of cases in which there is nothing to restrain competition; no hindrances to it either in the nature of the case or in artificial obstacles; yet in which the result is not determined by competition, but by custom or usage; competition either not taking place at all, or producing its effect in quite a different manner from that which is ordinarily assumed to be natural to it.

Competition, in fact, has only become in any considerable degree the governing principle of contracts at a comparatively modern period. The farther we look back into history, the more we see all transactions and engagements under the influence of fixed customs. The reason is evident. Custom is the most powerful protector of the weak against the strong; their sole protector where there are no laws or government adequate to the purpose. Custom is a barrier which, even in the most oppressed condition of mankind, tyranny is forced in some degree to respect. To the industrious population, in a turbulent military community, freedom of competition is a vain phrase; they are never in a condition to make terms for themselves by it; there is always a master who throws his sword into the scale, and the terms are such as he imposes. But though the law of the strongest decides, it is not the interest nor in general the practice of the strongest to strain that law to the utmost, and every relaxation of it has a tendency to become a custom, and every custom to become a right. Rights thus originating, and not competition in any shape, determine, in a rude state of society, the share of the produce enjoyed by those who produce it.

Prices, whenever there was no monopoly, came earlier under the influence of competition, and are much more universally subject to it, than rents: but that influence is by no means, even in the present activity of mercantile competition, so absolute as is sometimes assumed.

The wholesale trade, in the great articles of commerce, is really under the dominion of competition. There, the buyers as well as sellers are traders and manufacturers, and their purchases are not influenced by indolence or vulgar finery, but are business transactions. In the wholesale markets, therefore, it is true as a general proposition that there are not two prices at one time for the same thing: there is at each time and place a market price, which can be quoted in a price-current. But retail price, the price paid by the actual consumer, seems to feel very slowly

148

and imperfectly the effect of competition; and when competition does exist, it often, instead of lowering prices, merely divides the gains of the high price among a greater number of dealers. The influence of competition is making itself felt more and more through the principal branches of retail trade in the large towns and the rapidity and cheapness of transport, by making consumers less dependent on the dealers in their immediate neighbourhood, are tending to assimilate more and more the whole country to a large town: but hitherto it is only in the great centres of business that retail transactions have been chiefly, or even much, determined by competition. Elsewhere it rather acts, when it acts at all, as an occasional disturbing influence; the habitual regulator is custom, modified from time to time by notions existing in the minds of purchasers and sellers, of some kind of equity or justice.

In many trades the terms on which business is done are a matter of positive arrangement among the trade, who use the means they always possess of making the situation of any member of the body who departs from its fixed customs, inconvenient or disagreeable. It is well known that the bookselling trade was, until lately, one of these, and that, notwithstanding the active spirit of rivalry in the trade, competition did not produce its natural effect in breaking down the trade rules. All professional remuneration is regulated by custom. The fees of physicians, surgeons, and barristers, the charges of attorneys, are nearly invariable. Not certainly for want of abundant competition in those professions, but because the competition operates by diminishing each competitor's chance of fees, not by lowering the fees themselves.

Since custom stands its ground against competition to so considerable an extent, even where, from the multitude of competitors and the general energy in the pursuit of gain, the spirit of competition is strongest, we may be sure that this is much more the case where people are content with smaller gains, and estimate their pecuniary interest at a lower rate when balanced against their ease or their pleasure. I believe it will often be found, in Continental Europe, that prices and charges, of some or of all sorts, are much higher in some places than in others not far distant, without its being possible to assign any other cause than that it has always been so: the customers are used to it, and acquiesce in it. An enterprising competitor, with sufficient capital, might force down the charges, and make his fortune during the process; but there are no enterprising competitors; those who have capital prefer to leave it where it is, or to make less profit by it in a more quiet way.

Frank H. Knight

(1885-1992)

The University of Chicago has long been a bastion of independent, liberal thinking and has had a succession of iconoclastic and brilliant thinkers who had important roles in economics. The first of these was J. Laurence Laughlin, who founded the economics department, then called "political economy," at the University in 1892. The second was Frank Knight, whose work provided new insight into competition, risk, and the role of uncertainty in economics. His writing was broadly philosophical and it placed economics within a larger liberal tradition. He was concerned with such issues as the relationship between economics and religion and the family.

In this selection he briefly summarizes how a market system works "in a fairly tolerable way," and he adds the qualifications that all good economists add to a description of a market: Knight calls it the "task of putting the complex and unlovely flesh and viscera of reality upon this clean white skeleton of abstract principle."

Frank Knight. 1933. *The Economic Organization*. New York: Harper and Row, Publishers, pp. 31-36.

The Price System and the Economic Process

Modern Economics Organization: an "Automatic" System

One of the most conspicuous features of organization through exchange and free enterprise, and one most often commented upon, is the absence of conscious design or control. It is a social order, and one of unfathomable complexity, yet constructed and operated without social planning or direction, through selfish individual thought and motivation alone. No one ever worked out a plan for such a system, or willed its existence; there is no plan of it anywhere, either on paper or in anybody's mind, and no one directs its operations. (This is true just insofar as the social order is in fact one of exchange and enterprise. We do have a large and increasing amount of deliberate planning and control in modern society, but this means precisely the substitution of "political" for economic methods of organization.) Yet in a fairly tolerable way, "it works", and grows and changes. We have an amazingly elaborate division of labor, yet each person finds his own place in the scheme; we use a highly involved technology with minute specialization of industrial equipment, but this too is created, placed and directed by individuals, for individual ends, with little thought of larger social relations or any general social objective. Innumerable conflicts of interest are constantly resolved, and the bulk of the working population kept generally occupied, each person ministering to the wants of an unknown multitude and having his own wants satisfied by another multitude equally vast and unknown—not perfectly indeed, but tolerable on the whole, and vastly better than each could satisfy his wants by working directly for himself. To explain the mechanism of this cooperation, unconscious and unintended, between persons whose feelings are often actually hostile to each other, is the problem of economic science. It is both a challenge to the intellectual interest, and of surpassing practical importance: for the workings of the system must be understood, if the action which society, in its self-conscious aspect is constantly taking in regard to it, is to result in good rather than harm.

Price, the Guide and Regulator. The Price System

The economic organization is built up and controlled, in a way familiar in its broad outlines to everyone, through the impersonal forces of *price*. The principles on which it operates are facts universally familiar; yet in their application to the practical problems of improving the working of the system, these principles not only become complicated, but run counter to natural and established ways of thinking. Many popular beliefs regarding economics and the effects of legislation are fallacies which when put into practice tend to impoverish the nation. On a general understanding of the fundamental laws of price relations, and on their thoughtful application in measures of public policy, rests all hope for prosperity under democratic institutions, all hope for efficiency in industry and a progressively more equitable distribution of the burdens and benefits of social cooperation in economic life.

The general theory of the system of free enterprise, as stated above, is simple. People get their "living" by selling productive power, meaning their own personal services or the use of property which they own, to industrial establishments, for money, and buying with the money the means of satisfying their wants and needs. They buy from industrial establishments also, generally from different ones than those to which they sell their own services, and generally through the medium of merchants or dealers. Industrial enterprises, reciprocally, buy productive services (of person and property) from individuals, use them to "produce" the means of want-satisfaction, and sell these to individuals. It is always to be kept in mind that our social organization is not simply and solely one of free enterprise. In agriculture particularly, in the professions largely, and in some other fields less extensively, we have production carried on the "handicraft" principle; the family is the unit and uses its own productive power to make a product, which it sells in the market. Other productive operations are carried on by governmental agencies, which operate in various relations with the public and there are also some "cooperative" establishments. The typical modern business enterprise, however, is the corporation, an impersonal organization, which does buy or hire most of the productive power used in making the products which it sells. The process tends to be obscured by the fact that production of most things is divided into a great number of stages and branches, carried on in different establishments. Any single establishment commonly buys not only raw productive power, but various "products" of other establishments, together with some productive power, with which it turns out another "product", which in turn is probably not ready to satisfy wants, but is sold to still other establishments as "raw material". All these details will come in for discussion presently. In the meantime, it is possible to think of business establishments as a group, buying productive power from individuals, making products in the final sense, and selling these to individuals for "consumption" in satisfying their wants.

. . . . [T]he general interest requires that the available productive power of society at large be used to create the means of satisfying the more important wants, as far as it will go, that it be used as efficiently as possible, that the total output of industry or social income be distributed equitably among the people, and that the productive equipment itself be maintained and reasonably improved. The general theory of free enterprise from this point of view—the provision made in such a system for realizing these objectives—can be stated briefly. Production is motivated and controlled by the consumers' expenditure of income. Each person being free to spend his money as he pleases, the presumption is that he will know the relative importance of his own various wants and will buy goods accordingly. Producers will then be compelled to furnish the things most in demand. They are placed in competition with each other; the establishment which conforms best to the wishes of consumers can sell its product at the highest prices, and one which does not produce things in demand may not be able to sell its wares at all. Whenever too much of anything is being made, in proportion to its importance to consumers, its price falls, and the price of things relatively short in supply rises. Producers therefore find it profitable to utilize productive power to make the things the public needs, or wants, in the correct proportions.

Moreover, producers are in competition in the purchase of productive power, and their means for purchasing are derived from the sale of products. Those who make products most in demand can pay higher prices for labor, materials, etc., and it is assumed that those who furnish these things will sell them to those who offer to pay most. Thus it is not a matter of choice with the producer. He is literally compelled to meet the consumers' demands as accurately as his competitors do, or he cannot secure productive power, and cannot remain in business.

In the same way, the competition of producers tends to force them to be as *efficient* as possible in the conduct of their operations. For those who succeed in turning out the largest quantity of any commodity with the use of a given amount of productive power can pay most for it, and force less efficient competitors either to adopt more efficient methods or to go out of business. Thus every detail in the production process is constantly subjected to a ruthless process of selection in a struggle for existence, and an irresistible pressure is brought to bear toward the use of productive power both in the "best" direction and in accord with methods of the highest possible efficiency.

The payments made by producers for productive power, including labor and the use of capital and natural resources, constitute the incomes of individuals. Competition of producers, and the effort of each individual to secure as large an income as he can in exchange for the services he furnishes to production, *tend* to make these payments equal to the full value of every service in its most productive use. Thus the distribution of income is worked out on the principle of paying each individual in accord with his contribution to the total social product, as measured by the amount consumers are willing to pay. Consumers also compete with each other, those who will pay the most for any product get it, and this competition tends to assure to the individual who furnishes any productive service a payment for its use equal to the value of the most valuable contribution which that service can be made to yield. The relation of the system to the fourth primary task of organization, that is, to maintenance and progress, can only be mentioned here. It is surely evident that rich rewards are waiting for those who can introduce improved methods of production, or bring new resources into use, while those who only patiently accumulate capital to make possible the increase and improvement of productive equipment in its commonest forms are rewarded with interest on savings.

Principles versus Facts: Explanation versus Justification or Criticism

Such is the enterprise system in a brief "airplane" view, and according to the accepted theories of economics, which are undoubtedly sound if not pushed beyond such an outline of fundamental tendencies. In such a view, the system appears both extremely simple and altogether beneficent. But when these few abstract principles are clothed with the concrete facts of life, which is the task of economic science, it quickly develops that economic relations are far from simple and the results achieved [are] not only far from ideal in the sense of creating universal happiness but also far from what we have a reasonable right to expect. Our task of putting the complex and often unlovely flesh and viscera of reality upon this clean white skeleton of abstract principle must be carried out in several stages. Only a few of the earlier stages can be sketched in this volume, and we must be concerned primarily with the more general sources of error in understanding the way in which the system actually works. ....

John Kenneth Galbraith

(1908-)

This is the third selection from this author's works that appears in this book, and you have already been introduced to him.

Galbraith is known most widely for his popular writing. It is often forgotten that before he began writing for the lay public, he wrote on technical issues in economics. When he found that his technical writing was not influencing the profession, he turned to popular writing. In this selection we see some of his more technical work. It was written in 1948 as part of a general survey. It is a discussion of the evolution of monopoly theory and in it he gives you some background of the tools of monopolistic competition.

Note that when Galbraith refers to "the depression" or "the Great Depression," he means the depression that began late in 1929 and lasted till about 1941.

John Kenneth Galbraith. 1948. "Monopoly and the Concentration of Economic Power," in *A Survey of Contemporary Economics,* edited by H. S. Ellis. Homewood: Irwin, pp. 99-103.

The Development of Monopoly Theory

Excluding only the issues associated with fiscal policy and the level and stability of employment, no problem attracted more attention from economists during the [1930s] than that of monopoly. As usual, the sources of this interest are traceable in part to ideas and in part to circumstance. Several years before the depression started, certain long-held and vital assumptions concerning the structure of the typical market were undergoing re-examination. The results became apparent at a time when economists everywhere were looking for an interpretation of the current crisis in capitalist society. A retrospect on monopoly, in its theoretical and applied aspects, properly begins, therefore, with a review of the ideas which accounted for the original revival of interest. It is appropriately followed by a consideration of the effect of these ideas as they were carried into the world of policy and politics.

* * * *

The first influential new step in the field of ideas was the publication in 1926 by Piero Sraffa of his now famous article,"The laws of returns under competitive conditions". Subject to qualifications, the tendency at the time Mr. Sraffa's article appeared was to recognize the limiting case of monopoly, but to assume, in general, a rule of competition. Competition was not assumed to be perfect. Those already in the business might variously obstruct the entry of newcomers. Or entry might be rendered difficult by the prestige associated with trademarks and trade names. Imperfect knowledge of opportunities might interfere. Decreasing costs were deemed an especially serious handicap for the newcomer, who, because he was new, was likely to be small. If large scale and accompanying requirements in capital and organization brought substantial economies, the small newcomer was faced with an organic handicap. Nevertheless, these barriers, though widely recognized, were conventionally assumed to be of secondary effect. They were frictions that muddled and at times diverted but did not check the great underlying current which was toward a competitive equilibrium. Given that equilibrium, there was a presumption, again subject to many dissenting voices, that economic resources would be employed with maximum efficiency and the product so distributed as to maximize satisfactions. Sraffa attacked the assumption that the "frictions" were in fact a secondary and fugitive phenomenon. He argued they were stable and indeed cumulative and yielded a solution consistent not with a competitive, but a monopolistic equilibrium. He argued that monopoly, not free competition, was the more appropriate assumption in market theory.

153

In 1932-33 Mrs. Robinson and Professor Chamberlin produced the two books that were to become the texts for the revived interest in monopoly. The first leaned heavily on Sraffa; the second has a more independent genesis. Both had a prompt and enthusiastic reception. This is not difficult to explain. For years there had been marked discontent with the accustomed assumptions and the standard analysis of competitive and monopolized markets. Discussion and teaching had too long centered on what, too obviously, were limiting cases. Even (or perhaps especially) students were reluctant to accept the results as descriptive of the real world. The new work had the great advantage, from the viewpoint of marketability, of adding something new to something old, and of adding almost precisely what the customers wanted. Both books were solidly in the tradition of Marshallian partial equilibrium analysis; and in the United States and the United Kingdom this had become not only an utterly respectable but an all but impregnable tradition in economic thought. The inhabitants of this citadel, although never too hospitable to strangers, were bound to accept old inhabitants armed with familiar weapons even though they used these weapons in a seemingly dangerous way. Both Professor Chamberlin and Mrs. Robinson offered an organized, intellectually palatable approach to the middle ground between monopoly and competition—an obvious antidote to the existing uneasiness. In this respect their contribution was sharply distinguished from that of Marshall, J. M. Clark, and others who had delved but briefly into this intermediate area, from that of teachers who had warned their students that the old categories were inadequate, and from that of Cournot, Edgeworth, and Bowley who, at most, had offered a smattering of mostly improbable solutions to mostly improbable situations.

In retrospect the most important contribution of Professor Chamberlin and Mrs. Robinson was to emancipate the analysis of markets from the inadequate categories of competition (impaired by sundry frictions) and single-firm monopoly. Almost at once duopoly, oligopoly, and the purposeful differentiation of products became accredited and very useful categories in market analysis.

This liberalization of market categories was more important than the theory that explored them. Professor Chamberlin did make a notable refinement in the existing concept of competition. Where previously competition had often been loosely identified by the terms of rivalry in the market—conditions of entry, the energy and knowledge of participants, and the like—he, in effect, derived its character from the competitive equilibrium it was assumed to bring about. The concept of pure competition was thereby confined to markets where the demand for the product of the individual seller was infinitely elastic at the ruling price. This was a good deal more rigorous than existing definitions; it had, as I shall argue presently, important practical consequences.

Both Professor Chamberlin and Mrs. Robinson also made the marginal revenue curve a standard tool of market analysis and Professor Chamberlin's theory of monopolistic competition—of competition between numerous sellers differentiated by location, personality, or physical or psychic differences in their product—brought the vast phenomenon of merchandising and advertising within the scope of theoretical analysis. For the purposes of the present essay, however, it was the area of failure rather than achievement of the new work that is of prime significance. Without much doubt the dominant market of modern capitalism is not one made up of many sellers offering either uniform or differentiated products. Rather it is a market of few sellers, that is: oligopoly. Apart from consumers' goods, the counterpart of few buyers associated with many or few sellers is also a common phenomenon. Where sellers are few the product is automatically identified with its vendor and hence there is always a measure of differentiation—the elasticity of substitution between products of a few sellers can never be quite perfect. But the ruling characteristic is the fewness of the sellers.

In dealing with small numbers or oligopoly, Professor Chamberlin, who went farthest with the problem on a general theoretical level, did little more than resurrect the engaging but largely irrelevant novelties of Cournot and Edgeworth. This was a failure of prime importance —one that economists were, on the whole, slow to recognize. The failure was inevitable. Success, by familiar standards, implied a determinate solution. One certain fact about oligopoly (and its counterpart on the buyer's side of the market) is that the entire market solution can be altered unilaterally by any single participant. This is at once the simplest and the most critical distinction between oligopoly and pure competition. It also means that the methodological device by which the competitive market has been analysed, that is, laying down general assumptions about the group response of numerous individuals to common stimuli, is inadmissible. Rather the assumptions must be sufficiently comprehensive to cover the behavior pattern of each participant in the market. Even though it is assumed that the possible individual behavior patterns and resulting market solutions are almost infinitely numerous, and the assumption that all individuals will seek maximum pecuniary return (as distinct from non-pecuniary prestige, expression of individuality, etc.) is questionable. Edgeworth and Cournot and, in that tradition, Chamberlin, merely derived the market solution that followed from two or three out of a near infinity of possible behavior combinations. It follows that they were not offering a theory of duopoly or oligopoly but displaying a few samples. Little progress has been made to an analysis of oligopoly by this route and little could be expected.

The importance of oligopoly in the world as it exists was highlighted, almost simultaneously with the appearance of Professor Chamberlin's and Mrs. Robinson's books, by [Adolph] Berle and [Gardiner] Means's mammoth study of the modern corporation. This study was also launched well prior to the Great Depression; its inspiration, Professor Berle stated in the preface, was the Wall Street boom and the attendant pyramiding of industrial oligarchies. But it was not Professor Berle's interesting and erudite study of the changing property rights of the individual security holder but Gardiner C. Means's statistics on the industrial predominance of the nation's 200 largest non-financial corporations that captured popular attention. These, he estimated, had combined assets at the beginning of 1930 of $81 billion, or about half of all assets owned by corporations. Although open to challenge as to detail, his calculations buttressed his contention that "the principles of duopoly have become more important than those of free competition". The book had a popular as well as academic audience and the figure of "200" became a magic symbol in subsequent investigations of economic power.

The new market categories, plus the evidence of Berle and Means and of the scholar's own eyes as to the need for them, set the stage for the revived interest in monopoly and its allied issues. One must also emphasize the *esprit* which Chamberlin's and Robinson's works gave to students of the field. Even though they substituted a new set of frustrations for the old ones, the new ones were welcome. It has been suggested that the most revolutionary feature of the monopolistic competition theories [was] the unprecedented pace at which they conquered their audience. Neither Chamberlin nor Robinson was destroyed and redestroyed as was Keynes a few years later. Their most effective critic, Professor Schumpeter, centered his attacks not on the validity of their analysis *per se* [in themselves] but more generally on the notion that it much affected the assessment of capitalist reality. Rarely in economics have ideas had such an enthusiastic and uncritical welcome.

C. Northcote Parkinson

(1909-1993)

C. Northcote Parkinson was an English economist who was educated at three British universities and then taught at several British universities and the University of Malaya, as well as briefly in the United States at the University of Illinois and the University of California. He was a wide-ranging author and wrote on naval history, military history, economic history, international relations, and political thought. His great wit combined with his economic training moved him to a high level of economic fame: he has a law named after him—Parkinson's Law. Most of you will probably have heard that law: Work expands to fit the time allotted to it. Here we see its source.

It is characteristic of economists that they have a cynical attitude toward bureaucracy. In this selection we see that cynicism coming through but we also see some deep insight into the nature of organizations and management. Notice as you read this selection that Parkinson's Law follows directly from economists' rational choice theory applied in a specific institutional framework.

C. Northcote Parkinson. 1957. *Parkinson's Law and Other Studies in Administration*. New York: Houghton Mifflin Company, Chapter One.

Parkinson's Law or the Rising Pyramid

Work expands so as to fill the time available for its completion. General recognition of this fact is shown in the proverbial phrase "It is the busiest man who has time to spare." Thus, an elderly lady of leisure can spend the entire day in writing and dispatching a postcard to her niece at Bognor Regis [a small town in England. An hour will be spent in finding the postcard, another in hunting for spectacles, half an hour in a search for the address, an hour and a quarter in composition, and twenty minutes in deciding whether or not to take an umbrella when going to the mailbox in the next street. The total effort that would occupy a busy man for three minutes all told may in this fashion leave another person prostrate after a day of doubt, anxiety, and toil.

Granted that work (and especially paper work) is thus elastic in its demands on time, it is manifest that there need be little or no relationship between the work to be done and the size of the staff to which it may be assigned. A lack of real activity does not, of necessity, result in leisure. A lack of occupation is not necessarily revealed by a manifest idleness. The thing to be done swells in importance and complexity in a direct ratio with the time to be spent. This fact is widely recognized, but less attention has been paid to its wider implications, more especially in the field of public administration. Politicians and taxpayers have assumed (with occasional phases of doubt) that a rising total in the number of civil servants must reflect a growing volume of work to be done. Cynics, in questioning this belief, have imagined that the multiplication of officials must have left some of them idle or all of them able to work for shorter hours. But this is a matter in which faith and doubt seem equally misplaced. The fact is that the number of the officials and the quantity of the work are not related to each other at all. The rise in the total of those employed is governed by Parkinson's Law and would be much the same whether the volume of the work were to increase, diminish, or even disappear. The importance of Parkinson's Law lies in the fact that it is a law of growth based upon an analysis of the factors by which that growth is controlled.

The validity of this recently discovered law must rest mainly on statistical proofs, which will follow. Of more interest to the general reader is the explanation of the factors underlying the general tendency to which this law gives definition. Omitting technicalities (which are numerous) we may distinguish at the outset two motive forces. They can be represented for the present purpose by two almost axiomatic statements, thus: (1) "An official wants to multiply subordinates, not rivals" and (2) "Officials make work for each other."

To comprehend Factor 1, we must picture a civil servant, called A, who finds himself overworked. Whether this overwork is real or imaginary is immaterial, but we should observe, in passing, that A's sensation (or illusion) might easily result from his own decreasing energy: a normal symptom of middle age. For this real or imagined overwork there are, broadly speaking, three possible remedies. He may resign; he may ask to halve the work with a colleague called B; he may demand the assistance of two subordinates, to be called C and D. There is probably no instance in history, however, of A choosing any but the third alternative. By resignation he would lose his pension rights. By having B appointed, on his own level in the hierarchy, he would merely bring in a rival for promotion to W's vacancy when W (at long last) retires. So A would rather have C and D, junior men, below him. They will add to his consequence and, by dividing the work into two categories, as between C and D, he will have the merit of being the only man who comprehends them both. It is essential to realize at this point that C and D are, as it were, inseparable. To appoint C alone would have been impossible. Why? Because C, if by himself, would divide the work with A and so assume almost the equal status that has been refused in the first instance to B; a status the more emphasized if C is A's only possible successor. Subordinates must thus number two or more, each being thus kept in order by fear of the other's promotion. When C complains in turn of being overworked (as he certainly will) A will, with the concurrence of C, advise the appointment of two assistants to help C. But he can then avert internal friction only by advising the appointment of two more assistants to help D, whose position is much the same. With this recruitment of E, F, G, and H the promotion of A is now practically certain.

Seven officials are now doing what one did before. This is where Factor 2 comes into operation. For these seven make so much work for each other that all are fully occupied and A is actually working harder than ever. An incoming document may well come before each of them in turn. Official E decides that it falls within the province of F, who places a draft reply before C, who amends it drastically before consulting D, who asks G to deal with it. But G goes on leave at this point, handing the file over to H, who drafts a [memo] that is signed by D and returned to C, who revises his draft accordingly and lays the new version before A.

What does A do? He would have every excuse for signing the thing unread, for he has many other matters on his mind. Knowing now that he is to succeed W next year, he has to decide whether C or D should succeed to his own office. He had to agree to G's going on leave even if not yet strictly entitled to it. He is worried whether H should not have gone instead, for reasons of health. He has looked pale recently—partly but not solely because of his domestic troubles. Then there is the business of F's special increment of salary for the period of the conference and E's application for transfer to the Ministry of Pensions. A has heard that D is in love with a married typist and that G and F are no longer on speaking terms—no one seems to know why. So A might be tempted to sign C's draft and have done with it. But A is a conscientious man. Beset as he is with problems created by his colleagues for themselves and for him—created by the mere fact of these officials' existence—he is not the man to shirk his duty. He reads through the draft with care, deletes the fussy paragraphs added by C and H, and restores the thing back to the form preferred in the first instance by the able (if quarrelsome) F. He corrects the English—none of these young men can write grammatically—and finally produces the same reply he would have written if officials C to H had never been born. Far more people have taken far longer to produce the same result. No one has been idle. All have done their best. And it is late in the evening before A finally quits his office and begins the return journey [home]. The last of the office lights are being turned off in the gathering dusk that marks the end of another day's administrative toil. Among the last to leave, A reflects with bowed shoulders and a wry smile that late hours, like gray hairs, are among the penalties of success.

From this description of the factors at work the student of political science will recognize that administrations are more or less bound to multiply. Nothing has yet been said, however, about the period of time likely to elapse between the date of A's appointment and the date from which we can calculate the pensionable service of H. Vast masses of statistical evidence have been collected and it is from a study of this data that Parkinson's Law has been deduced. Space will not allow of detailed analysis but the reader will be interested to know that research began in the British Navy Estimates. These were chosen because the Admiralty's responsibilities are more easily measurable than those of, say, the Board of Trade. The question is merely one of numbers and tonnage. Here are some typical figures. The strength of the Navy in 1914 could be shown as 146,000 officers and men, 3249 dockyard officials and clerks, and 57,000 dockyard workmen. By 1928 there were only 100,000 officers and men and only 62,439 workmen, but the dockyard officials and clerks by then numbered 4,558. As for warships, the strength in 1928 was a mere fraction of what it had been in 1914—fewer than 20 capital ships in commission as compared with 62. Over the same period the Admiralty officials had increased in number from 2,000 to 3,569, providing (as was remarked) "a magnificent navy on land." These figures are more clearly set forth in tabular form.

ADMIRALTY STATISTICS

Year	Capital ships in commission	Officers and men in R.N. [Royal Navy]	Dockyard workers	Dockyard officials and clerks	Admiralty officials
1914	62	146,000	57,000	3,249	2,000
1928	20	100,000	62,439	4,558	3,569
Increase or Decrease	=-67.74%	=-31.5%	=9.54%	=40.28%	=78.45%

The criticism voiced at the time centered on the ratio between the numbers of those available for fighting and those available only for administration. But that comparison is not to the present purpose. What we have to note is that the 2,000 officials of 1914 had become the 3,569 of 1928; and that this growth was unrelated to any possible increase in their work. The Navy during that period had diminished, in point of fact, by a third in men and two-thirds in ships. Nor, from 1922 onward, was its strength even expected to increase; for its total of ships (unlike its total of officials) was limited by the Washington Naval Agreement of that year. Here we have then a 78 per cent increase over a period of fourteen years; an average of 5.6 per cent increase a year on the earlier total. In fact, as we shall see, the rate of increase was not as regular as that. All we have to consider, at this stage, is the percentage rise over a given period.

Can this rise in the total number of civil servants be accounted for except on the assumption that such a total must always rise by a law governing its growth? It might be urged at this point that the period under discussion was one of rapid development in naval technique. The use of the flying machine was no longer confined to the eccentric. Electrical devices were being multiplied and elaborated. Submarines were tolerated if not approved. Engineer officers were beginning to be regarded as almost human. In so revolutionary an age we might expect that storekeepers would have more elaborate inventions to compile. We might not wonder to see more draughtsmen on the payroll, more designers, more technicians and scientists. But these, the dockyard officials, increased only by 40 per cent in number when the men of Whitehall increased their total by nearly 80 per cent. For every new foreman or electrical engineer at Portsmouth there had to be two more clerks at Charing Cross. From this we might be tempted to conclude, provisionally, that the rate of increase in administrative staff is likely to be double that of the technical staff at a time when the actually useful strength (in this case, of seamen) is being reduced by 31.5 per cent. It has been proved statistically, however, that this last percentage is irrelevant. The officials would have multiplied at the same rate had there been no actual seamen at all. It would be interesting to follow the further progress by which the 8,118 Admiralty staff of 1935 came to number 33,788 by 1954. But the staff of the Colonial Office affords a better field of study during a period of imperial decline.

* * * *

No attempt has been made to inquire whether departments *ought* to grow in size. Those who hold that this growth is essential to gain full employment are fully entitled to their opinion. Those who doubt the stability of an economy based upon reading each other's [memos] are equally entitled to theirs. It would probably be premature to attempt at this stage any inquiry into the quantitative ratio that should exist between the administrators and the administered. Granted, however, that a maximum ratio exists, it should soon be possible to ascertain by formula how many years will elapse before that ratio, in any given community, will be reached. The forecasting of such a result will again have no political value. Nor can it be sufficiently emphasized that Parkinson's Law is a purely scientific discovery, inapplicable except in theory to the politics of the day. It is not the business of the botanist to eradicate the weeds. Enough for him if he can tell us just how fast they grow.

Ronald Coase
(1910-)

Most economists would be happy to have written an article that is considered a true classic. Ronald Coase, the British economist, has written two—this one on the nature of the firm, and "The Problem of Social Cost." Both stem from the same questioning approach to economics. Coase did not simply assume markets exist; he asked what were the economic conditions under which markets would come into, and go out of, existence.

Coase was educated in Britain, but he soon moved to the U.S. He taught at the University of Chicago where he was one of the originators of the law-and-economics movement. He won a Nobel prize in 1991 for work on the theory of firms and markets.

In this selection from "The Nature of the Firm," he argues that the task of economists is to discover why a firm emerges at all in a specialized exchange economy. He argues that this occurs because there is a cost of using the price mechanism and firms, utilizing transactions that would not exist without them, gives us goods at lower costs. As you read the selection, you will find it useful to try to fit the reasoning in it with the reasoning in the previous piece, by C. Northcote Parkinson, and think about their consistency and their differences.

Ronald Coase. 1937. "The Nature of the Firm." *Economica*, New Series 4, pp. 386-405.

The Nature of the Firm

Economic theory has suffered in the past from a failure to state clearly its assumptions. Economists in building up a theory have often omitted to examine the foundations on which it was erected. This examination is, however, essential not only to prevent the misunderstanding and needless controversy which arise from a lack of knowledge of the assumptions on which a theory is based, but also because of the extreme importance for economics of good judgment in choosing between rival sets of assumptions. For instance, it is suggested that the use of the word "firm" in economics may be different from the use of the term by the "plain man." Since there is apparently a trend in economic theory towards starting analysis with the individual firm and not with the industry, it is all the more necessary not only that a clear definition of the word "firm" should be given but that its difference from a firm in the "real world," if it exists, should be made clear. Mrs. Robinson has said that "the two questions to be asked of a set of assumptions in economics are: Are they tractable? and: Do they correspond with the real world?" Though, as Mrs. Robinson points out, "More often one set will be manageable and the other realistic," yet there may well be branches of theory where assumptions may be both manageable and realistic. It is hoped to show in the following paper that a definition of a firm may be obtained which is not only realistic in that it corresponds to what is meant by a firm in the real world, but is tractable by two of the most powerful instruments of economic analysis developed by Marshall, the idea of the margin and that of substitution, together giving the idea of substitution at the margin. Our definition must, of course, "relate to formal relations which are capable of being conceived exactly."

It is convenient if, in searching for a definition of a firm, we first consider the economic system as it is normally treated by the economist. Let us consider the description of the economic system given by Sir Arthur Salter. "The normal economic system works itself. For its current operation it is under no central control, it needs no central survey. Over the whole range of human activity and human need, supply is adjusted to demand, and production to consumption, by a process that is automatic, elastic and responsive." An economist thinks of the economic system as being co-ordinated by the price mechanism and society becomes not an organization but an organism. The economic system "works itself."

* * * *

In view of the fact that while economists treat the price mechanism as a coordinating instrument, they also admit the co-ordinating function of the "entrepreneur," it is surely important to enquire why co-ordination is the work of the price mechanism in one case and of the entrepreneur in another. The purpose of this paper is to bridge what appears to be a gap in economic theory between the assumption (made for some purposes) that resources are allocated by means of the price mechanism and the assumption (made for other purposes) that this allocation is dependent on the entrepreneur-co-ordinator. We have to explain the basis on which, in practice, this choice between alternatives is effected.

Our task is to attempt to discover why a firm emerges at all in a specialized exchange economy. The price mechanism (considered purely from the side of the direction of resources) might be superseded if the relationship which replaced it was desired for its own sake. This would be the case, for example, if some people preferred to work under the direction of some other person. Such individuals would accept less in order to work under someone, and firms would arise naturally from this. But it would appear that this cannot be a very important reason, for it would rather seem that the opposite tendency is operating if one judges from the stress normally laid on the advantage of "being one's own master." Of course, if the desire was not to be controlled but to control, to exercise power over others, then people might be willing to give up something in order to direct others; that is, they would be willing to pay others more than they could get under the price mechanism in order to be able to direct them. But this implies that those who direct pay in order to be able to do this are not paid to direct, which is clearly not true in the majority of cases. Firms might also exist if purchasers preferred commodities which are produced by firms to those not so produced; but even in spheres where one would expect such preferences (if they exist) to be of negligible importance, firms are to be found in the real world. Therefore there must be other elements involved.

The main reason why it is profitable to establish a firm would seem to be that there is a cost of using the price mechanism. The most obvious cost of "organizing" production through the price mechanism is that of discovering what the relevant prices are. This cost may be reduced but it will not be eliminated by the emergence of specialists who will sell this information. The costs of negotiating and concluding a separate contract for each exchange transaction which takes place on a market must also be taken into account. Again, in certain markets, e.g., produce exchanges, a technique is devised for minimizing these contract costs; but they are not eliminated. It is true that contracts are not eliminated when there is a firm but they are greatly reduced. A factor of production (or the owner thereof) does not have to make a series of contracts with the factors with whom he is co-operating within the firm, as would be necessary, of course, if this co-operation were as a direct result of the working of the price mechanism. For this series of contracts is substituted one [contract]. At this stage, it is important to note the character of the contract into which a factor enters that is employed within a firm. The contract is one whereby the factor, for a certain remuneration (which may be fixed or fluctuating), agrees to obey the directions of an entrepreneur within certain limits. The essence of the contract is that it should only state the limits to the powers of the entrepreneur. Within these limits, he can therefore direct the other factors of production.

There are, however, other disadvantages—or costs—of using the price mechanism. It may be desired to make a long-term contract for the supply of some article or service. This may be due to the fact that if one contract is made for a longer period, instead of several shorter ones, then certain costs of making each contract will be avoided. Or, owing to the risk attitude of the people concerned, they may prefer to make a long rather than a short-term contract. Now, owing to the difficulty of forecasting, the longer the period of the contract is for the supply of the commodity or service, the less possible, and indeed, the less desirable it is for the person purchasing to specify what the other contracting party is expected to do. It may well be a matter of indifference to the person supplying the service or commodity which of several courses of action is taken, but not to the purchaser of that service or commodity. But the purchaser will not know which of these several courses he will want the supplier to take. Therefore, the service which is being provided is expressed in general terms, the exact details being left until a later date. All that is stated in the contract is the limits to what the persons supplying the commodity or service is expected to do. The details of what the supplier is expected to do [are] not stated in the contract but [are] decided later by the purchaser. When the direction of resources (within the limits of the contract) becomes dependent on the buyer in this way, that relationship which I term a "firm" may be obtained. A firm is likely therefore to emerge in those cases where a very short-term contract would be unsatisfactory. It is obviously of more importance in the case of services—labor—than it is in the case of the buying of commodities. In the case of commodities, the main items can be stated in advance and the details which will be decided later will be of minor significance.

We may sum up this section of the argument by saying that the operation of a market costs something and by forming an organization and allowing some authority (an "entrepreneur") to direct the resources, certain marketing costs are saved. The entrepreneur has to carry out his function at less cost, taking into account the fact that he may get factors of production at a lower price than the market transactions which he supersedes, because it is always possible to revert to the open market if he fails to do this.

Sir John Hicks
(1904-1989)

One of the giants in the field of economics was J.R. Hicks. He extended technical economics in a variety of directions, contributing to both microeconomics and macroeconomics. Two of his books, The Theory of Wages *(1932, revised 1963) and* Value and Capital *(1939), developed the neoclassical theory of distribution to its logical conclusion and his work on macroeconomics developed a model that is used in intermediate macroeconomics. Hicks won a Nobel prize in 1972.*

In this selection from his Theory of Wages, *Hicks specifies the conditions under which a firm will hire workers. It was an early clear statement of the marginal conditions for equilibrium in the resource market. Notice as you read it that after going through the analytics, Hicks carefully limits the direct applicability of the analysis, stating that "the real labor market is scarcely ever in equilibrium in the sense considered here."*

John R. Hicks. 1932. *The Theory of Wages.* London: Macmillan & Co., Ltd., pp. 4-9, 14-19.

Wage Theory: Basic Forces

The interaction of supply and demand on the labor market is a problem which will have to occupy a good deal of our attention. All buying and selling have some features in common; but nevertheless differences do exist between the ways in which things are bought and sold on different markets. Organized produce markets differ from wholesale trade of the ordinary type; both of these differ from retail trade, and from sale by tender or by auction. The labor market is yet another type. It has been the usual practice of economists to concentrate their attention on those features of exchange which are common to all markets; and to dismiss the differences between markets with a brief reminder that markets may be more or less "perfect." There is little doubt that in doing so they did seize on the really significant thing; the general working of supply and demand is a great deal more important than the differences between markets. But this course meant the almost complete neglect of some factors which appear at first sight very important indeed; the fact that they are really less important than those aspects which were discussed was rarely demonstrated clearly.

When an attempt is made to apply to the labor market the ordinary principles of price determination—without making allowance for the type of market—the result appears at first sight very odd. Wages, say the textbooks, tend to that level where demand and supply are equal. If supply exceeds demand, some men will be unemployed, and in their efforts to regain employment they will reduce the wages they ask to that level which makes it just worthwhile for employers to take them on. If demand exceeds supply, employers will be unable to obtain all the labor they require, and will therefore offer higher wages in order to attract labor from elsewhere.

Now this, as I hope to make abundantly clear, is quite a good simplified model of the labor market. So far as general tendencies are concerned, wages do turn out on the whole very much as if they were determined in this manner. . . .

We can begin by confining our attention to a labor market in equilibrium. Let us suppose that a level of wages is fixed so that demand and supply balance, and thus there is no tendency for wages to rise or to fall. Let us suppose, further, that this balancing of demand and supply is brought about, not by compensating fluctuations of the demand from particular firms, but by the demand from each firm being stationary, because no employer has any incentive to vary the number of men he takes on. It is necessary for us to adopt this abstract and rigorous conception of equilibrium, since otherwise we should not be effectively ruling out the difficulties of change, but should still be faced with very much the same kind of problem which confronts us in the case of a rise or fall in wages.

We have thus to examine the conditions of full equilibrium in the labor market, assuming the supply of laborers given, and their efficiencies given and equal. This enables us finally to isolate the pure problem of demand. It is true that we only achieve this isolation at the expense of a series of highly artificial assumptions; but in economics, as in other sciences, abstraction is usually the condition of clear thinking. The complications created by the things we have left out can be reintroduced later.

Conditions of Equilibrium

The first of the necessary conditions of equilibrium is that every man should receive the same wage—subject at any rate to allowances for "other advantages" and possibly for costs of movement (but these things also we neglect at present). If wages are not equal, then it will clearly be to the advantage of an employer who is paying a higher level of wages to dismiss his present employees, and to replace them by other men who had been receiving less. If he offers a wage somewhere between the two previously existing levels, he will both lower his own costs (and consequently improve his own situation) and successfully attract the new men, since he is offering them a higher wage than they received before. So long as such transfers can be made advantageously to both parties entering upon the new contract, there is no equilibrium; since someone can always disturb it to his own advantage. Equal wages are a necessary condition of equilibrium in a market governed by our present assumptions.

The second condition is much more critical. The only wage at which equilibrium is possible is a wage which equals the value of the marginal product of the laborers. At any given wage it will pay employers best to take on that number of laborers which makes their marginal product—that is to say, the difference between the total physical product which is actually secured and that which would have been secured from the same quantity of other resources if the number of laborers had been increased or diminished by one—equal in value to the wage. In this way the demand for labor of each employer is determined, and the total demand of all employers is determined from it by addition. Since in equilibrium it is necessary that the total demand should equal the total supply, the wage must be that which just enables the total number of laborers available to be employed. This must equal the value of the marginal product of the laborers available.

The conventional proof of the marginal productivity proposition is simple enough. It follows from the most fundamental form of the law of diminishing returns that an increased quantity of labor applied to a fixed quantity of other resources will yield a diminished marginal product. Thus, if the employer were to take on a number of laborers so large that their marginal product was not worth the wage which has to be paid, he would soon find that the number was excessive. By reducing the number he employed, he would reduce his total production, and therefore (under competitive conditions) his gross receipts. But at the same time he would reduce his expenditure, and since the wage was higher than the marginal product, he would reduce his expenditure more than his receipts, and so increase his profits. Similarly, he would not reduce his employment of labor to such a point as would make the wage less than the marginal product; for by so doing he would be reducing his receipts more than his expenditure, and so again diminishing his profits. The number of laborers which an employer will prefer to take on is that number which makes his profits a maximum, and that number is given by the equality of wages to the marginal product of the labor employed.

It is thus clear that the wage at which equilibrium is possible will vary in the opposite direction to changes in the total number of laborers available. If the number of laborers available on the market had been larger, the wage must have been lower; since the additional product secured by the employment of one of these extra laborers would be worth less than the previously given wage, and consequently it would not pay to employ these men unless the wage level was reduced. If the number had been less, employers would have had an incentive to demand more laborers at the given wage than would actually have been available, and their competition would therefore force up the level of wages. The only wage which is consistent with equilibrium is one which equals the value of the marginal product of the available labor.

This "Law of Marginal Productivity" is regarded by most modern economists as the most fundamental principle of the theory of wages. . . .

When an entrepreneur has to choose between two different methods of producing a given output, he may be expected to choose that which costs least. For, at any rate in the first place, anything which reduces his costs will raise his profits. If employers are not using the cheapest method of production available to them, they have an incentive to change; and so there is no equilibrium.

It is this condition of minimum cost of production per unit of output which leads us directly to the law of marginal productivity. For if we suppose the prices of all the factors of production to be given, the "least cost" combination of factors will be given by the condition that the marginal products of the factors are proportional to their prices. If the marginal product of factor A divided by the price of A is greater than marginal product of factor B divided by the price of B, then this means that it will be to the advantage of the entrepreneur to use a method of production which uses a little more of A and a little less of B, since in that way he will get a larger product for the same expenditure, or (what comes to the same thing) he will get an equal product at a lower cost.

This condition of the proportionality of marginal products is simply another means of expressing the necessity that the method employed in a position of equilibrium should be the cheapest method of reaching the desired result. No new principle whatever is introduced; so that in practical applications we can work with the condition of minimum cost, or with the condition of the proportionality of marginal products—whichever seems more significant in the particular case.

It must, however, be observed that the above condition only states that the marginal products are proportional to the prices of the factors—it does not say that the prices *equal* the values of the marginal products. So far as the choice of methods of production is concerned, it appears that the prices of the factors might exceed, or all fall short of, the values of the marginal products—so long as they do it in the same proportion. But if this were to be the case, it would be possible for the entrepreneur to increase his profits by expanding or contracting production without changing his methods. The condition of equality between price and cost of production would not be satisfied.

When we allow for the variability of methods of production, there is thus another way in which changes in wages may affect the demand for labor. A rise in wages will make labor expensive relatively to other factors of production, and will thus encourage entrepreneurs to use methods which employ less labor and more of these other factors. And this evidently applies in exactly the same way to industry as a whole, as it does to particular industries. The more extensive the rise in wages the more substitution will take place. For exactly the same reason, a fall in wages will lead to substitution in the reverse direction.

The law of marginal productivity, in its usual form, is simply a convenient means whereby the statement of the two tendencies we have been discussing can be combined. On the one hand, the returns to other resources than labor tend to equality in their different applications (the tendency which alone is taken account of in the formulation of "net productivity"); on the other hand, employers can modify the methods which they employ in their businesses, and the relative profitability of different methods depends on the relative prices of the factors of production. For some purposes it is convenient to use the conventional formulation, which brings together the two tendencies, and enables us to manipulate them together; but for a good many other purposes it is convenient to treat them separately.

There can be no full equilibrium unless the wages of labor equal its marginal product; since, if this equality is not attained, it means that someone has open to him an opportunity of gain which he is not taking. Either employers will be able to find an advantage in varying the methods of production they use, or investors and other owners of property will be able to benefit themselves by transferring the resources under their control from one branch of production to another. But we cannot go on from this to conclude that this equality of wages and marginal products will actually be found in practice; for the real labor market is scarcely ever in equilibrium in the sense considered here. In actual practice, changes in methods are continually going on; and resources are continually being transferred from one industry to another, or new resources being put at the disposal of industry, which are not uniformly distributed among the various branches of production. This ceaseless change is partly a consequence of changes in the ultimate determinants of economic activity—those things which we have to take as the final data of economic enquiry—changes in tastes, changes in knowledge, changes in the natural environment, and in the supply and efficiency of the factors of production generally. As these things change, so the marginal product of labor changes with them; and these changes in marginal productivity exert pressure, in one direction or the other, upon the level of wages.

David Ricardo

(1772-1823)

In most history of thought books, David Ricardo is seen as the successor of Adam Smith, the preeminent British economist of the era. A stockbroker by trade, he produced economic writing that was highly abstract and often difficult to follow. But that very abstraction made his writing seem insightful, and it cleared up a number of questions that had vexed economists. Ricardo is most famous for his theory of rent, which provided the basis, later, for the marginal productivity theory of neoclassical writers. Interestingly, the limitation on land that existed in England was not the case in the United States because in the United States land was relatively free in the West.

This selection gives you a good sense of Ricardo's writing. It is one of the earliest clear statements of what rent is and of how the marginal product of land will determine the price of land, providing rent to all other users.

As you read this selection, it will be useful to remember that the symbol £ denotes a unit of English money (like the U.S. $). Also, he discusses "corn," by which term the English mean grain, in terms of a unit of measurement, the "quarter." We have substituted the word "measure" for "quarter" rather than go through all the calculations to translate this into a specific term current readers would quickly grasp (one quarter = 8 bushels; one bushel = 2150.4 cubic inches, and on and on).

David Ricardo. 1817. *Principles of Political Economy and Taxation*. London: J. Murray.

Rent

Rent is that portion of the produce of the earth which is paid to the landlord for the use of the original and indestructible powers of the soil. It is often, however, confounded with the interest and profit of capital, and, in popular language, the term is applied to whatever is annually paid by a farmer to his landlord. If, of two adjoining farms of the same extent, and of the same natural fertility, one had all the conveniences of farming buildings, and, besides, were properly drained and manured, and advantageously divided into hedges, fences, and walls, while the other had none of these advantages, more remuneration would naturally be paid for the use of one, than for the use of the other; yet in both cases the remuneration would be called rent. But it is evident, that a portion only of the money annually to be paid for the improved farm, would be given for the original and indestructible powers of the soil; the other portion would be paid for the use of the capital which had been employed in ameliorating the quality of the land, and in erecting such buildings as were necessary to secure and preserve the produce. Adam Smith sometimes speaks of rent, in the strict sense to which I am desirous of confining it, but more often in the popular sense in which the term is usually employed. He tells us, that the demand for timber, and its consequent high price, in the more southern countries of Europe caused a rent to be paid for forests in Norway, which could before afford no rent. Is it not, however, evident, that the person who paid what he thus calls rent, paid it in consideration of the valuable commodity which was then standing on the land, and that he actually repaid himself with a profit, by the sale of the timber? If indeed, after the timber was removed, any compensation were paid to the landlord for the use of the land, for the purpose of growing timber or any other produce, with a view to future demand such compensation might justly be called rent, because it would be paid for the productive powers of the land; but in the case stated by Adam Smith, the compensation was paid for the liberty of removing and selling the timber, and not for the liberty of growing it.

On the first settling of a country, in which there is an abundance of fertile land, a very small proportion of which is required to be cultivated for the support of the actual population, or indeed can be cultivated with the capital which the population can command, there will be no rent; for no one would pay for the use of land, when there was an abundant quantity not yet appropriated, and, therefore, at the disposal of whosoever might choose to cultivate it.

If all land had the same properties, if it were unlimited in quantity, and uniform in quality, no charge could be made for its use, unless where it possessed peculiar advantages of situation. It is only, then, because land is not unlimited in quantity and uniform in quality, and because in the progress of population, land of an inferior quality, or less advantageously situated, is called into cultivation, that rent is ever paid for the use of it. When in the progress of society, land of the second degree of fertility is taken into cultivation, rent immediately commences on that of the first quality, and the amount of that rent will depend on the difference in the quality of those two portions of land.

When land of the third quality is taken into cultivation, rent immediately commences on the second, and it is regulated as before, by the difference in their productive powers. At the same time, the rent of the first quality will rise, for that must always be above the rent of the second, by the difference between the produce which they yield with a given quantity of capital and labor. With every step in the progress of population, which shall oblige a country to have recourse to land of a worse quality, to enable it to raise its supply of food—rent, on all the more fertile land, will rise.

Thus suppose land—No. 1, 2, 3—to yield with an equal employment of capital and labor, a net produce of 100, 90, and 80 [measures] of corn. In a new country, where there is an abundance of fertile land compared with the population, and where therefore it is only necessary to cultivate No. 1, the whole net produce will belong to the cultivator, and will be the profits of the stocks which he advances. As soon as population had so far increased as to make it necessary to cultivate No. 2, from which 90 [measures] only can be obtained after supporting the laborers, rent would commence on No. 1; for either there must be two rates of profit on agricultural capital, or 10 [measures], or the value of 10 [measures] must be withdrawn from the produce of No. 1, for some other purpose. Whether the proprietor of the land, or any other person, cultivated No. 1, these 10 [measures] would equally constitute rent; for the cultivator of No. 2 would get the same result with his capital, whether he cultivated No. 1, paying 10 [measures] for rent, or continued to cultivate No. 2, paying no rent. In the same manner it might be shown that when No. 3 is brought into cultivation, the rent of No. 2 must be 10 [measures], or the value of 10 [measures], whilst the rent of No. 1 would rise to 20 [measures]; for the cultivator of No. 3 would have the same profits whether he paid 20 [measures] for the rent of No. 1, 10 [measures] for the rent of No. 2, or cultivated No. 3 free of all rent.

It often, and, indeed commonly happens, that before No. 2, 3, 4, or 5, or the inferior lands are cultivated, capital can be employed more productively on those lands which are already in cultivation. It may perhaps be found, that by doubling the original capital employed on No. 1, though the produce will not be doubled—will not be increased by 100 [measures], it may be increased by 85 [measures]—and that this quantity exceeds what could be obtained by employing the same capital, on land No. 3.

In such case, capital will be preferably employed on the old land, and will equally create a rent; for rent is always the difference between the produce obtained by the employment of equal quantities of capital and labor. If with a capital of £1,000 a tenant obtain[s] 100 [measures] of wheat from his land, and by the employment of a second capital of £1,000, he obtain[s] a further return of 85, his landlord would have the power at the expiration of his lease, of obliging him to pay 15 [measures] or an equivalent value for additional rent, for there cannot be two rates of profit. If he is satisfied with a diminution of 15 [measures] in the return for his second £1,000 it is because no employment more profitable can be found for it. The common rate of profit would be in that proportion and if the original tenant refused, some other person would be found willing to give all which exceeded that rate of profit to the owner of the land from which he derived it.

If, then, good land existed in a quantity much more abundant than the production of food for an increasing population required, or if capital could be indefinitely employed without a diminished return on the old land, there could be no rise of rent; for rent invariably proceeds from the employment of an additional quantity of labor with a proportionally less return.

The exchangeable value of all commodities, whether they be manufactured, or the produce of the mines, or the produce of land, is always regulated, not by the less quantity of labor that will suffice for their production under circumstances highly favorable, and exclusively enjoyed by those who have peculiar facilities of production; but by the greater quantity of labor necessarily bestowed on their production by those who have no such facilities; by those who continue to produce them under the most unfavorable circumstances, the most unfavorable under which the quantity of produce required, renders it necessary to carry on the production.

It is true, that on the best land, the same produce would still be obtained with the same labor as before, but its value would be enhanced in consequence of the diminished returns obtained by those who employed fresh labor and stock on the less fertile land. Notwithstanding, then, that the advantages of fertile over inferior lands are in no case lost, but only transferred from the cultivator, or consumer, to the landlord, yet since more labor is required on the inferior lands, and since it is from such land only that we are enabled to furnish ourselves with the additional supply of raw produce, the comparative value of that produce will continue permanently above the former level, and make it exchange for more hats, cloth, shoes, and so forth, in the production of which no such additional quantity of labor is required.

The reason, then, why raw produce rises in comparative value, is because more labor is employed in the production of the last portion obtained, and not because a rent is paid to the landlord. The value of corn is regulated by the quantity of labor bestowed on its production on that quality of land, or with that portion of capital, which pays no rent. Corn is not high because a rent is paid, but a rent is paid because corn is high; and it has been justly observed, that no reduction would take place in the price of corn, although landlords should forego the whole of their rent. Such a measure would only enable some farmers to live like gentlemen, but would not diminish the quantity of labor necessary to raise raw produce on the least productive land in cultivation.

Nothing is more common than to hear of the advantages which the land possesses over every other source of useful produce, on account of the surplus which it yields in the form of rent. Yet when land is most abundant, when most productive, and most fertile, it yields no rent; and it is only when its powers decay, and less is yielded in return for labor, that a share of the original produce of the more fertile portions is set apart for rent. It is singular that this quality in the land, which should have been noticed as an imperfection, compared with the natural agents by which manufacturers are assisted, should have been pointed out as constituting its peculiar pre-eminence. If air, water, the elasticity of steam, and the pressure of the atmosphere, were of various qualities; if they could be appropriated, and each quality existed only in moderate abundance, they, as well as the land, would afford a rent, as the successive qualities were brought into use. With every worse quality employed, the value of the commodities in the manufacture of which they were used, would rise, because equal quantities of labor would be less productive. Man would do more by the sweat of his brow, and nature perform less; and the land would be no longer pre-eminent for its limited powers.

Frank H. Knight

(1885-1992)

Frank Knight was introduced earlier. This selection is from his book The Economic Organization *and discusses the role of economic profit in the economic process. Notice how he distinguishes monopoly gain from profit. He also explains that insurable risk does not lead to profit; it is only uninsurable risk that involves uncertainty that leads to profit.*

Frank H. Knight. 1951. *The Economic Organization*. New York: Kelley & Millman, Inc., pp. 118-21.

Profit

. . . Profit is a difference—positive in the case of "profit" and negative in the case of "loss"—between the income realized from the sale of a product and the total cost incurred in producing it, including in cost payment at the ordinary competitive rates for whatever personal service or use of his own property the producer himself puts into the productive operations, as well as his actual outlays for the services and property of other persons. Such differences arise because the process of distribution, or evaluating the productive services entering into a product, does not work with perfect accuracy. If this process did work with unfailing precision, the product value would be exactly distributed among the productive services, including those furnished by the owner of the business, and no profit or loss outside of payment for the owner's services would exist. The whole theory of normal price rests on this "tendency" of price and cost of production to be equal which is the negation of profit.

. . . [T]he reason for the inaccuracy of distribution and the occurrence of profit is essentially the inaccurate forecasting of demand by producers, and to a lesser degree the impossibility of predicting the physical result of a productive operation and so controlling it with precision. The latter cause applies especially to agriculture and industries affected by weather conditions. It is fairly apparent that if businessmen could foresee future conditions exactly, and if the relations between them were those of competition only, cost and price would always be equal: there would be no pure profit. We are concerned here with the first of these two phenomena, errors in estimating conditions and in making adjustments to them. The existence of conditions other than those of competition implies *monopoly gain,* a form of income often included under profit, but of a very different character from that now under discussion.

All that is here to be added to the discussion of the theory of profit [are] a few observations on the nature of risk and uncertainty or the reasons for inaccuracy in prediction. The first of these observations is that not all "risks" necessarily give rise to profit, or loss. Many kinds can be *insured against,* which eliminates them as factors of uncertainty. The principle of insurance is the application of the "law of large numbers," that in a large group of trials the proportion of occurrences to non-occurrences of a contingent event tends to be constant. The death of a particular individual, burning of a particular building, loss of a particular ship at sea, and so forth, is uncertain; but in a group of a hundred thousand similar cases the proportion of losses is very accurately predictable. There are many ways of applying this principle, in addition to the various forms of insurance called by the name. A large corporation, by broadening the scale of its operations, distributes and reduces its risks. Concentration of speculation in the hands of a professional class tends to make errors in judgment largely cancel out. The essential point for profit theory is that insofar as it is possible to insure by any method against risk, the cost of carrying it is converted into a constant element of expense, and it ceases to be a cause of profit and loss.

The uncertainties which persist as causes of profit are those which are uninsurable because there is no objective measure of the probability of gain or loss. This is true especially of the prediction of demand. It not only cannot be foreseen accurately, but there is no basis for saying that the probability of its being of one sort rather than another is of a certain value—as we can compute the chance that a man will live to a certain age. Situations in regard to which business judgment must be exercised do not repeat themselves with sufficient conformity to type to make possible a computation of probability.

It is further to be observed that a large part of the risks which give rise to profit are connected with progressive social change. Changes in demand and in methods of production, especially, cause large gains to some enterprises, and losses to others. And the work of exploring for and developing new natural resources is fraught with the greatest unpredictability, with corresponding frequency of large profits or losses. It is to be kept in mind that such changes do not merely "happen," giving rise to profit. The possibility of securing a profit and consequence of a change induces business men to make large expenditures in bringing about changes in every field. In the main, no doubt, changes thus induced are improvements, and represent real social progress. This is true of the discovery of natural resources and of more effective productive methods. It is not so certain in connection with the promotion of changes in wants. . . . The theory of individualism is especially weak at this point and . . . a large fraction of the political interference found necessary has to do with safeguarding the maintenance and improvement of society. Where distinctively human values are involved, the working of the profit motive is likely to give very unsatisfactory results.

The nature and source of *monopoly* [and *gain* are different]. . . . Where a producer can in any way prevent other persons from using productive resources in making a product equivalent to his own or can bar them from using especially effective processes, he can make a gain by restricting output. It is to be observed that any individual rendering a unique personal service—such as an artist, or a professional man with a reputation causing his services to be in special demand—has a monopoly of a very distinctive and secure variety. . . . [U]niqueness is the very essence of monopoly. The greater part of advertising represents an effort to build up an impression of uniqueness, to establish what may be called a "psychological" uniqueness, in particular products, and thus to secure a degree of monopoly power.

John Stuart Mill
(1806-1873)

You have been introduced to John Stuart Mill earlier. Here we have chosen a brief selection which Mill wrote in response to socialist writers who were arguing that private property was the root of the problems of capitalist society. Mill, who was sympathetic to the values and goals of the socialists, felt that a market economy based on private property offered the best hope for society, especially if there were population control and universal education.

John Stuart Mill. 1848 (1871). "Of Property," in *Principles of Political Economy, with some of their Applications to Social Philosophy*, Book II, Chapter 1. London: Longmans, Green, & Co., pp. 208-209.

Private Property Has Not Had Fair Trial

The principle of private property has never yet had a fair trial in any country; and less so, perhaps, in this country [England] than in some others. The social arrangements of modern Europe commenced from a distribution of property which was the result, not of just partition, or acquisition by industry, but of conquest and violence; and notwithstanding what industry has been doing for many centuries to modify the work of force, the system still retains many and large traces of its origin. The laws of property have never yet conformed to the principles on which the justification of private property rests. They have made property of things which never ought to be property, and absolute property where only a qualified property ought to exist. They have not held the balance fairly between human beings, but have heaped impediments upon some, to give advantage to others; they have purposely fostered inequalities, and prevented all from starting fair in the race. That all should indeed start on perfectly equal terms, is inconsistent with any law of private property; but if as much pains as has been taken to aggravate the inequality of chances arising from the natural working of the principle had been taken to temper that inequality by every means not subversive of the principle itself; if the tendency of legislation had been to favor the diffusion, instead of the concentration of wealth—to encourage the subdivision of the large masses, instead of striving to keep them together—the principle of individual property would have been found to have no necessary connection with the physical and social evils which almost all Socialist writers assume to be inseparable from it.

Private property, in every defense made of it, is supposed to mean the guarantee to individuals of the fruits of their own labor and abstinence. The guarantee to them of the fruits of the labor and abstinence of others, transmitted to them without any merit or exertion of their own, is not of the essence of the institution, but a mere incidental consequence, which, when it reaches a certain height, does not promote, but conflicts with the ends which render private property legitimate. To judge of the final destination of the institution of property, we must suppose everything rectified which causes the institution to work in a manner opposed to that equitable principle of proportion between remuneration and exertion, on which in every vindication of it that will bear the light, it is assumed to be grounded. We must also suppose two conditions realized, without which neither Communism nor any other laws or institutions could make the condition of the mass of mankind other than degraded and miserable. One of these conditions is universal education; the other, a due limitation of the numbers of the community. With these, there could be no poverty even under the present social institutions. . . .

Henry George
(1839-1897)

Every era has its lay economist, journalist, or businessperson who writes about economics and whose writing achieves a certain notoriety. Henry George was such a person (a newspaperman) in the last quarter of the 19th century. He developed the idea that ownership of land was the chief cause of poverty among people who did not own land, and he strongly advocated the taxation of land rental values as a way for government to obtain income.

It will likely be difficult reading for many of you, not so much because the ideas it discusses are difficult, but, rather, because of its literary style, which is somewhat dense, and because of some of the jumps in logic that he makes. We include it because (1) it is from an important popular book in the 1890s, and (2) because it ties together many of the ideas about factor payments and justice that the textbook touches on.

Henry George. 1879. *Progress and Poverty*. New York: Modern Library, pp. xii-xvii.

Progress and Poverty: Preface

Beginning with a brief statement of facts which suggest this inquiry I proceed to examine the explanation currently given in the name of political economy of the reason why in spite of the increase of productive power wages tend to the minimum of a bare living. This examination shows that the current doctrine of wages is founded upon a misconception; that, in truth, wages are produced by the labor for which they are paid and should other things being equal, increase with the number of laborers. Here the inquiry meets a doctrine which is the foundation and center of most important economic theories, and which has powerfully influenced thought in all directions—the Malthusian doctrine, that population tends to increase faster than subsistence. Examination, however, shows that this doctrine has no real support either in fact or in analogy, and that when brought to a decisive test it is utterly disproved.

Thus far the results of the inquiry, though extremely important, are mainly negative. They show that current theories do not satisfactorily explain the connection of poverty with material progress, but throw no light upon the problem itself, beyond showing that its solution must be sought in the laws which govern the distribution of wealth. It therefore becomes necessary to carry the inquiry into this field. A preliminary review shows that the three laws of distribution must necessarily correlate with each other, which as laid down by the current political economy they fail to do, and an examination of the terminology in use reveals the confusion of thought by which this discrepancy has been slurred over. Proceeding then to work out the laws of distribution, I first take up the law of rent. This, it is readily seen, is correctly apprehended by the current political economy. But it is also seen that the full scope of this law has not been appreciated, and that it involves as corollaries the laws of wages and interest—the cause which determines what part of the produce shall go to the land owner necessarily determining what part shall be left for labor and capital. Without resting here, I proceed to an independent deduction of the laws of interest and wages. I have stopped to determine the real cause and justification of interest, and to point out a source of much misconception—the confounding of what are really the profits of monopoly with the legitimate earnings of capital. Then returning to the main inquiry, investigation shows that interest must rise and fall with wages, and depends ultimately upon the same thing as rent—the margin of cultivation or point in production where rent begins. A similar but independent investigation of the law of wages yields similar harmonious results. Thus the three laws of distribution are brought into mutual support and harmony, and the fact that with material progress rent everywhere advances is seen to explain the fact that wages and interest do not advance.

What causes this advance of rent is the next question that arises, and it necessitates an examination of the effect of material progress upon the distribution of wealth. Separating the factors of material progress into increase of population and improvements in the arts, it is first seen that increase in population tends constantly, not merely by reducing the margin of cultivation, but by localizing the economies and powers which come with increased population, to increase the proportion of the aggregate produce which is taken in rent, and to reduce that which goes as wages and interest. Then eliminating increase of population, it is seen that improvement in the methods and powers of production tends in the same direction, and, land being held as private property, would produce in a stationary population all the effects attributed by the Malthusian doctrine to pressure of population. And then a consideration of the effects of the continuous increase in land values which thus spring from material progress reveals in the speculative advance inevitably begotten when land is private property a derivative but most powerful cause of the increase of rent and the crowding down of wages. Deduction shows that this cause must necessarily produce periodical industrial depressions, and induction proves the conclusion; while from the analysis which has thus been made it is seen that the necessary result of material progress, land being private property, is, no matter what the increase in population, to force laborers to wages which give but a bare living.

This identification of the cause that associates poverty with progress points to the remedy, but it is to so radical a remedy that I have next deemed it necessary to inquire whether there is any other remedy. Beginning the investigation again from another starting point, I have passed in examination the measures and tendencies currently advocated or trusted in for the improvement of the condition of the laboring masses. The result of this investigation is to prove the preceding one, as it shows that nothing short of making land common property can permanently relieve poverty and check the tendency of wages to the starvation point.

The question of justice now naturally arises, and the inquiry passes into the field of ethics. An investigation of the nature and basis of property shows that there is a fundamental and irreconcilable difference between property in things which are the product of labor and property in land; that the one has a natural basis and sanction while the other has none, and that the recognition of exclusive property in land is necessarily a denial of the right of property in the products of labor. Further investigation shows that private property in land always has, and always must, as development proceeds, lead to the enslavement of the laboring class; that land owners can make no just claim to compensation if society choose to resume its right; that so far from private property in land being in accordance with the natural perceptions of men, the very reverse is true, and that in the United States we are already beginning to feel the effects of having admitted this erroneous and destructive principle.

The inquiry then passes to the field of practical statesmanship. It is seen that private property in land, instead of being necessary to its improvement and use, stands in the way of improvement and use, and entails an enormous waste of productive forces; that the recognition of the common right to land involves no shock or dispossession, but is to be reached by the simple and easy method of abolishing all taxation save that upon land values. And this an inquiry into the principles of taxation shows to be, in all respects, the best subject of taxation.

A consideration of the effects of the change proposed then shows that it would enormously increase production; would secure justice in distribution; would benefit all classes; and would make possible an advance to a higher and nobler civilization.

The inquiry now rises to a wider field, and recommences from another starting point. For not only do the hopes which have been raised come into collision with the widespread idea that social progress is possible only by slow race improvement, but the conclusions we have arrived at assert certain laws which, if they are really natural laws, must be manifest in universal history. As a final test, it therefore becomes necessary to work out the law of human progress, for certain great facts which force themselves on our attention, as soon as we begin to consider this subject, seem utterly inconsistent with what is now the current theory. This inquiry shows that differences in civilization are not due to differences in individuals, but rather to differences in social organization; that progress, always kindled by association, always passes into retrogression as inequality is developed; and that even now, in modern civilization, the causes which have destroyed all previous civilizations are beginning to manifest themselves, and that mere political democracy is running its course toward anarchy and despotism. But it also identifies the law of social life with the great moral law of justice, and, proving previous conclusions, shows how retrogression may be prevented and a grander advance begun. This ends the inquiry. The final chapter will explain itself.

The great importance of this inquiry will be obvious. If it has been carefully and logically pursued, its conclusions completely change the character of political economy, give it the coherence and certitude of a true science, and bring it into full sympathy with the aspirations of the masses of men, from which it has long been estranged. What I have done in this book, if I have correctly solved the great problem I have sought to investigate, is, to unite the truth perceived by the school of Smith and Ricardo to the truth perceived by the schools of Proudhon and Lasalle; to show that *laissez faire* (in its full true meaning) opens the way to a realization of the noble dreams of socialism; to identify social law with moral law, and to disprove ideas which in the minds of many cloud grand and elevating perceptions. . . .

George Stigler

(1911-1992)

Another of the great Chicago economists was George Stigler, who taught at the University of Chicago at the same time as Milton Friedman. Friedman was relatively short, Stigler tall; and the two made quite a pair as they walked down the paths and halls of the University. While their sizes may have differed, their views did not. Both were libertarian, iconoclastic, and witty. Stigler wrote a variety of papers, mainly to economists, and these papers not only expounded economics but also explored the limits of economics, and what happens when economics is pushed too far.

Stigler is most known for his work on the economics of information and regulation where he emphasized the limits of political action. He won a Nobel prize in 1982. Stigler was known both for his brilliance as an economist and for his wit. In this satirical piece, which was written at a number of different, interwoven, levels, he talks about truth in the teaching of economics. But he has a more serious point to make, as becomes clear in his reference to Ralph Nader, the consumer advocate. The point is that laws and regulations have dynamic long-run effects. For example, when the truth in teaching law was built into expectations, students were forbidden to take notes—so that professors could introduce new ideas. And the longer the run, the greater the effects: notice the end of the piece, where Stigler essentially predicts that were such a law to be passed, universities would stop receiving tuition and instead finance themselves from government grants.

In the selection Stigler cites several imaginary court cases. It is not necessary to decipher the abbreviations in the citations or to try to look up the cases.

George Stigler. 1984. "A Sketch of the History of Truth in Teaching," in *The Intellectual and the Marketplace*, Enlarged Edition, Chapter 6. Cambridge, MA, and London, England: Harvard University Press, pp. 43-50.

A Sketch of the History of Truth in Teaching

The future is obscure, even to men of strong vision, and one would perhaps be wiser not to shoot arrows into it. For the arrows will surely hit targets that were never intended. Witness the arrow of consumerism.

It started simply enough: various people—and especially a young man named Nader—found automobiles less safe than they wished, and quite possibly than you would have wished. They demanded and in a measure obtained, if not safer cars, at least cars that were ostensibly safer. A considerable and expensive paraphernalia of devices became obligatory in new cars. These zealous patrons of the public furthermore insisted that defective products be corrected, and that damage arising in spite of the most conscientious efforts of the manufacturer should be his financial responsibility. Similar arrows were soon launched at a score of non vehicular industries.

This quiver of truth- and safety-minded arrows was thrown for a time at perfectly appropriate targets—businessmen accustomed to public abuse, who were naturally able to charge their customers for any amount of safety, frequent and successful lawsuits, and obloquy. But the arrows of reform pass through—if they hit at all—the targets at which they are aimed, and in 1973 they hit a professor. Evil day!

In that year a young man named Dascomb Henderson, a graduate of Harvard Business School (1969) and recently discharged as assistant treasurer of a respectable-sized corporation, sued his alma mater for imparting instruction since demonstrated to be false. This instruction—I will omit here its explicit and complex algebraic formulation—concerned the proper investment of working capital. One of Henderson's teachers at Harvard, a Professor Plessek, had thoroughly sold his students on a sure-fire method of predicting short-term interest rate movements, based upon a predictive equation incorporating recent movements of the difference between high- and low-quality bond prices, the stock of money (Plessek had a Chicago Ph.D.), the number of "everything is under control" speeches given by governors of the Federal Reserve Board in the previous quarter, and the full-employment deficit. It was established in the trial that the equation had worked tolerably well for the period 1960-1968 (and Henderson was exposed to this evidence in Plessek's course in the spring of 1969), but the data for 1969 and 1970, once analyzed, made it abundantly clear that the equation was capable of grotesquely erroneous predictions. Assistant treasurer Henderson, unaware of these later results, played the long-term bond market with his corporation's cash, and in the process the cash lost its surplus character. He was promptly discharged, learned of the decline of the Plessek model, and sued.

This was a new area of litigation, and Henderson's attorney deliberately pursued several lines of attack, in the hope that at least one would find favor with the court:

1. Professor Plessek had not submitted his theory to sufficient empirical tests. Had he tried it for the decade of the 1950s, he would have had less confidence in it.
2. Professor Plessek did not display proper scientific caution. Henderson's class notes recorded the sentence: "I'll stake my reputation as an econometrician that this model will not [engage in intercourse with] a portfolio manager." This was corroborated, with a different verb, by a classmate's notes.
3. Professor Plessek should have notified his former students once the disastrous performance of his theory in 1969 and 1970 became known.
4. Harvard University was grossly negligent in retaining (and hence certifying the professional competence of) an assistant professor whose work had received humiliating professional criticism (Journal of Business, April 1972). Instead, he had been promoted to associate professor in 1972.

The damages asked were $500,000 for impairment of earning power and $200,000 for humiliation.

Harvard and Professor Plessek asked for dismissal of the suit, claiming that it was frivolous and unfounded. Universities and teachers could not be held responsible for honest errors, or all instruction would be brought to a stop. Universities and professors could not be asked to disseminate new knowledge to previous students—this would be intolerably costly. In the lower court these defenses prevailed, and Judge MacIntosh (Harvard, LL.B. 1938) asserted that university instruction and publication were preserved from such attacks by the First Amendment, the principle of academic freedom, an absence of precedent for such a complaint, and the established unreliability of academic lectures. On appeal, however, Judge Howlson (Yale, LL.B. 1940) remanded the case for trial on the merits, and in the course of reversing Judge MacIntosh's decision, remarked: "It seems paradoxical beyond endurance to rule that a manufacturer of shampoos may not endanger a student's scalp but that a premier educational institution is free to stuff his skull with nonsense."

As the reader will know, Harvard and Professor Plessek won the case on the merits, but by a thin and foreboding margin. Only the facts that (1) the Plessek equation, as of 1969, looked about as good as most such equations, and (2) the plaintiff could not reasonably be expected to be informed of the failure of the equation as soon as two years after it was discovered—the lag in publication alone is this long—excused the errant professor. As for Harvard, it would have shared responsibility for the undisputed damage to the plaintiff if Plessek had been of slightly lower quality. So held the court of last resort, in a decision that professors read as carefully as a hostile book review.

The university world received the decision with what an elderly Englishman would call concern and I would call pandemonium. Professional schools—medicine as well as business—were quick to realize its implications. Within a breathless three weeks, a professor at Cornell's medical school had sent an explicit retraction of his treatment of Parkinson's disease to the last decade's graduates of the school. This proved to be only the first of a torrent of such actions; but well before that torrent had climaxed, at least ninety-five suits against universities and teachers had been filed. Along with the "recalls," as the retractions were called in honor of their automobile antecedents, the learned journals were flooded with statements of "errata" and confessions of error. A fair number of academic reputations fell suddenly and drastically.

The subsequent, explosively rapid expansion of litigation directed at error in teaching is not for this nonlegal writer to report. Many years and cases were required before a reasonably predictable set of rights and responsibilities could be established, and a man may find much to be angry about in these cases, whatever his position. That the lazy or stupid student was entitled to an exhaustive explanation for his failure in a course *(Anderson v. Regents,* 191 Cal. 426) was an intolerably expensive aberration—especially when the teacher was required to present a tape recording of the explanation. That a professor could not be held responsible for error in a field where truth and error frequently exchanged identities *(Neal v. Department of Sociology,* 419 Mich. 3), on the other hand, inevitably raised a challenge to the field to justify its existence. Rather than pursue either the main line of decisions or the aberrations, it seems preferable to look at the eventual effects of truth in teaching upon the universities. A conscientious observer must be cautious in his interpretation of the effect even though the present essay is clearly exempt from challenge *(President Bowen v. Assistant Professor Holland,* 329 N.J. 1121, a tenure case)—so the following remarks are best viewed as plausible hypotheses.

In general, the new responsibility rested heavily upon those most able to bear it: those fields in which classification of given material as true or excusably false versus inexcusably false was easiest to establish with near unanimity. Theological schools were virtually exempted, and, oddly enough, also computer science. Mathematics was exempted because one could always look up the answer, and political science because one couldn't. The branch of economics dealing with how to enrich a new nation ("economic development" was the title) was actually forbidden by the courts, on the ground that no university could pay for the damage its teachers did.

In those subjects where truth in teaching bore most heavily—those where incorrect knowledge was costly and demonstrable, as medicine, chemistry, and tax law— the classroom became a very different place. Students were *forbidden* by most universities to take notes, which were instead supplied by the teacher, and the sneaky device of a tape recorder with hidden microphone was combated vigorously, if not always successfully. Harvard's defense proved to have content: teachers were unwilling to introduce new ideas, but it can be argued that the net balance was favorable—much ancient nonsense also vanished, and courses often were completed in two weeks.

The learned journals underwent a remarkable transformation. Let me quote the introductory paragraph of an article on the nature of short-run price fluctuations in commodity prices *(Review of Economics and Statistics,* August 1978):

> The present essay presents a theory, with corroborating though inadequate evidence, that there is a set of nonrandom shortrun movements in the price of "wheat." (The actual commodity analyzed is secret but will be revealed to professors on written waiver of responsibility.) The present essay is concerned only with methodology. Only the crudest beginning has been made, and it would be irresponsibly rash to venture money on the hypothesis. Also, the hypothesis is virtually identical with Reslet's (1967); I contribute chiefly a more powerful statistical technique (due to S. Stigler 1973), which has its own limitations. The regressions have been calculated three times, on different computers, with similar results.[1] The author will welcome, but not be surprised at, valid criticisms of the paper.

The superscript 1 referred to a footnote inserted by the editor of the Review: "The Board of Overseers of Harvard University expresses concern at the measure of nonrandomness in the residuals, which, if the author were a Harvard professor, would require a full departmental review of the manuscript." No wonder one scholar complained that there was more warning against reading his article than against smoking marijuana cigarettes!

The longer-term effects of truth in teaching are another story, which I shall not seek even to summarize here. The historic step was the creation in 1981 of the Federal Bureau of Academic Reading, Writing, and Research (BARWR). This body soon established licenses for participation in scholarly activities, and the license became a prima facie defense against the charge of incompetence. No university that employed an unlicensed teacher could receive federal grants, which by 1985 averaged 99.7 percent of university revenue.

The BARWR has instituted rigorous standards for the conduct of learned journals and is now inquiring into the possibility of establishing subject matters (for example, communistic theory) that are prima facie evidence of incompetence.

John Stuart Mill

(1806-1873)

We've given you some background on John Stuart Mill in some of the other selections from Mill. His work, in many ways, represents a high point in classical economic writing which integrated social and political issues into its themes. Of all his writings none was received with greater hostility than The Subjection of Women *published in 1869. Mill completed this work two years after the death of his wife, Harriet Taylor, but waited nine years before publishing it because of its then controversial nature. At the time the thought that the two sexes should be considered equal was seen as almost heresy to the established order.*

John Stuart Mill. 1869. *The Subjection of Women*. London: Longman's Green Reader and Dyer, pp. 219, 262-65, 316-17.

The Subjection of Women

The object of this Essay is to explain as clearly as I am able, the grounds of an opinion which I have held from the very earliest period when I had formed any opinions at all on social or political matters, and which, instead of being weakened or modified, has been constantly growing stronger by the progress of reflection and the experience of life. That the principle which regulates the existing social relations between the two sexes—the legal subordination of one sex to the other—is wrong in itself, and now one of the chief hindrances to human improvement; and that it ought to be replaced by a principle of perfect equality, admitting no power or privilege on the one side, nor disability on the other.

The very words necessary to express the task I have undertaken, show how arduous it is. But it would be a mistake to suppose that the difficulty of the case must lie in the insufficiency or obscurity of the grounds of reason on which my conviction rests. The difficulty is that which exists in all cases in which there is a mass of feeling to be contended against. So long as an opinion is strongly rooted in the feelings, it gains rather than loses in stability by having a preponderating weight of argument against it. For if it were accepted as a result of argument, the refutation of the argument might shake the solidity of the conviction; but when it rests solely on feeling, the worse it fares in argumentative contest, the more persuaded its adherents are that their feeling must have some deeper ground, which the arguments do not reach; and while the feeling remains, it is always throwing up fresh intrenchments of argument to repair any breach made in the old. And there are so many causes tending to make the feelings connected with this subject the most intense and most deeply-rooted of all those which gather round and protect old institutions and customs, that we need not wonder to find them as yet less undermined and loosened than any of the rest by the progress Of the great modern spiritual and social transition; nor suppose that the barbarisms to which men cling longest must be less barbarisms than those which they earlier shake off.

* * * *

... [D]oes he hug himself in the consciousness of the power the law gives him, exact its legal rights to the utmost point which custom (the custom of men like himself) will tolerate, and take pleasure in using the power, merely to enliven the agreeable sense of possessing it. What is more; in the most naturally brutal and morally uneducated part of the lower classes, the legal slavery of the woman, and something in the merely physical subjection to their will as an instrument, causes them to feel a sort of disrespect and contempt towards their own wife which they do not feel towards any other woman, or any other human being, with whom they come in contact; and which makes her seem to them an appropriate subject for any kind of indignity. Let an acute observer of the signs of feeling, who has the requisite opportunities, judge for himself whether this is not the case: and if he finds that it is, let him not wonder at any amount of disgust and indignation that can be felt against institutions which lead naturally to this depraved state of the human mind.

We shall be told, perhaps, that religion imposes the duty of obedience; as every established fact which is too bad to admit of any other defense, is always presented to us as an injunction of religion. The Church, it is very true, enjoins it in her formularies, but it would be difficult to derive any such injunction from Christianity. We are told that St. Paul said, "Wives, obey your husbands": but he also said, "Slaves, obey your masters." It was not St. Paul's business, nor was it consistent with his object, the propagation of Christianity, to incite anyone to rebellion against existing laws. The Apostle's acceptance of all social institutions as he found them, is no more to be construed as a disapproval of attempts to improve them at the proper time, than his declaration, "The powers that be are ordained of God," gives his sanction to military despotism, and to that alone, as the Christian form of political government, or commands passive obedience to it. To pretend that Christianity was intended to stereotype existing forms of government and society, and protect them against change, to reduce it to the level of Islamism or of Brahminism. It is precisely because Christianity has not done this, that it has been the religion of the progressive portion of mankind, and Islamism, Brahminism, etc. have been those of the stationary portions or rather (for there is no such thing as a really stationary society) of the declining portions. There have been abundance of people, in all ages of Christianity, who tried to make it something of the same kind, to convert us into a sort of Christian Mussulmans, with the Bible for a Koran, prohibiting all improvement: and great has been their power, and many have had to sacrifice their lives in resisting them. But they have been resisted, and the resistance has made us what we are, and will yet make us what we are to be.

After what has been said respecting the obligation of obedience, it is almost superfluous to say anything concerning the more special point included in the general one—a woman's right to her own property; for I need not hope that this treatise can make any impression upon those who need anything to convince them that a woman's inheritance or gains ought to be as much her own after marriage as before. The rule is simple: whatever would be the husband's or wife's if they were not married, should be under their exclusive control during marriage; which need not interfere with the power to tie up property by settlement, in order to preserve it for children. Some people are sentimentally shocked at the idea of a separate interest in money matters, as inconsistent with the ideal fusion of two lives into one. For my own part, I am one of the strongest supporters of community of goods, when resulting from an entire unity of feeling in the owners, which makes all things common between them. But I have no relish for a community of goods resting on the doctrine, that what is mine is yours, but what is yours is not mine; and I should prefer to decline entering into such a compact with anyone, though I were myself the person to profit by it.

This particular injustice and oppression to women, which is, to common apprehensions, more obvious than all the rest, admits of remedy without interfering with any other mischiefs: and there can be little doubt that it will be one of the earliest remedied. Already, in many of the new and several of the old States of the American Confederation, provisions have been inserted even in the written Constitutions, securing to women equality of rights in this respect: and thereby improving materially the position, in the marriage relation, of those women at least who have property, by leaving them one instrument of power which they have not signed away, and preventing also the scandalous abuse of the marriage institution, which is perpetrated when a man entraps a girl into marrying him without a settlement, for the sole purpose of getting possession of her money. When the support of the family depends, not on property, but on earnings, the common arrangement, by which the man earns the income and the wife superintends the domestic expenditure, seems to me in general the most suitable division of labour between the two persons. If, in addition to the physical suffering of bearing children, and the whole responsibility of their care and education in early years the wife undertakes the careful and economical application of the husband's earnings to the general comfort of the family; she takes not only her fair share, but usually the larger share, of the bodily and mental exertion required by their joint existence. If she undertakes any additional portion, it seldom relieves her from this, but only prevents her from performing it properly. The care which she is herself disabled from taking of the children and the household, nobody else takes; those of the children who do not die, grow up as they best can, and the management of the household is likely to be so bad, as even in point of economy to be a great drawback from the value of the wife's earnings. In an otherwise just state of things, it is not, therefore, I think, a desirable custom, that the wife should contribute by her labour to the income of the family. In an unjust state of things, her doing so may be useful to her, by making her of more value in the eyes of the man who is legally her master; but, on the other hand, it enables him still farther to abuse his power, by forcing her to work, and leaving the support of the family to her exertions, while he spends most of his time in drinking and idleness. The *power* of earning is essential to the dignity of a woman, if she has not independent property. But if marriage were an equal contract, not implying the obligation of obedience; if the connexion were no longer enforced to the oppression of those to whom it is purely a mischief, but a separation, on just terms (I do not now speak of a divorce), could be obtained by any woman who was morally entitled to it; and if she would then find all honourable employments as freely open to her as to men; it would not be necessary for her protection, that during marriage she should make this particular use of her faculties. Like a man when he chooses a profession, so, when a woman marries, it may in general be understood that she makes choice of the management of a household, and the bringing up of a family, as the first call upon her exertions, during as many years of her life as may be required for the purpose; and that she renounces, not all other objects and occupations, but all which are not consistent with the requirements of this. The actual exercise, in a habitual or systematic manner, of outdoor occupations, or such as cannot be carried on at home, would by this principle be practically interdicted to the greater number of married women. But the utmost latitude ought to exist for the adaptation of general rules to individual suitabilities; and there ought to be nothing to prevent faculties exceptionally adapted to any other pursuit, from obeying their vocation notwithstanding marriage: due provision being made for supplying otherwise any falling-short which might become inevitable, in her full performance of the ordinary functions of mistress of a family. These things, if once opinion were rightly directed on the subject, might with perfect safety be left to be regulated by opinion, without any interference of law.

* * * *

. . . [W]hich it so often condemns them, by forbidding them to exercise the practical abilities which many of them are conscious of, in any wider field than one which to some of them never was, and to others is no longer, open. If there is anything vitally important to the happiness of human beings, it is that they should relish their habitual pursuit. This requisite of an enjoyable life is very imperfectly granted, or altogether denied, to a large part of mankind; and by its absence many a life is a failure, which is provided, in appearance, with every requisite of success. But if circumstances which society is not yet skillful enough to overcome, render such failures often for the present inevitable, society need not itself inflict them. The injudiciousness of parents, a youth's own inexperience, or the absence of external opportunities for the congenial vocation, and their presence for an uncongenial, condemn numbers of men to pass their lives in doing one thing reluctantly and ill, when there are other things which they could have done well and happily. But on women this sentence is imposed by actual law, and by customs equivalent to law. What, in unenlightened societies, colour, race, religion, or in the case of a conquered country, nationality, are to some men, sex is to all women; a peremptory exclusion from almost all honourable occupations, but either such as cannot be fulfilled by others, or such as those others do not think worthy of their acceptance.

Sufferings arising from causes of this nature usually meet with so little sympathy, that few persons are aware of the great amount of unhappiness even now produced by the feeling of a wasted life. The case will be even more frequent, as increased cultivation creates a greater and greater disproportion between the ideas and faculties of women, and the scope which society allows to their activity.

When we consider the positive evil caused to the disqualified half of the human race by their disqualification—first in the loss of the most inspiriting and elevating kind of personal enjoyment, and next in the weariness, disappointment, and profound dissatisfaction with life, which are so often the substitute for it; one feels that among all the lessons which men require for carrying on the struggle against the inevitable imperfections of their lot on earth, there is no lesson which they more need, than not to add to the evils which nature inflicts, by their jealous and prejudiced restrictions on one another. Their vain fears only substitute other and worse evils for those which they are idly apprehensive of: while every restraint on the freedom of conduct of any of their human fellow-creatures (otherwise than by making them responsible for any evil actually caused by it), dries up *pro tanto* [by just that much] the principal fountain of human happiness, and leaves the species less rich, to an inappreciable degree, in all that makes life valuable to the individual human being.

Jack Hirshleifer

(1925-)

From the 1950s through the 1970s, there were two schools that were known for their strong support of markets and opposition to regulation. These schools were the University of Chicago and the University of California at Los Angeles (UCLA). Milton Friedman and George Stigler were at the University of Chicago, Armen Alchian and Jack Hirshleifer were at UCLA. In this satirical piece Hirshleifer responds to critics of the market economy who argue that it creates false wants and then fulfills them by extending the argument to many more goods. (One such critic was John Kenneth Galbraith in "The Dependence Effect," earlier in this book.) The point at issue is, of course, where to draw the line.

Regulation of wants is a slippery slope, and Hirshleifer and other libertarians believe that once society starts down that slope, it will go much further than makes sense.

In the article, "SS" is a reference to the secret police of Adolf Hitler's dictatorship in Nazi Germany.

Jack Hirshleifer (under the pen name "Sir Epicure Mammon"). 1959. "The Sumptuary Manifesto." *Journal of Law and Economics*, Vol. II. October, pp. 120-23.

The Sumptuary Manifesto

Consumption . . . is a seamless web. If we ask about the chromium, we must ask about the cars. The questions that are asked about one part can be asked about all parts. The automobiles are too heavy, and they use irreplaceable lead? One can ask with equal cogency if we need to make all the automobiles that we now turn out . . . .

As with automobiles, so with everything else. In an opulent society the marginal urgency of all kinds of goods is low. It is easy to bring our doubts and questions to bear on the automobiles. But the case is not different for (say) that part of our food production which contributes not to nutrition but to obesity, that part of our tobacco which contributes not to comfort but to carcinoma and that part of our clothing which is designed not to cover nakedness but to suggest it. . . .

It is also suggested that uninhibited consumption has something to do with individual liberty. If we begin interfering with consumption, we shall be abridging a basic freedom.

I shan't dwell long on this. That we make such points is part of the desolate modern tendency to turn the discussion of all questions, however simple and forthright, into a search for the violation of some arcane principle, or to evade and suffocate common sense by verbose, incoherent, and irrelevant moralizing. Freedom is not much concerned with tail fins or even with automobiles. Those who argue that it is identified with the greatest possible range of choice of consumers' goods are only confessing their exceedingly simple-minded and mechanical view of man and his liberties.

Our Peerless Leader

Accordingly, and with a view to liberating mankind from their insane preoccupation with material comforts of low marginal urgency, the SUMPTUARY SOCIETY (SS) has been formed to DEMAND that this nation immediately and without exception declare it to be a CAPITAL OFFENSE to:

1. Live in a dwelling unit of more than 400 square feet.
2. Own an automobile with wheelbase over 72 inches.
3. Drive an automobile using gasoline of higher octane rating (and lead content) than standard fuel of the year 1923.
4. Drink whiskey aged more than 60 days.

5. Smoke more than ten cigarettes in one day.
6. Possess clothing in excess of, if a male, 1 coat, 2 pairs of shoes, 2 pairs of socks, 2 suits, 4 shirts, 3 handkerchiefs, 1 tie, 1 hat, 1 pair of rubbers, and 1 change of underwear. If a female, the same rules will apply with appropriate modifications (for example, jackets will button on the left instead of the right).
7. Appear in public clean-shaven (if a male).

Furthermore, it will be declared an exceptionally HEINOUS offense punishable by boiling in oil to:

1. Possess more than two of the following: eye-level kitchen range, refrigerator with across-the-top freezing compartment, combination washer-dryer, two-tone auto paint job, Waring blender, chafing dish, or double-ended egg cup.
2. Be detected reading [George] Orwell's *1984*, a book known to have low marginal usefulness, and whose production consumes irreplaceable timber, ink, glue, and lead type.

The following remarks are directed to sympathetic citizens who may not have fully grasped the logic underlying the reconstruction of our greedy wasteful society on sumptuary principles.

The most crucial point to appreciate is that the principles of the SS must be distinguished from a bleak Puritanism which would leave life joyless and empty. Under the false Puritan ideal, the individual was to be restrained from pursuit of the illusory goal of material pleasure by self-discipline. With our deeper knowledge today, of course, we are aware that the internal conflicts thus set up are psychologically damaging. The principles of the SS, in contrast, are to be enforced by a psychologically sound and healthy method, the method of (in the words of our PEERLESS LEADER) social responsibility. That is to say, through detectives, policemen, judges, and wardens. Furthermore, any residue of frustrations suffered by unreconstructed individuals will be more than compensated by the wholesome (and non-material-consuming) glee in their work which society's guardians may be expected to take.

The second point to realize is that our PEERLESS LEADER has declared certain forms of consumption to be innocuous or even praiseworthy: education, health, good government, clean countryside, and orchestras are specifically commended as having "rather small materials requirements." Of course, under sumptuary principles unaccompanied vocalists are even superior to orchestras, while among orchestras those employing expensive material-consuming mechanical aids like the piano, violin, and French horn should probably be eschewed in favor of those relying on simple instruments like the harmonica, ocarina, and kazoo. We may similarly reason that clean surroundings are best achieved by a man with bag and pointed stick; the tendency toward mechanization of garbage-handling is to be deplored, however creditable the object.

The modern sumptuary philosophy is an outgrowth—the culmination and crowning achievement of twentieth century economic science. We place particular importance, therefore, upon matters of economic policy, especially when these are regarded (in the words of our PEERLESS LEADER) as "instruments of social control." Our program includes the following DEMANDS:

1. *Farm price supports at 200 per cent of parity*. Our PEERLESS LEADER (also known as the FEARLESS FRIEND OF THE FARM BLOC) himself refuted those who would have reduced price support from 90 per cent of parity, showing the enormous contribution these support payments have made to agricultural progress and technological innovation. Still more progress could be anticipated with prices at 200 per cent of parity. This

arrangement has the unique sumptuary advantage that improvements of production techniques do not lead to any increase in consumption. Furthermore, the unconsumed produce may be used as fertilizer to restore or even increase the quality of the soil—a vital component of our "resource base" for the future.

2. *Price ceilings on everything not price-supported*. To allow markets to go uncontrolled would be to "ascribe a magical automatism" to the price system.

3. *A food excise tax proportioned to calorie content; personal taxes based on avoirdupois or volume displacement*. The anti-corpulence program of the SS is based, of course, upon the concern of our PEERLESS LEADER with the problem of obesity. Our slogan: Fine the fat, stick the stout, and plunder the plump.

4. *A yardage tax on clothing materials*.

5. *A universal protective—nay, prohibitive—tariff*. For, if it is wrong for us to overconsume our own irreplaceable materials, how much worse to use our economic power to rob poorer nations of their limited heritage.

No thinking man today will be swayed by the FAKE FREEDOM ISSUE raised by our enemies, the so-called libertarians or voluntarists. To paraphrase our PEERLESS LEADER, true consumer's freedom gives no one license to buy autos with tail fins—anymore than true freedom of speech gives any misguided person a "right" to propagandize against the views of the SS.

Milton Friedman
(1912-)

More than just about any other economist, Milton Friedman has spanned the domain of economics from popular literature to theoretical literature, from macro theory to micro theory. Friedman attended Columbia University and played a significant role in the re-establishment of classical economics. He also has been a forceful spokesman for the use of economic reasoning for microeconomic problems. In the 1950s his was one of the few voices arguing strongly for classical liberalism—what today is sometimes called conservatism.

Friedman's argument here is that economic freedom is a prerequisite for political freedom, and if a society loses its economic freedom, it will quickly lose its political freedom.

Note that when Friedman talks about being "compelled by law to devote something like 10 per cent of his income to the purchase of a particular kind of retirement contract, administered by the government," he means the social security tax. In the same paragraph Friedman describes the Amish sect who refused to pay the tax and the severe penalties the government imposed. There was so much adverse publicity of this event in American life that Congress changed the law, meaning that the Amish and other recognized sects who are religiously adverse to the social security concept do not have to obtain social security numbers and do not have to pay the tax, providing they also refuse the benefits when they would otherwise be eligible.

Milton Friedman. 1962. *Capitalism and Freedom*. Chicago: University of Chicago Press, Chapter 1, pp. 7-10.

The Relation between Economic Freedom and Political Freedom

It is widely believed that politics and economics are separate and largely unconnected; that individual freedom is a political problem and material welfare an economic problem; and that any kind of political arrangements can be combined with any kind of economic arrangements. The chief contemporary manifestation of this idea is the advocacy of "democratic socialism" by many who condemn out of hand the restrictions on individual freedom imposed by "totalitarian socialism" in Russia, and who are persuaded that it is possible for a country to adopt the essential features of Russian economic arrangements and yet to ensure individual freedom through political arrangements. The thesis of this chapter is that such a view is a delusion, that there is an intimate connection between economics and politics, that only certain combinations of political and economic arrangements are possible, and that in particular, a society which is socialist cannot also be democratic, in the sense of guaranteeing individual freedom.

Economic arrangements play a dual role in the promotion of a free society. On the one hand, freedom in economic arrangements is itself a component of freedom broadly understood, so economic freedom is an end in itself. In the second place, economic freedom is also an indispensable means toward the achievement of political freedom.

The first of these roles of economic freedom needs special emphasis because intellectuals in particular have a strong bias against regarding this aspect of freedom as important. They tend to express contempt for what they regard as material aspects of life, and to regard their own pursuit of allegedly higher values as on a different plane of significance and as deserving of special attention. For most citizens of the country, however, if not for the intellectual, the direct importance of economic freedom is at least comparable in significance to the indirect importance of economic freedom as a means to political freedom.

The citizen of Great Britain, who after World War II was not permitted to spend his vacation in the United States because of exchange control, was being deprived of an essential freedom no less than the citizen of the United States, who was denied the opportunity to spend his vacation in Russia because of his political views. The one was ostensibly an economic limitation on freedom and the other a political limitation, yet there is no essential difference between the two.

The citizen of the United States who is compelled by law to devote something like 10 per cent of his income to the purchase of a particular kind of retirement contract, administered by the government, is being deprived of a corresponding part of his personal freedom. How strongly this deprivation may be felt and its closeness to the deprivation of religious freedom, which all would regard as "civil" or "political" rather than "economic", were dramatized by an episode involving a group of farmers of the Amish sect. On grounds of principle, this group regarded compulsory federal old age programs as an infringement of their personal individual freedom and refused to pay taxes or accept benefits. As a result, some of their livestock were sold by auction in order to satisfy claims for social security levies. True, the number of citizens who regard compulsory old age insurance as a deprivation of freedom may be few, but the believer in freedom has never counted noses.

A citizen of the United States who under the laws of various states is not free to follow the occupation of his own choosing unless he can get a license for it, is likewise being deprived of an essential part of his freedom. So is the man who would like to exchange some of his goods with, say, a Swiss for a watch but is prevented from doing so by a quota. So also is the Californian who was thrown into jail for selling Alka Seltzer at a price below that set by the manufacturer under so-called "fair trade" laws. So also is the farmer who cannot grow the amount of wheat he wants. And so on. Clearly, economic freedom, in and of itself, is an extremely important part of total freedom.

Viewed as a means to the end of political freedom, economic arrangements are important because of their effect on the concentration or dispersion of power. The kind of economic organization that provides economic freedom directly, namely, competitive capitalism, also promotes political freedom because it separates economic power from political power and in this way enables the one to offset the other.

Historical evidence speaks with a single voice on the relation between political freedom and a free market. I know of no example in time or place of a society that has been marked by a large measure of political freedom, and that has not also used something comparable to a free market to organize the bulk of economic activity.

Because we live in a largely free society, we tend to forget how limited is the span of time and the part of the globe for which there has ever been anything like political freedom: the typical state of mankind is tyranny, servitude, and misery. The nineteenth century and early twentieth century in the Western world stand out as striking exceptions to the general trend of historical development. Political freedom in this instance clearly came along with the free market and the development of capitalist institutions. So also did political freedom in the golden age of Greece and in the early days of the Roman era.

History suggests only that capitalism is a necessary condition for political freedom. Clearly it is not a sufficient condition. Fascist Italy and Fascist Spain, Germany at various times in the last seventy years, Japan before World Wars I and II, tzarist Russia in the decades before World War I—are all societies that cannot conceivably be described as politically free. Yet, in each, private enterprise was the dominant form of economic organization. It is therefore clearly possible to have economic arrangements that are fundamentally capitalist and political arrangements that are not free.

Abba Lerner
(1903-1982)

One of the most lively set of debates in the 1950s was between Abba Lerner and Milton Friedman. Whereas Friedman was a classic libertarian, Lerner was an admixture of various views: he strongly advocated the market, but simultaneously held strong socialist leanings. He learned his economics from two conservatives: Lionel Robbins and F. A. Hayek, but he quickly switched to Keynesianism in macro. In micro, he became associated with market socialism—using the market to allocate goods, but using political means to determine the distribution of those goods.

In this selection, which is a review of Friedman's Capitalism and Freedom *(from which the previous selection in this book was taken), we see Lerner at his best. We also see a discussion of Friedman's chapters in which differences are matters of degree and slight interpretation and can have various levels. Notice that Lerner says he enthusiastically supports Friedman 90 percent of the time, but that in Lerner's view Friedman pushes the argument too far.*

Abba Lerner. 1963. "Review of *Capitalism and Freedom* by Milton Friedman." *American Economic Review*, pp. 639-61.

Review of *Capitalism and Freedom* by Milton Friedman

This rewrite of lectures and articles by Milton Friedman is largely a defense of liberalism against "liberalism"—that is, (to spell it out since the quotation marks are easily transposed) of nineteenth-century European liberalism's concern for individual freedom against twentieth-century American "liberals." To these he refers (quoting Schumpeter) as "the enemies of the system of private enterprise [who] have thought it wise to appropriate its label" (p. 5), and he characterizes them by their readiness to rely on the state for the furtherance of welfare and equality.

Although Friedman is no more against welfare than the "liberals" are against freedom, he seems to have reacted so strongly against the failure of many "liberals" to understand the nature, the merits, and the potentialities of the market system, and their consequent tendency, in or out of season, to cry "there ought to be a law," that he tends to cry "never, never pass a law—well, hardly ever!" In this he is buttressed by a deep political pessimism about the inevitable corruption of even the best-intentioned government action by narrow partisan interests. The result is that although he erects his system on an unimpeachable framework that all "liberals" as well as all liberals would accept—recognizing that a case may be made for government intervention whenever the market system fails to work satisfactorily by reason of monopoly or "neighborhood effects" (divergence between private and social benefits or costs)—his pessimistic antigovernmentism leads him to some strange extremes.

Thus, he is against fair employment practices legislation (FEPC) because by admitting the government into that area one opens the way to unfair employment practices legislation like the Nuremberg laws (UEPC?). (He does *not* object to government enforcing honest labeling on the grounds that this would open the way to enforcing or protecting dishonest labeling.) His treatment of racial and other discrimination as a matter of taste whose gratification is legitimate (however bad the taste) would be applicable, and not merely elegant, if the resulting supply of black, white, and mixed schools or housing had no great "neighborhood effect" in depriving Negroes of reasonable facilities. His displeasure with the Keynesian concentration on fiscal policy (a result of its development at a time when monetary policy was not working well or was being worked very badly) leads him to declare the belief that "a rise in government expenditures relative to tax receipts, even when financed by borrowing, is *necessarily* expansionist" (page 82) to be based on one or the other of two extreme assumptions; either a liquidity elasticity of infinity (the liquidity trap) or an investment elasticity of zero (collapse of confidence). But although one of these extreme assumptions is required for the belief that *monetary policy* is completely ineffective, neither is really necessary for the belief that expansionary *fiscal policy* "is *necessarily* expansionist." All that is needed is the rejection of the opposite extreme assumption of an unchangeable velocity of circulation. Friedman himself judges that "$100 increase in government expenditures can on the average be expected to add just about $100 to income" (page 84), so that, unless the government expenditures have no value whatsoever, they would bring about a significant expansion not only of employment but also of useful output. Nor would Friedman deny that in time of less than average prosperity the multiplier would be greater than unity. Nevertheless, he concludes that the belief that expansionary fiscal policy can relieve depression is "economic mythology" (*ibid.*).

And yet in spite of these and a few other extravagances, *Capitalism and Freedom* is an important and valuable book with which as a liberal "liberal" I find myself in enthusiastic agreement some 90 per cent of the time. For the book powerfully demonstrates an impressive number of ways in which both freedom and welfare could be increased by a fuller utilization of the price mechanism. In some cases this could be achieved by freeing the price mechanism from governmental or private hindrances that have outlived any justifications they may once have had; in other areas, like education, by developing new institutions (for providing security of investment in human capital) that would permit the competitive price mechanism to begin to operate in them. Annoyance with Friedman's antigovernment complex should not be permitted to obscure the legitimacy and the persuasiveness of his plea for permitting private enterprise to compete freely with government enterprise in such activities as schooling or mail delivery, or his arguments against price supports, tariffs and import restrictions, output restrictions, rent and wage controls, and the ICC's perversion from combating railroad monopolies to enforcing general transportation monopolies. He provides a beautiful analysis of the American Medical Association's self-virtuous conspiracy against the American public. Particularly welcome is his treatment of the control of money, even though it suffers from his inability to credit governmental authority with the power to learn to avoid even "inexcusable" misjudgments, and his chapter on international trade and financial arrangements, where he deserves special praise for his unflinching courage in demonstrating how any compromise on the unpopular cause of flexible exchanges endangers all the popular aspects of free trade and sentimental internationalism.

Every liberal, "liberal," or simple decent fellow interested in public affairs can gain much by reading this book and even more by rereading any part that may repel him. The antigovernment extravagances that I have perhaps overemphasized in this review are to be deplored less for the (to my mind) bad advice to which they lead than for their inhibitory effect on potential readers of an important book that will provoke much thinking and rethinking.

George Stigler
(1911-1992)

You were introduced to George Stigler earlier. Here we see another demonstration of Stigler's wit. This time it is the market itself and "economic reforms" that are being lampooned. His point, again, is that policies, even ones that introduce markets, have long-run consequences, many of which will not have been predicted. Thus one should undertake policy very carefully.

Note that all the professors in this piece have been invented by Stigler, except for "Hutchins," to whom the imaginary professor Seguira is compared. Robert Hutchins was considered an upstart because he was appointed president of the University of Chicago at the age of 30. In his long career there (1929-1951), he instituted many novel (at the time) educational experiments, such as abolishing football and fraternities and changing the emphasis of the curriculum, many of which flourished and are still influential today.

George Stigler. 1984. *The Intellectual and the Marketplace.* Cambridge: Harvard University Press, Chapter 1, pp. 3-9.

An Academic Episode

I had been proposing a favorite thesis: that our universities are run in reverse. While a man is still young and energetic and curious, he is required to teach so many elementary courses and read so many examinations—and scrub so many floors at home—that he can do no research. Even his summers must be spent earning more money. When he gets older, his teaching load is cut in half and his paperwork is delegated to assistants and his salary doubles. But by then he is usually beyond creative work, and develops his bridge game or gardening skills. Pinzio, the venerable head of Romance Languages, agreed that there was much truth in the indictment, but thought that any remedy would be worse than the disease. He related the following story.

About thirty years ago a young man named Seguira became the rector of a university in a South American country in which his father had recently financed a successful revolution. Seguira, who previously had been quite the gay young blade, surprised everyone when he immediately settled down to become a serious-minded reformer—a sort of Latin Hutchins. He began casting about for reform, of which—Pinzio said—the university could stand a good deal, and eventually hit upon the merit system. He soon issued the following regulations.

In June of each year any member of the faculty could challenge the person immediately above him a rank to a competitive examination. The examination was to be made up and graded by a group of impartial professors in the United States. (Seguira told Pinzio that this country had been chosen in order to make bribery more expensive.) If the challenger won, he would exchange position and salary with his former superior. Thus an able graduate student could in successive years become an instructor, an assistant professor, an associate professor, and a professor.

There was a terrible uproar, and some shrill glee, when this announcement came out. Some of the older men were very bitter, and emphasized the fact that the rectorship was not included in the competition. But most of the younger members of the faculty were delighted at the prospect, Pinzio among them.

The announcement was made in September, and some very desirable effects were observed during the first year. The physicist Antonio bought a new pair of spectacles so he could once again read small print. Cardan the economist, who had been spending most of his time running a noodle factory, engaged an assistant professor (who could not challenge him for two years) to tutor him in the developments that had occurred in the field of economics during the previous fifteen years. The senior professor in chemistry announced in December, once he fully understood the plan, that for reasons of health he was retiring the next June, and several others followed him.

The library experienced an unprecedented rush. Learned journals—especially American—came out of dusty stacks, and hot disputes raged over the attempts of some men to draw out all of the modern treatises in a field. This, indeed, was the one clear disadvantage of the reform: men began to hoard knowledge. Few were willing to discuss their field except with better-informed people, and the exceptions were attributed to deceit as often as to arrogance. The graduate students suffered most: Filipo devoted his year course in the advanced theory of functions to a review of Euclid; Danto succeeded in getting many economics students to read Alfred instead of Adam Smith; and Ricardo reviewed the Baconian theory, in painstaking detail, in his course on Shakespeare.

Yet the results of the competitions the following June were generally conceded to be beneficial. Several men began rapid, if overdue, movement toward retirement. Rumor had it that the unsuccessful and incompetent associate professor Jordan, whose wife was the daughter of the chairman of his department, was contemplating divorce. Pinzio became an associate professor.

Seguira in particular was delighted with the outcome. But he was worried by the tendency of teachers to devote their graduate courses to empty and irrelevant subjects; so he amended the regulations to grant five points (in a hundred) to a teacher for each of his students who won a challenge. This new rule led to careful calculation: would five points outweigh a superior performance by the student in the examination? The general belief was that professors gained, and assistant professors lost, by careful instruction. The scheme led to some paradoxes the following year: Dourni was challenged by seven of his graduate students and all got higher grades in the examination, but his thirty-five point bonus kept his position for him.

By the next autumn another unanticipated result of the reform became apparent. There was a precipitous fall in enrollments of graduate students, and it was soon discovered that all who could afford it had gone to the United States for graduate work. Seguira shared the professor[s'] indignation at this maneuver, and vowed to amend the regulations the following spring. But meanwhile a heavy gloom settled on the staff: Were not the migratory students virtually studying the examination questions?

The gloom was justified by the fact. Of the sixty-one students who spent the year in the United States, forty-six won their challenge the following spring. Nor were the results so generally approved as the year before. It is true that several fossils continued their steady march to the museum, and several able young men moved up another rank (Pinzio among them). But Storeo, the brilliant young astronomer, was defeated by a mediocre graduate student who—with the examiner—had spent the year studying some obscure variable stars. And Birnii fell because his magisterial command of political theory did not extend to the details of the New England township.

Seguira was in a quandary. To rule out migration was to invite charges of provincialism and inbreeding; to permit it on the current scale was to destroy graduate study. He finally devised a compromise: the examinations would be given by professors chosen at random from the United States, England, France, Sweden, and Germany. Now if a graduate student went abroad, four times out of five he would guess the wrong country. The amendment did stop the mass migration, but it had its own embarrassments: one sociologist had the same examination question, by chance, in two consecutive years, and each time gave the same answer. The first year he received an ignominious flunk (from Stockholm), and the second year he was offered a professorship (at Harvard).

And as the scheme entered its third year, a further effect could no longer be overlooked. Research had almost stopped. Once observed, of course, it was easy to explain. A man was likely to pass the examination with high marks if he knew what others were doing; it did not help his chances materially to do something himself. The faculty was becoming extremely well-read, and extremely unenterprising. The most prominent exceptions showed the advisability of the rule. Therespi had continued his careful researches on the fruit fly and lost in two challenges. Laboro had finished the seventh volume of his monumental history of South America, and flunked the question on the Crusades.

Another year and some serious faculty losses were required to arouse Seguira to the importance of this problem. Once persuaded, he issued still another amendment: a man was to receive two points for each article, and seven for each book. He wanted to restrict these bonuses only to current publications, but the opposition was too strong. Even the younger men, especially the successful younger men, were complaining of the baneful effects of insecurity of tenure. And it was pointed out that definitive works required time—perhaps even two years. Seguira compromised by including all works published within the previous decade.

The calculations of the faculty now became even more complex. A book (seven points), or the training of a superior student (five points)? The writing of the book might require three years, but the points were received every year thereafter, whereas the student might eventually leave. The answers at which the faculty finally arrived were various. Cimoor, whose father owned a publishing house, succeeded in getting out two books within the first year, and so influential was his father that many of the reviews were neutral. The political scientist Broze withdrew a book already in page proof, and published the nineteen chapters as nineteen articles. This, however, occasioned less complaint than Cardan's publication of a book of readings. But still, research revived somewhat.

This sequence of felt difficulty and hopeful amendment, Pinzio said, might have gone on as long as the unstable political foundations of Seguira's position permitted, had not two developments come to pass. The first was the sudden dawning on Seguira that this patchwork of rules was gradually obliterating the whole purpose of his reforms. This was brought home during the next annual competition, when four professors came out of unwilling retirement and three, with the aid of their writings of previous years, began again to climb the academic ladder. This particular development, of course, could be dealt with through a new rule—but where was it leading?

The conjunction of the second event proved decisive. Shortly after this awakening, Seguira received an invitation from the towering University of South America to become its rector. The regents wrote that his reputation for originality and enterprise was international, and that the success of his experiments indicated the need for a wider field of application. He accepted the new position, as much as a refuge as a promotion.

And what happened to Seguira? we demanded, and to the university? Seguira became as conservative as his reputation would allow, Pinzio assured us. And the merit system? Only one more amendment was added: a man could receive a permanent bonus of any number of points the department chairman deemed fit, when an offer was received from another university.

Thomas R. Malthus

(1766-1834)

Malthus was an English clergyman who thought deeply about economic problems and is best known for his Essay on the Principle of Population, *from which this selection is taken. Unlike most classical economists, Malthus saw the possibility that gluts (depressions) could exist and argued that position strongly. The essential argument presented in this essay is that population growth can and will outstrip the food supply. This argument has entered the language with the term "Malthusian doctrine."*

His suggestion that population ought to be controlled was very striking at the time. He was born with a cleft palate and a harelip and, as one of his contemporaries observed, he spoke in a "tremulous stammering voice, seemingly little fitted for the utterance of any doctrine which could be deemed dangerous to social welfare."

Malthus wrote his first version of the Essay *in 1798, but for the so-called second edition (1803) he revised the work so extensively that it is really a new book. The work went through many editions, but it never again was substantially revised as far as the selection here is concerned.*

Thomas Malthus. 1803 (14th edition: 1826). *An Essay on the Principle of Population*. London: J.M. Dent, pp. 1-24 *passim*.

The Theory of Population

In an inquiry concerning the improvement of society, the mode of conducting the subject which naturally presents itself, is, (1), to investigate the causes which have hitherto impeded the progress of mankind towards happiness; and (2), to examine the probability of the total or partial removal of these causes in the future. The principal object of this essay is to examine the effects of one great cause intimately united with the very nature of man. That is the constant tendency of all animated life to increase beyond the nourishment provided for it.

Through the animal and vegetable kingdoms Nature has scattered the seeds of life abroad with the most profuse and liberal hand. If the germs of existence contained in the earth could freely develop themselves, they would fill millions of worlds in the course of a few thousand years. Necessity, that imperious, all-pervading law of nature restrains them and man alike within prescribed bounds.

The effects of nature's check on man are complicated. Impelled to the increase of his species by an equally powerful instinct, reason interrupts his career, and asks whether he may not bring beings into the world, for whom he cannot provide the means of support. If he hear not this suggestion, the human race will be constantly endeavoring to increase beyond the means of subsistence. But as, by that law of our nature which makes food necessary to the life of man, population can never actually increase beyond the lowest nourishment capable of supporting it, a strong check on population, namely, the difficulty of acquiring food, must be constantly in operation. This difficulty must fall somewhere, and must necessarily be severely felt in some or other of the various forms of misery by a large portion of mankind. This conclusion will sufficiently appear from a review of the different states of society in which man has existed. But the subject will be seen in a clearer light if we endeavor to ascertain what would be the natural increase in population, if left to exert itself with perfect freedom.

Many extravagant statements have been made of the length of the period within which the population of a country can double. To be perfectly sure we are far within the truth, we will take a slow rate, and say that population, when unchecked, goes on doubling itself every 25 years, or increases in a geometrical ratio. The rate according to which the productions of the earth may be supposed to increase, it will not be so easy to determine. However, we may be perfectly certain that the ratio of their increase in a limited territory must be of a totally different nature from the ratio of the increase in population. A thousand millions are just as easily doubled every 25 years by the power of population as a thousand. But the food will by no means be obtained with the same facility. Man is confined in room. When acre has been added to acre until all the fertile land is occupied, the yearly increase in food must depend upon the melioration of the land already in possession. This is a fund which, from the nature of all soils, instead of increasing must be gradually diminishing. But population, could it be supplied with food, would go on with unexhausted vigor, and the increase in one period would furnish a power of increase in the next, and this without any limit. If it be allowed that by the best possible policy the average produce could be doubled in the first 25 years, it will be allowing a greater increase than could with reason be expected. In the next 25 years it is impossible to suppose that the produce could be quadrupled. It would be contrary to our knowledge of the properties of land.

Let us suppose that the yearly additions which might be made to the former average produce instead of decreasing as they certainly would do, were to remain the same; and that the product of the land might be increased every 25 years, by a quantity equal to what it at present produces. The most enthusiastic speculator can not suppose a greater increase than this. Even then the land could not be made to increase faster than in an arithmetical ratio. Taking the whole earth, the human species would increase as the numbers 1, 2, 4, 8, 16, 32, 64, 128, 256, and subsistence as 1, 2, 3, 4, 5, 6, 7, 8, 9. In two centuries the population would be to the means of subsistence as 256 to 9; in three centuries as 4,096 to 13, and in two thousand years the difference would be almost incalculable.

In this supposition, no limits whatever are placed to the produce of the earth. It may increase forever and be greater than any assignable quantity; yet still the power of population, being in every period so much greater, the increase of the human species can only be kept down to the level of the means of subsistence by the constant operation of the strong law of necessity, acting as a check upon the greater power.

But this ultimate check to population, the want of food, is never the immediate check except in cases of famine. The latter consists in all those customs and all those diseases, which seem to be generated by a scarcity of the means of subsistence; and all those causes which tend permanently to weaken the human frame. The checks may be classed under two general heads—the preventative and the positive.

The preventative check, peculiar to man, arises from his reasoning faculties, which enable him to calculate distant consequences. He sees the distress which frequently presses upon those who have large families; he cannot contemplate his present possessions or earnings, and calculate the amount of each share, when they must be divided, perhaps, among seven or eight, without feeling a doubt whether he may be able to support the offspring which probably will be brought into the world. Other considerations occur. Will he lower his rank in life, and be obliged to give up in great measure his former habits? Does any mode of employment present itself by which he may reasonably hope to maintain a family? Will he not subject himself to greater difficulties and more severe labor than in his present state? Will he be able to give his children adequate educational advantages? Can he face the possibility of exposing his children to poverty or charity, by his inability to provide for them? These considerations prevent a large number of people from pursuing the dictates of nature.

The positive checks to population are extremely various, and include every cause, whether arising from vice or misery, which in any degree contributes to shorten the natural duration of human life. Under this head may be enumerated all unwholesome occupations, severe labor, exposure to the seasons, extreme poverty, bad nursing of children, great towns, excesses of all kinds, the whole train of common diseases, wars, plagues, and famines.

The theory of population is resolvable into three propositions: (1) Population is necessarily limited by the means of subsistence. (2) Population invariably increases where the means of subsistence increase, unless prevented by some very powerful and obvious checks. (3) These checks which keep population on a level with the means of subsistence are all resolvable into moral restraint, vice, and misery.

Frédéric Bastiat

(1801-1850)

Frédéric Bastiat was a French economist, known for journalistic writing in favor of free trade and the economics of Adam Smith, and for his forceful disagreement with Ricardian economics.

Note that this piece was written before the day of electric light. Among the terms that may be unfamiliar to you is "snuffers," which are used to snuff, or put out, candles. Also, the author speaks of an increase in the use of tallow (for candles) leading to the necessity of an increase in the number of cattle and sheep. The connection is that tallow is made from the fat of these animals. Similarly, when he speaks of the increase in whale fisheries, the connection is that whale oil was used in oil lamps. The discussion of Lisbon oranges can be more clearly understood if one remembers that Lisbon, the capital of Portugal, is in a warm, sunny climate where oranges may be matured, as compared to Paris where oranges must be brought in and then artificially ripened.

Frédéric Bastiat. 1845 (reprinted 1882). "Petition From the Manufacturers of Candles, Wax Lights, Lamps, Chandeliers, Reflectors, Snuffers, Extinguishers; and From the Producers of Tallow, Oil, Resin, Alcohol, and Generally of Everything Used for Lights." *Economic Sophisms*. New York: G.P. Putnam's Sons.

Petition of the Candlemakers

Petition from the manufacturers of candles, wax lights, lamps, chandeliers, reflectors, snuffers, extinguishers; and from the producers of tallow, oil, resin, alcohol, and generally of everything used for lights.

To the Honorable the Members of the Chamber of Deputies:

GENTLEMEN—You are in the right way: you reject abstract theories; abundance, cheapness, concerns you little. You are entirely occupied with the interest of the producer, whom you are anxious to free from foreign competition. In a word, you wish to secure the *national market* to *national labor.*

We come now to offer you an admirable opportunity for the application of your—what shall we say? your theory? no, nothing is more deceiving than theory—your doctrine? your system? your principle? But you do not like doctrines; you hold systems in horror; and, as for principles, you declare that there are no such things in political economy. We will say, then, your practice; your practice without theory, and without principle.

We are subjected to the intolerable competition of a foreign rival, who enjoys, it would seem, such superior facilities for the production of light, that he is enabled to *inundate* our *national market* at so exceedingly reduced a price, that, the moment he makes his appearance, he draws off all custom for us; and thus an important branch of French industry, with all its innumerable ramifications, is suddenly reduced to a state of complete stagnation. This rival, who is no other than the sun, carries on so bitter a war against us, that we have every reason to believe that he has been excited to this course by our perfidious neighbor England. (Good diplomacy this, for the present time!) In this belief we are confirmed by the fact that in all his transactions with that proud island, he is much more moderate and careful than with us.

Our petition is, that it would please your honorable body to pass a law whereby shall be directed the shutting up of windows, dormers, skylights, shutters, curtains, *vasistas, oeil-de-boeufs,* in a word, all openings, holes, chinks, and fissures through which the light of the sun is used to penetrate into our dwellings, to the prejudice of the profitable manufactures which we flatter ourselves we have been enabled to bestow upon the country; which country cannot, therefore, without ingratitude, leave us now to struggle unprotected through so unequal a contest.

We pray your honorable body not to mistake our petition for a satire, nor to repulse us without at least hearing the reasons which we have to advance in its favor.

And first, if, by shutting out as much as possible all access to natural light, you thus create the necessity for artificial light, is there in France an industrial pursuit which will not, through some connection with this important object, be benefited by it?

If more tallow be consumed, there will arise a necessity for an increase of cattle and sheep. Thus artificial meadows must be in greater demand; and meat, wool, leather, and above all, manure, this basis of agricultural riches, must become more abundant.

If more oil be consumed, it will cause an increase in the cultivation of the olive tree. This plant, luxuriant and exhausting to the soil, will come in good time to profit by the increased fertility which the raising of cattle will have communicated to our fields.

Our heaths will become covered with resinous trees. Numerous swarms of bees will gather upon our mountains the perfumed treasures which are now cast upon the winds, useless as the blossoms from which they emanate. There is, in short, no branch of agriculture which would not be greatly developed by the granting of our petitions.

Navigation would equally profit. Thousands of vessels would soon be employed in the whale fisheries, and hence would arise a navy capable of sustaining the honor of France, and of responding to the patriotic sentiments of the undersigned petitioners, candle merchants, and so forth.

But what words can express the magnificence which Paris will then exhibit! Cast an eye upon the future and behold the gildings, the bronzes, the magnificent crystal chandeliers, lamps, reflectors, and candelabra, which will glitter in the spacious stores, compared with which the splendor of the present day will appear trifling and insignificant.

There is none, not even the poor manufacturer of resin in the midst of his pine forest, nor the miserable miller in his dark dwelling, but who would enjoy an increase of salary and of comforts.

Gentlemen, if you will be pleased to reflect, you cannot fail to be convinced that there is perhaps not one Frenchman, from the opulent stockholder of Anzin down to the poorest vender of matches, who is not interested in the success of our petition.

We foresee your objections, gentlemen; but there is not one that you can oppose to us which you will not be obliged to gather from the works of the partisans of free trade. We dare challenge you to pronounce one word against our petition, which is not equally opposed to your own practice and the principle which guides your policy.

Do you tell us, that if we gain by this protection, France will not gain, because the consumer must pay the price of it?

We answer you:

You have no longer any right to cite the interest of the consumer. For whenever this has been found to compete with that of the producer, you have invariably sacrificed the first. You have clone this to *encourage labor,* to *increase the demand for labor.* The same reason should now induce you to act in the same manner.

You have yourselves already answered the objection. When you were told, the consumer is interested in the free introduction of coal, iron, corn, wheat, cloths, and so forth, your answer was, Yes, but the producer is interested in their exclusion. Thus, also if the consumer is interested in the admission of light, we, the producers, pray for its interdiction.

You have also said, the producer and the consumer are one. If the manufacturer gains by protection, he will cause the agriculturist to gain also; if agriculture prospers, it opens a market for manufactured goods. Thus we, if you confer upon us the monopoly of furnishing light during the day, will as a first consequence buy large quantities of tallow, coals, oil, resin, wax, alcohol, silver, iron, bronze, crystal, for the supply of our business; and then we and our numerous contractors having become rich, our consumption will be great, and will become a means of contributing to the comfort and competency of the workers in every branch of national labor.

Will you say that the light of the sun is a gratuitous gift, and that to repulse gratuitous gifts is to repulse riches under pretense of encouraging the means of obtaining them?

Take care—you carry the death blow to your own policy. Remember that hitherto you have always repulsed foreign produce *because* it was an approach to a gratuitous gift, and *the more in proportion* as this approach was more close. You have, in obeying the wishes of other monopolists, acted only from a *half-motive;* to grant our petition there is a much *fuller inducement.* To repulse us, precisely for the reason that our case is a more complete one than any which have preceded it, would be to lay down the following equation: $+X+=-$; in other words, it would be to accumulate absurdity upon absurdity.

Labor and nature concur in different proportions, according to country and climate, in every article of production. The portion of nature is always gratuitous; that of labor alone regulates the price. If a Lisbon orange can be sold at half the price of a Parisian one, it is because a natural and gratuitous heat does for the one what the other only obtains from an artificial and consequently expensive one.

When, therefore, we purchase a Portuguese orange, we may say that we obtain it half gratuitously and half by the right of labor; in other words, at *half-price* compared with those of Paris.

Now it is precisely on account of this *demi-gratuity* (excuse the word) that you argue in favor of exclusion. How, you say, could national labor sustain the competition of foreign labor, when the first has everything to do, and the last is rid of half the trouble, the sun taking the rest of the business upon himself? If then the *demi-gratuity* can determine you to check competition, on what principle can the *entire gratuity* be alleged as a reason for admitting it? You are no logicians if, refusing the demi-gratuity as hurtful to human labor, you do not a *fortiori,* and with double zeal, reject the full gratuity.

Again, when any article, as coal, iron, cheese, or cloth, comes to us from foreign countries with less labor than if we produced it ourselves, the difference in price is a *gratuitous gift* conferred upon us; and the gift is more or less considerable, according as the difference is greater or less. It is the quarter, the half, or the three quarters of the value of the produce, in proportion as the foreign merchant requires the three quarters, the half, or the quarter of the price. It is as complete as possible when the producer offers, as the sun does with light, the whole in free gift. The question is, and we put it formally, whether you wish for France the benefit of gratuitous consumption, or the supposed advantages of laborious production. Choose, but be consistent. And does it not argue the greatest inconsistency to check as you do the importation of coal, iron, cheese, and goods of foreign manufacture, merely because and even in proportion as their price approaches *zero,* while at the same time you freely admit, and without limitation, the light of the sun, whose price is during the whole day at *zero?*

Adam Smith
(1723-1790)

In the introductory section you saw one selection from Adam Smith's Wealth of Nations *(1776). Here, you see another. It is a short selection that captures Smith's argument that it is best to rely on the market to translate individuals' actions into actions for the general good, rather than to rely on individuals' beneficence.*

Adam Smith. 1776 (6th edition: 1791). *An Inquiry into the Nature and Causes of the Wealth of Nations.* London: A. Strahan.

Restraints on Trade and the Invisible Hand

The produce of industry is what it adds to the subject or materials upon which it is employed. In proportion as the value of this produce is great or small, so will likewise be the profits of the employer. But it is only for the sake of profit that any man employs a capital in the support of industry; and he will always, therefore, endeavour to employ it in the support of that industry of which the produce is likely to be of the greatest value, or to exchange for the greatest quantity either of money or of other goods.

But the annual revenue of every society is always precisely equal to the exchangeable value of the whole annual produce of its industry, or rather is precisely the same thing with that exchangeable value. As every individual, therefore, endeavours as much as he can both to employ his capital in the support of domestic industry, and so to direct that industry that its produce may be of the greatest value; every individual necessarily labors to render the annual revenue of the society as great as he can. He generally, indeed, neither intends to promote the public interest, nor knows how much he is promoting it. By preferring the support of domestic to that of foreign industry, he intends only his own security; and by directing that industry in such a manner as its produce may be of the greatest value, he intends only his own gain, and he is in this, as in many other cases, led by an invisible hand to promote an end which was no part of his intention. Nor is it always the worse for the society that it was no part of it. By pursuing his own interest he frequently promotes that of the society more effectually than when he really intends to promote it. I have never known much good done by those who affected to trade for the public good. It is an affectation, indeed, not very common among merchants, and very few words need be employed in dissuading them from it.